CULTURE AND SOCIAL CHANGE

CULTURE AND SOCIAL CHANGE

Social Movements in Québec and Ontario

Edited by Colin Leys & Marguerite Mendell

BLACK ROSE BOOKS

Montréal/New York

BLACK ROSE BOOKS No. V177
Hardcover ISBN: 1-895431-29-8
Paperback ISBN: 1-895431-28-X
Library of Congress Catalog No. 92-70625

Canadian Cataloguing in Publication Data

Main entry under title:
Culture and social change

ISBN: 1-895431-29-8 (bound) — ISBN: 1-895431-28-X (pbk.)

1. Social change. 2. Social movements. I. Leys, Colin, 1931- . II. Mendell, Marguerite, 1947-

HM201.C84 1992   303.48'4   C92-090132-8

Cover Illustration: Robert Darrel

Mailing Address

BLACK ROSE BOOKS
C.P. 1258
Succ. Place du Parc
Montréal, Québec
H2W 2R3 Canada

BLACK ROSE BOOKS
340 Nagel Drive
Cheektowaga, New York
14225 USA

A publication of the Institute of Policy Alternatives of Montréal (IPAM)

Printed in Canada

TABLE OF CONTENTS

LIST OF CONTRIBUTORS

Laurie Adkin teaches Political Science at the University of Alberta, Edmonton.

Gregory Baum teaches Religious Studies at McGill University, Montréal.

John Clark is Chair of Ontario Coalition Against Poverty.

Micheline De Séve teaches Political Science at the Université du Québec à Montréal.

Jean-Pierre Deslauriers teaches Social Work at the Université du Québec à Hull.

Louis Fravreau teaches Social Work at the Université du Québec à Hull.

Mona Josée Gagnon teaches Sociology at the Université de Montréal.

Henri Lustiger-Thaler teaches Sociology at Concordia University, Montréal.

Michael McConkey has a Ph.D. from McGill University and is currently an unemployed counter-hegemonic intellectual in Toronto.

Joe Mihevc is City Councilor, City of York, Toronto, and teaches Religious Studies at St. Michael's College, University of Toronto.

Gregor Murray teaches Industrial Relations at Université Laval.

Serge Quenneville is advisor for the environment, C.S.N Service de génie industriel.

Rosemary Warskett is a Ph.D candidate, Department of Sociology, Carleton University, Ottawa, and lecturer at Labour College of Canada.

* * *

Colin Leys has an M.A. in Philosophy, Politics and Economics from Oxford University, and teaches Political Studies at Queen's University.

Marguerite Mendell holds a Ph.D. in Economics from McGill University and is principal at the School of Community and Public Affairs, Concordia University, Montréal, where she also teaches Political Economy.

PREFACE AND ACKNOWLEDGMENTS

This book grew out of a series of workshops sponsored by the Karl Polanyi Institute of Political Economy at Concordia University and the Group for the Study of National and International Development at Queen's University in 1989-91. The aim was to bring together scholars and activists to discuss the fate of the socialist project in light of their knowledge of, and experience in the social movements in Québec and Ontario. The need to rethink the nature of the socialist project had been clear for at least a decade, but the unfolding transformation of "actually existing socialism" in the USSR and Eastern Europe at the end of the 1980s gave it new urgency. Another aim was to cross the language and cultural barrier separating progressive activists and scholars in Québec and English Canada, and where possible to use the differences between Québec and Ontario as a context for comparison. The focus on social movements was due to our conviction that any renewed progressive project must ultimately reflect their experience and practice.

The success of these workshops led us to invite a still broader group of people to contribute to this volume. Its conception and development owes a considerable debt, however, to many participants in the original workshops whose presentations are not included here, to all of whom we wish to extend our thanks: Chris de Bresson, Dan O'Meara, Jorge Niosi, Robert Shenton, Marc Lesage, Roberta Hamilton, Jean-Marc Piotte, Heather-Jon Maroney, Elaine Stavro-Pearce, Jean-Guy Vaillancourt, José Prades, Luc Gagnon, Maurice Boutin, Pierre Goldberger, and Marsha Hewitt.

We are grateful to the governments of Québec and Ontario for financial support over the two years 1989-91 through their programme of inter-university cooperation between Québec and Ontario; to the Douglas Coldwell Foundation for a timely and generous grant towards the cost of editing; and to Professor Charles L. Bertrand, former Dean of Arts and Sciences at Concordia University for his personal participation and financial support.

Our thanks are also due to Rev. George Topp, S.J. and Daniel Salée for translation; Janet Dorocynski for editorial assistance; and Denise Stobbe and Bernice Gallagher for secretarial assistance.

Special thanks are due to Dimitri Roussopoulos for his encouragement and invaluable personal involvement in the final shaping of the project. In addition, our debt to the dedicated contribution of Ana Gómez at all stages of the project is too great to be recorded in words.

Colin Leys and Marguerite Mendell

Capitalism, Socialism, Culture and Social Movements

The meaning and the prospects of the socialist project at the end of the twentieth century in both Québec and Ontario raises fundamental questions. The necessary information required for such an investigation can be found by exploring the interplay of culture and structure in the politics of some of the most important social movements — the labour movement, the women's movement, the ecology movement and religious movements. It is not proposed that a definitive conclusion is expected to be found within the experiences of these particular social movements occurring in the early 1990s; however, for advanced industrial countries such as Canada, the answers to the question of what, if anything, can or must replace capitalism can hardly be looked for elsewhere than in such movements and the interaction between them.

This is not to say that the different kinds of movements occurring in other parts of the world — be they national, religious, socialist, or other — have not also had a profound impact on determining the content of a new anti-capitalist, post-capitalist project. Nor are the more progressive political parties (including social democratic and green parties) in countries such as Canada irrelevant, for they too, are based in social movements. All of these various movements contribute to the understanding and to the formulating of socialism's future. The meaning and the prospects of socialism have become problematic as a result of both fundamental social changes and specific political experiences; it seems unlikely that a new project can be expected to emerge otherwise than through reflection on the experiences of these movements and the challenges they pose to previous patterns of thought.

RETHINKING SOCIALISM

Three main attitudes towards socialism are possible in the 1990s. The first is that the socialist project inherited from the late nineteenth century remains by and large as valid as ever, in spite of both Stalinist deformations and social-democratic compromises. Most of the old or "revolutionary" left in the advanced capitalist countries and in the underdeveloped countries adhere to this general position. The second attitude is based on the belief that the project is definitively over, discredited and *dépassé*. The international capitalist class and the media they own adopt this attitude, as does a large part of the intelligentsia in Eastern Europe and the USSR. Those who take on the third attitude believe that the need to solve the acute human problems posed by capitalism remains as strong as ever; but that the modern development of capitalism on the one hand, and the experience of "actually existing socialisms" on the other, have made it necessary to rethink, in a more or less radical fashion, what "socialism" now *means*, what needs to be accomplished, and what tactics should be employed to achieve these goals.

It is from this last perspective that this book has been written. The authors do not believe that capitalism, organised on a global scale and increasingly free from effective political control, is compatible with civilised life. Like Karl Polanyi, they are convinced that the "self-regulating" market, which controls almost all societies, inexorably and continuously transforms and destroys the societies and the natural environments in which it operates.

Polanyi argued that the West had twice confronted the threat posed by the "self-regulating market," and had twice organised countermovements to operate it in the interest of a stable, tolerably egalitarian, humane and liberal social order. The first of these countermovements occurred in the 1880s and 1890s, and the second, after the bitter experience of the Slump, in the "Keynesian Welfare State," developed during and after World War II.[1] Today, the restraints have once again been largely cast off, at a time when capital is organised transnationally to a degree that increasingly outstrips the regulative reach of any supranational agency, not to mention all national ones. Although it is probable that capital can increase production in the USSR and in the countries of Eastern Europe, such an occurrence would most likely also create new problems of inequality, social dislocation, unemployment, and new forms of powerlessness.

The advanced capitalist countries are also experiencing menacing strains: "good" new jobs are not being created,[2] and fewer people have full-time, well-paid work with good holidays, pensions and other benefits; the income and welfare provided by the State is also increasingly said to be an unaffordable burden on production and revenues, and to be a handicap in competition with other countries which provide even less. In the USA itself, average real incomes have been falling for more than a decade and they show no promise of improving.[3] As a result, inner-city, ethnic, gender and other forms of deprivation are unlikely to be seriously reduced.

Moreover, the decline of public schooling, and the displacement of reading by increasingly commercially-oriented television, is reducing the capability of the majority in the "advanced" capitalist countries to take part in political and cultural life other than as spectators. Instead, they are increasingly absorbed in a shallow and alienated culture of consumption which is essentially a loss of citizenship, of a sense of individual efficacy in social decision-making. Fundamental human needs and values are debated less and less in the context of social and political choices. The boundaries of the personal sphere of efficacy shrink, while the world of "politics" and "the economy" has become the increasingly distant domain of professional politicians, economists and technocrats.

The process is also encouraged by a culture which attributes to the sciences, particularly to economics, a privileged understanding of reality, and a mythic objectivity and neutrality. In the world of science and technology, there is no place for the systematic posing of questions of morality and social values. Such issues are generally left to be posed, after frequently irreversible decisions have been made, by "outside" groups of so-called "dissenters" and "protesters," whose status is clearly revealed by their labels alone. These issues are then left to become perhaps nothing more than the subject of pseudo-authoritative media "investigations."

Indeed, the most powerful aspect of the once again dominant ideology of the market is the popular belief that there is no choice, that there is no alternative to the economic and growth- and profit-orientated tech-nocratic policies being pursued by States everywhere. "Morality" and "choice" are instead increasingly left to the realm of television evangelism and soap operas, in both of which they are above all presented as being *personal* topics. This privatisation of moral issues increases peoples' burden of guilt and responsibility for the problems of existence, while inhibiting their ability either to understand or to solve them. Problems such as poverty, loneliness, violence and drug-abuse are automatically referred to the sphere of individual choice, an approach energetically promoted by neoconservative parties and governments. President Bush demonstrated this attitude with his short-lived "crusade" against drugs.

Exceptions exist, generally due to disasters such as Three Mile Island, Chernobyl, or AIDS. These may permit "outsiders," such as those mobilised in the "new social movements," to temporarily play a part in policy deter-mination. However, the women's movement's message that the personal *is* political, or the ecology movement's themes of democratisation, decentralisation and self-determination, have generally not yet made many inroads into a power-structure for which these ideas are really anathema, even though official rhetoric may say otherwise.

> As for the rest of the world, the poor and forsaken are still condemned to live in a world of terrible injustices, crushed by unreachable and apparently unchangeable economic magnates on which the political authorities, even when formally democratic, nearly always depend. In such a world, the idea that the hope of revolution is spent...is to close one's eyes so as not to see. Are the democracies that govern the world's richest countries capable of solving the problems that communism has failed to solve?...Democracy, let us admit it, has overcome the challenge of

historical communism. But what means and what ideals does it
have to confront the very problems out of which the communist
challenge was born?[4]

Those who are unwilling to treat this question as purely rhetorical dare
not minimise the difficulty of answering it. Many of the ideas of the
orthodox Marxist tradition have been severely discredited, and not merely
by association with Stalinist dogma, bureaucratic inefficiency and repression. "Revisionists" sympathetic to Marx's aims, such as Alec Nove or Jon
Elster, have identified serious gaps and dangerously utopian assumptions
in his thought.[5] Also, at a practical level, fundamental contradictions and
weaknesses have become evident in some central ideas of socialism, such
as collective ownership and control of production, State-provided welfare
(housing, transport, education), State macro-economic management and
income redistribution. Problems have also been exposed in the idea of
political centralisation as a means of offsetting private economic power,
and in the idea that national, regional, gender, ethnic, religious and other
particular identities can and should be subordinated to that of Socialist
Man or Woman. Indeed, a multitude of additional problems contribute to
the creation of a very long list that shows little hope of being shortened: the
classic agencies of collective action, the labour movement and the mass
party, have lost their original vitality, which was based on active mass
memberships and the devotion of large voluntary cadres.[6] It is hard to
envisage the forms which a movement for major social reform and transformation might now take.

Although capitalism shows no signs of being able to solve this increasingly intractable list of problems, the socialist approach is far from being as
wholly negative as current neoliberal triumphalism proclaims it to be.
Nevertheless, the challenge remains, and it is not simply a question of
arriving at new solutions. The scale and complexity of the problems, not to
mention the rapidity of the transformations produced by contemporary
technology as a result of continuous shifts in corporate competitive
strategies, makes the idea of a new socialist "programme" premature if not
positively anachronistic. As Laurie Adkin says in chapter five of this book,
it is not even clear that the word "socialism" can any longer denote or
connote the essential shifts that are called for:

> Rethinking socialism could even mean re-thinking everything
> that we ever meant by this idea, with a view to transcending it, not
> just revamping it; at the least it means recognising that there will
> be 'many socialisms,' reflecting the diversity of people, of cultures
> and their corresponding individual histories and institutions.[7]

This does not suggest the validity of the "rejection of class theory," the
idea that distinctive social classes are formed by capitalism and play crucial
roles in politics. However, it does suggest rejecting the idea that only

classes play crucial roles — an idea that could only have seemed plausible at a very particular juncture of Western European history. As Polanyi wrote almost half a century ago, "actually class interests offer only a limited explanation of long-run movements in society...The fate of classes is much more often determined by the needs of society than the fate of society is determined by the needs of classes...."[8] This book studies the interplay of class and non-class social movements from this perspective.

THE CULTURAL DIMENSION OF MODERN CAPITALISM

One of the issues that confronts any attempt to address the problems presented by capitalism in an industrialised country such as Canada is the analytic weakness of the Marxian tradition with regard to "culture." Capitalism has not mutated into something else; on the contrary, its current extension to all quarters of the earth, its steady transformation into commodities of activities that were formerly outside, or only partially subordinated to its logic ("services"), and its increasingly rapid substitution of science and technology for living labour (productivity increases), all conform perfectly to Marx's understanding of its natural history. However, the contemporary forms of consciousness produced by capitalism in the West, and its deepest psychological effects — in short, its cultural dimension — lie beyond the scope of Marx's vision. Except for the Frankfurt School, Marxists have paid little attention to how the logic of capitalist development meshes or conflicts with logics of behaviour stemming from other dimensions of human life, such as emotions, spirituality, familiality, sexuality, intellect, and so on. These alternative dimensions could never change as fast as a mode of production, perhaps they are even completely static.

The orthodox tradition derived from the Second International was especially reductionist in this sense, as it tended to treat culture as "a decorative addendum to the 'hard world' of production and things, the icing on the cake of the material world.!"[9] This was curious, given the early German Social Democrats' exemplary attention to the development of a socialist culture for the German working class, and the rich cultural backgrounds of so many of its leaders; but certainly the tendency was to consider culture as causally derivative from the social relations of "material production." To think otherwise was to risk being "idealistic."

A variety of reasons have now caused the study of culture to become a major preoccupation for the left, one of them being that political life in countries of advanced technology has become overly dependent on and conducted through visual media. Another is that contemporary production and marketing strategies involve plucking the sub-cultures out of the mass culture, or at least of taking just enough cultural signs from particular groups of potential consumers to constitute profitable market "niches."[10] The result is that media advertising (for which the information or entertainment offered is intended primarily to create audiences, not the other way round) more and more deliberately *makes* culture, rather than merely seeking to exploit it: art imitating life imitating art has become normal. In this situation, treating culture as marginal, or as a mere epiphenomenon of "material forces," is more impossible that ever.

A further reason, which should be compelling to the most die-hard "materialist," is that not only has the production of information and images become the fastest growing industry; material production itself has become increasingly dependent on science and technology — which are self-evidently not themselves simple consequences of previous production, but vary critically from country to country on account of factors which, based on any definition of the term, are *cultural*.

An influential group of theorists, many of them former socialists, have of course gone further. According to Lyotard, Derrida, Baudrillard and others, we who live in the industrial West are now living in a "postmodern" society in which the idea of collective action by unified historical subjects (for example, by people who consistently think and act so as to achieve a particular set of goals) no longer convinces or works because it no longer corresponds to reality (if it ever did). The idea of a "metanarrative" such as socialism, purporting to interpret all of history in the light of the universal criteria of progress is, according to this view, a mistake, and has lost its power to arouse popular action. This is unfortunate for those who do not feel satisfied with the status quo: as Sabina Lovibond says, "how can anyone ask me to say goodbye to 'emancipatory metanarratives' when my own emancipation [as a woman] is still such a patchy, hit-and-miss affair?"[11] It is even more unfortunate for those in less developed countries who, so far from being emancipated, are hungry, unemployed, oppressed and hopeless.

It is not the intent of this book to discuss the significance of the current power and excitement concerning the post-structuralist school of thought to which the postmodernist thesis belongs. We can only register the critical distance which it seems to us necessary to adopt in relation to it. It is, first, not a social-scientific tendency, but a philosophy, a doctrine, that denies the possibility of having a scientific understanding of social (not to mention global) reality; it specifically denies that it makes sense to speak of "a reality" in the sense in which social science seeks to understand it. Postmodernism may be understood only as an ideology, a way of grasping the world as it is experienced, a way that may be penetrating and useful, but one that more or less fails to acknowledge its own social determination and which is therefore contradictory, incomplete and problematic. In addition, the social determinants of this ideology are not hard to seek: they evidently lie in the way contemporary life in the advanced capitalist countries affects, above all, the intellectual strata to which postmodernist thinkers belong.

In many respects the "reading" of contemporary life under advanced capitalism which the postmodernist literature puts forward is compelling — the "waning of affect," historical amnesia, the commodification of art, the hyperreality of media-mediated public and aesthetic life, and so on. However, from none of this is it necessary to conclude, as these theorists have tended to suggest, that the idea of a unified historical subject is no longer meaningful, that universalistic ideals are at best illusory and at worst "terroristic," and that collective action for social change is impossible. Both the basis on which these claims rest — impressionistic but sweeping assertions about social life, and declaratory interpretations of them — and the arcane forms of expression in which they are often couched, should make us aware of their ideological nature.

Two hypotheses suggest themselves in this regard. One is that intellectuals, especially in academia, have largely lost the influence they seemed to enjoy during the rise and ascendancy of social democracy. In the age of neoliberalism and the already virtually unconstrained operation across national boundaries of multinational corporate capital, we no longer have even the illusion that our work or ideas are practically influential. The social democratic parties are largely out of office and, in the effort to regain office, have swallowed a large part of the neoliberal creed. It is also clear that any national government, of any political stripe, has less and less effective power to affect the prime determinants of the national well-being. The impotence which post-modernism presents as a general feature of the human condition is in this sense a real phenomenon of recent political life, and one especially painful to erstwhile progressive social scientists and social philosophers.

The second hypothesis is at a more abstract level: it is that the condition to which post-modernism responds, in its critique or celebration of the depthless, historyless, alienated life-world of contemporary consumer society, is the beginning of that very *dissolution of society* by the "self-regulating" market of which Polanyi wrote. It is the expression, in the form of an ideology of human impotence, of the progressive dissolution of what is local, historical, personal, comprehensible and authentic in our lives, as market forces are allowed relentlessly to remake our jobs, our cities, our tastes, our family structures, even our language, at ever-increasing speed. This is occurring to the point where it is no longer merely true that our world is utterly different from that in which our parents grew up, it is almost as different from that in which we grew up ourselves. And even more than this, it is a world in which the alienation which Hegel and Marx first grasped as the hall-mark of bourgeois society is becoming rapidly total — in Polanyi's words, "a social dislocation of stupendous proportions."[12] In other words, what postmodernists present as the human condition may well be the first stage of the experience of the dissolution of society in the countries of advanced capitalism, as artists and filmmakers and architects and other intellectuals see and feel it. What these people are responding to, then, is not an illusion; what must be rejected is only the pessimistic, passive and even reactionary conclusions they invite us to draw from what they see. In order to do this, however, we too must learn to operate on the terrain on which their ideas have been developed — the terrain of culture.

An indepth understanding of the concept of culture is necessary for us to accomplish this goal. The broad definition of culture proposed for anthropology by Tylor in 1871 — the "capabilities and habits acquired by man (sic) as a member of society" — might seem at first sight too all-encompassing (apart, that is, from its implicit exclusion of women...).[13] On the other hand it is narrower than some contemporary conceptualisations which see culture as the ideational dimension of all human practices. For anthropologists, at least in the 1950s, culture was not "behaviour in all its concrete completeness" but consisted only of the norms and standards of behaviour, ideologies justifying or rationalising behaviour, general principles of selectivity or ordering in terms of which patterns of behaviour are reducible to "parsimonious generalisation."[14] Culture was also *learned* behaviour, embodied in patterns of varying degrees of "primacy," from such "basic" and long-lived patterns as the alphabet, plough agriculture, monotheism or gender identities, to more secondary and more easily changed patterns such as constitutions or fashions. At a given moment culture is, in this view, "a precipitate of the history of a particular group;" of its past choices, conscious or unconscious. "Culture is this precipitate present in persons, shaping their perceptions of events, other persons, and the environing situation in ways not wholly determined by biology and environmental press. Culture is the intervening variable between the human "organism" and the "environment."[15]

This definition of culture includes *economic* life, the "production of goods and things" which, according to this view, is firmly embedded in society's cultural norms. The economy is a "cultural design of persons and goods," a symbolic system in which no object has any meaning outside the cultural significance assigned to it, in which needs themselves are culturally defined. The observation by contemporary students of advanced capitalist societies that we consume *symbols* as much as products has long been recognized not only by anthropologists, who have explained the cultural resistance to modernity in non-capitalist society, but by development economists fully aware of the need to destroy such resistance, a resistance to the threatened "liquidation of every and any cultural institution in an organic society."[16] To acknowledge that "the elemental force of culture contact which revolutionized the colonial world, is the same which, a century ago, created the dismal scenes of early capitalism," is also to recognise the cultural annihilation being wrought by contemporary capitalism in the advanced societies of the West.

However, it is one thing to recognise the centrality of "culture" in social change, another to decide how to theorise its relationship to social "structures." The so-called "pattern theory" of cultural anthropology did not "decide in advance which aspects of culture and society are most likely to form basic patterns — they may be matters of religion, technological invention, or ideas," and allowed for "cultural drift," such as changes in culture arising from causes internal to it.[17] In opposition, social anthropologists following Malinowski and Radcliffe-Brown held that so-cial relations had "basic explanatory value."

In spite of the ambiguity of some of the language used, the parallel with the debate between historical materialism and its opponents is clear enough: "the pattern theory subordinates social structure to culture, and the structural theory reverses the subordination."[18] Many anthropologists, it seems, have tended to settle for interdependence, with an agnostic attitude on the issue of priority; this is also perhaps the dominant tendency among those working in the Marxist tradition today. Although the sphere of culture, consciousness and ideology is seen as ultimately more depend-ent on the dominant relations of material production than the other way around, it is not merely an automatic reflector, and does have significant influence. Marx and Engels insisted, "Empirical observation must in each separate instance bring out empirically, and without any mystification and speculation, the connection of the social and political structure with production."[19] A good case can be made for saying that they took the same open-minded view of the connection between all of these and culture, or consciousness.[20] With regards to this view we need to discover, in any given situation, just how "cultural factors" interact with the "economic movement" (to adopt Engels's terminology in his famous letter to Conrad Schmidt of 1890) in order to work out how to bring about social change.

Post-structuralists consider the problem, as it has been outlined in the preceding paragraphs, to be false. There are no structures, to be contrasted with cultures; to have meaning, all behaviour involves participation in some system of signs, of which language is the most complex kind. The meanings of signs are given by the differences between the signifiers, not by their relationships to the real world.[21] Therefore, all human behaviour, insofar as it has meaning, has a "textual" as well as a material (or physical) nature; and insofar as it is the object of any reflection, this dimension is linguistic (for example, it could have meaning through a purely non-lin-guistic system of signification, such as music, but insofar as we have knowledge or even ideas *about* it, this knowledge of these ideas require language). To speak, then, of any pattern of behaviour as constituting a "structure" cannot mean that it is not also linguistic, let alone that it has some extra-linguistic grounding in reality that makes it somehow prior to, or more ultimate than, any other behaviour. Conversely, to characterise any behaviour as "cultural" cannot mean that it is less material, let alone less grounded in "reality" than any other. All behaviour is both material and linguistic, and if any of it is more enduring than any other it is not because it is more "material."

According to this view, the problem of analyzing the relationship between structure and culture is falsely posed. It is not a question of explaining the puzzling fact that patterns of behaviour which seem primarily mental, conceptual, linguistic, or the like, do not always, or perhaps ever, behave as pure epiphenomena of other patterns that appear to be primarily material. Instead, they often seem to offer, as a minimum, a good deal of "resistance" to the latter (the false problem posed by Marxists, or structural anthropologists). Nor is it a question of explaining the reverse — for example, how social structures are governed or determined by people's cultures, or systems of belief (the false problem posed by the pattern theory anthropologists). Rather, the dichotomy of "structure" and "culture" should be abandoned. In its place we must put a problematic of "discourses," in which all material practices occur, and ask in respect of each of them what their relations are to other "adjacent" discourses, what pressures they exert on each other that bring about changes.

Thus instead of asking how, for instance, the "national culture" of either Québec, feminism or ecologism, affects the "structure" of trade unionism, we should ask how the discourse of industrial organization and these other discourses intersect with each other, in a way that is simultaneously material and conceptual. Although this may at first appear to be less simple than the structuralist problematic, we should remember that the problem of all the structuralist approaches is that they tend to founder in long lists of exceptions and residual elements. These lists resist inclusion in all theories which seek to classify, in effect, some patterns or domains of behaviour as structures and others as cultures, and which understand their relations in terms of the dominance of the one sort over the other. In addition, we should reflect that the post-structuralist approach can be empowering: discourses are fields for ideological-material *action*, for what Laclau and Mouffe call "hegemonic articulations."

In connection with this view, accepting that the trade union movement, or even something as apparently "fundamental" as the prevailing pattern of family life, is a discourse like any other field of meaningful behaviour, may seem to "demote" it from the somehow superior status of a "structure." However, attributing the status of "structure" to the trade union movement or the family has not guaranteed either of them any noticeable immunity to erosion and weakening, and nothing is lost by giving it up. In a different way though, acknowledging that what used to be thought of as cultural is always also material, and vice versa, widens the options for possible intervention. It is no longer necessary to think, for instance, that the interests of workers can be defended only by protecting the "structures" of trade union organization against erosion by changes in the surrounding "culture;" one might instead be ready to accept quite drastic changes in the discourse (and hence the practices) of trade unionism, while also putting serious effort into bringing about critical changes (for workers' interests) in the discourse (and hence practices) of nationalism, ecologism, feminism, an so on.

While the post-structuralist position is epistemologically plausible it remains to be seen whether it is compatible with the requirements of practical and collective political action. Most critics have felt at least a severe tension between the two, and post-structuralist theorists have not been notable for their engagement in collective projects for political change, even if it is a mistake to represent them (as some opponents have) as *ipso facto* nihilists or reactionaries. We must continue to try to think and to act with the conceptual tools we have. Most people still use the terms "structures" and "cultures" to refer, roughly speaking, to domains in which the linguistic/ideational dimension is respectively less and more palpable; and since, in order to act politically, we need general causal theories of some sort (in order to decide what to act upon), a general conceptualisation of this kind may not be inappropriate, provided we do not reify what we choose to consider "structural," and overlook the materiality of what we choose to call "cultural."[22]

With respect to this book, this might be summed up by saying that the socialist project has always implied the possibility of subordinating the relations of *production* to relations of *politics* which are self-evidently profoundly *cultural*. In any given country capitalist development involves the reorganization of relations of production, which entails replacing the culture (for example, the ideas and values) that formed part of the old relations of production with the supremacy of the market; the same is true for any post-capitalist project. If we do not think the supremacy of the market is ultimately compatible with any tolerable form of social life, the development of a new culture (new discourse/practices) embodying this refusal, and displaying the culture of capitalism, is essential. In short we must accept that "culture," however conceptualised, is a crucial terrain of political thought and action.

It must be noted that this book does not presuppose any of the analyses currently on offer which suggest a particular line of response to the current moment of capitalist reconstruction. The "radical democracy" school, for example, that looks to a "plurality" of "popular-democratic" subjects — women, youth, gays, blacks, muslims, ecologists, etc — to transform society through a plethora of interlinked struggles for the democratisation of all spheres of life, including economic life, may have merit.[23] However, the general standpoint of this book is more agnostic. It is that an important mutation of capitalism has certainly been occurring, in the context of a major political defeat for anti-capitalist forces in both the West and the East; that the immediate task is to support, but at the same time to try to learn from, the experience of the organisations and movements, old and new, that have been most active in the resistance to capitalism and reaction in this period; and that this needs to be done with particular attention to the role of culture, considered as both "products of action and conditioning elements of further action."[24]

OLD AND NEW SOCIAL MOVEMENTS

A new social project, adequate to the challenge posed by capitalism at the end of the twentieth century, cannot be expected to emerge otherwise than from the experience of both the older progressive social movements and their organisations (above all labour unions and socialist parties), and the new social movements that have emerged in Western societies since the late 1960s. In describing and analyzing the new social movements in their relation to older ones, Claus Offe's work is in a class of its own, and provides the essential context for the studies that form the empirical focus of this book.[25] Offe shows conclusively that the "new social movements" (in particular, the ecology movement; the feminist and other human rights movements based on sex, race, age, language, religion, etc; the pacificist and peace movements; and movements for alternative ways of producing and distributing goods) were not, as many social scientists maintained, manifestations of anomic behaviour on the part of marginal, nostalgic, pre-modern and deviant groups. On the contrary, they have been predominantly initiated and led by elements of the most "modern" strata in contemporary industrial society, the service sector and public sector "new middle class." Moreover, they offer a modern and highly rational critique of modernisation, which appeals most powerfully to two other social categories which are particularly affected by the most recent manifestations of modernisation: "peripheral" or "decommodified" groups such as students and single parents, and other clients of the bureaucratic State; and some elements of the old middle class, such as farmers, who are particularly affected by the reach, penetration and seeming irresponsibility of the modern State.

While Offe does not doubt that the new identities and sensibilities formed under late capitalism provide some of the impetus for the formation of the new social movements, he argues that their origin is primarily to be sought in the limitations of the "old" political "paradigm" developed under social democracy, the Keynesian welfare State. The key to this paradigm was the incorporation of the working class into the official system of State management of the economy, in return for limiting its objectives to strictly economic matters, and its channels of self-expression to specialised representative organisations based on hierarchy and control. This, however, left private capital largely in control of the sphere of civil society, while failing to provide any legitimate channels for popular control. The new social movements, consequently, came into being to

> claim a type of issue for themselves, one that is neither 'private'... nor 'public'...but which consists in collectively 'relevant' side-effects of either private or institutional-political actors for which these actors, however, cannot be held responsible or made responsive by legal or institutional means.[26]

The new social movements are distinguished by their refusal of internal specialisation and hierarchy, and their parallel refusal to abide by the established political "rules of the game," or to work through the established political institutions which they see as the source of the problem. They also lack a specific class character, either in their composition or in their goals. They protest, they demand, they reject compromise, and they refuse also to see any one "field" or arena of social conflict as fundamental or primary, as in the orthodox Marxist conception: they do not believe that there is only one way in which the course of history can be changed.

These characteristics, and especially the ability to tolerate a wide variety of beliefs and attitudes among their members, through focusing on single issues and through having at most a rudimentary system of membership and other organisational rules, combines with several trends of modern capitalism, Offe believes, to give the new social movements a strong chance of growth and durability. In this respect they stand in sharp contrast with the older social movements, especially the labour movement, which are being undermined by the current processes of capitalist restructuring.[27] Offe even speculates that the prospects of continuing growth for the new movements, arising from the inherent tendencies of modern capitalism (to marginalise former workers, to alienate and to control new groups, and to pose catastrophic threats to social values and even survival which States and party politics show no signs of being able to identify and avert), parallel the growth prospects of the proletariat in the nineteenth century, which gave hope and weight to the emerging organisations of the working class at that time.

Be that as it may, the evidence continues to support Offe's general analysis. It is impossible to think about a new post-capitalist project without focusing as much on the new social movements as on the old. As Offe himself notes, however, the new social movements, in spite of their continued importance (which the recent neoliberal backlash has underlined as much as it has checked), have not yet formulated, let alone initiated, a collective project of general social change. In most cases these movements lack "a coherent set of ideological principles and interpretations of the world from which an image of a desirable arrangement of society could be derived and the steps toward transformation could be deduced."[28] It seems likely that this will have to be the work of individuals and groups connected to these movements, and so capable of drawing on their insights and their ethical and emotional strengths — which are those of some of the best educated and most perceptive members of their societies — yet also standing, for this purpose, somewhat outside them.[29]

It is also improbable that the "old paradigm" of politics can be overcome without an *alliance*, and perhaps ultimately a fusion, with elements drawn from the older social movements as well as the new. Here again, Offe has succinctly charted the ground: the need for an alliance between the new social movements (the "new paradigm") and elements in the "older" left, capable of detaching themselves from the limitations of the old paradigm, transcending its horizons. As Offe points out, the pressure to try to "restore growth" (and hence employment) in face of the crisis facing advanced capitalist countries under the global restructuring (relocation and robotisation) of capital is all too likely to pull the labour movement and the social-democratic parties back into the "old paradigm." The result is that an alliance with the new social movements, and a transformation of the "new paradigm" into a force capable of radical change, is frustrated.[30]

However, if enough elements in progressive political parties are themselves drawn towards the new social movements and their agendas; if the "crisis" is revealed as too endemic and deep for a "normalisation" of the old type to seem any longer possible; and if the ideologies of the new social movements strike a chord in the "folk memories" of the old left, re-awakening their engagement with the radical humanistic vision that animated them in the formative years of the working class; on these conditions an alliance, or fusion, around a new collective project is possible.[31]

Some people (including several contributors to this volume) argue that this is actually occurring and that Offe's fear that this tendency may be reversed in the face of economic crisis is misplaced: working class communities have changed, and a new balance of social forces is unlikely to formulate its demands in terms which do not reflect this new social reality. The restructuring of capital has contributed to a fragmentation of the working class itself whose social, political and cultural space has moved beyond the shop floor.[32] Conversely, as David Plotke points out, those who interpret new social movements and the broader issues which they address as a "post-materialist" response to primarily "cultural" deprivations do not recognize the extent to which these groups, however diverse, are a response to the failure of traditional social democratic parties and the labour movement to secure or protect quite basic *material* needs of people (women, blacks, gays, and many others) who were essentially ignored by the politics of the "old paradigm."[33] Moreover, their struggles have been highly *political*: in spite of their tendency to reject the established political process and its boundaries,

> ...they become involved with the national and local state, with legislatures and courts, with all the routine forms of political decision-making...The pure movements of (cultural) resistance, for which politics means only the affirmation of identity against intrusion, could not really last for long.[34]

According to this view, then, the gulf between the new and the old social movements is less wide than the *discourses* of either have been apt to suggest. On the one hand, the social bases of the old movements are being penetrated and their consciousness is being restructured in ways that make them much more prone to remobilisation around the characteristic themes of the new movements; on the other hand, the new social movements are increasingly forced to confront the need for a more systematic conception of politics. A "radical democratic pluralism" is being sought within this convergence, one which would strengthen the various social movements involved through "durable alliances," that would nonetheless resist becoming hegemonised by any one element in these alliances.

One may wonder how far this perspective is wishful thinking; how far it presents as already happening what is really only one among other possibilities at the present time; whether, without "any means of subsuming diverse objectives and self-conceptions in an enduring [ideological and organisational] unity" (such as a political party),[35] it is possible to imagine overcoming the global power of private capital, transcending its "cruel, destructive" logic as the driving force of social change. Nonetheless it is on this terrain, this field of interaction and struggle, that the question must be worked out; and it is this terrain, therefore, that is explored in the chapters which follow.

* * *

In the current triumphalist discourse of the right, traditional left politics — from Marxism through social democracy to anarchism — are no more than history. However, any informed and serious reflection strongly suggests, on the contrary, the increasing relevance of these different critiques of capitalist development, which are less incompatible with each other than dogmatic and sectarian exponents of them were inclined to believe in the past. How far the legacy of established schools of thought contains theortical elements necessary to a renewed socialist project is the concern of the first two chapters in the book.

Turning to the social movements themselves, a number of central themes are apparent in every sector. How fast and easily have the "old" social movements, above all, the trade union movement, been adapting to the rapidly changing situation at the end of the century? In the first place, they are confronted with radical and adverse changes due to the global restructuring of capital, free trade, and a new onslaught by management and neoliberal governments on their past gains. On the other hand, they are being forced to adapt to a range of competing demands from new social movements. How readily are the unions responding to the concerns of women? How easily has the traditional strategy of bargaining for wages and job security been adapted to encompass concerns of the environmental movement? In the face of all these stresses, a key question is how far the unions can be expected to develop the capacity to create the new social identities that are needed if an effective resistance is to be offered to the growing destruction of society by the market.

As for the new social movements, how far are we dealing with "single issue" groups that tend to dissolve once "their" demands are met, or once "their" dissenting discourse becomes incorporated or coopted by the dominant social forces and the State? How far are the new social movements genuinely empowering people in their workplaces, at home or in other collective spaces in such a way as to generate a new political culture, a "paradigm shift" which carries forward many of the values of the old left but is free from some of its constraining practices and assumptions?

The authors do not minimise the problems faced by the movements they describe, such as the divisions within the feminist movement over the national question in Québec, for example, or the tension between militancy and cooptation caused by State policies in the field of social services, for the urban and community movements.

Significant differences are apparent between Québec and Ontario with respect to a number of these issues. An interesting one concerns the role of progressive movements within the Churches. In Québec, the small but effective left opposition within the Catholic Church has succeeded in maintaining close ties with secular popular movements, whereas, in Ontario the inter-Church coalition, a much larger movement, appears to be threatened by the fact that it feels increasingly obliged to speak out on domestic problems, as opposed to those of the Third World. It is also striking that this pan-Canadian movement based in Ontario lacks a francophone component, despite the formal representation of the Catholic Church. On the other hand, the experience of urban political activists in the two provinces reveals a significant common pattern of response on the part of metropolitan governments which have tried to absorb the growing power of popular and community movements by adopting their democratic discourse while robbing them of any real power. The fact that these movements have understood this is an important step in their own development.

It is hard to read the chapters which follow without being convinced of the gradual, if sometimes painful, emergence of an increasingly coherent shared set of ideas and strategies transcending the various sectors of activism and struggle in Québec and Ontario. Some authors are optimistic and see the tensions between old strategies and practices and the need for new social and political practices as creative. Others, a minority, are less optimistic in face of the strength of the political forces disposed of by capital. However, one cannot read these chapters without being impressed by the energy and resilience currently displayed by the diverse movements described.

The question remains, however, whether the vitality and creativity of these movements, and their capacity to break down longstanding barriers between "old" and "new" movements are grounds for hope and optimism as the force and scale of globalization undermines new and old strategies at every level — international, national and local. Whichever stance we adopt, the culture of opposition represented by these movements must be taken seriously.

February, 1992

NOTES

1. Polanyi, Karl. *The Great Transformation.* Boston: Beacon Press, 1944.
2. *Good Jobs, Bad Jobs: Employment in the Service Economy,* Economic Council of Canada, Ottawa 1990.
3. Real weekly earnings in the private sector fell by 15% over the years 1972 (the historic peak) to 1988 (US Department of Labour, Bureau of Labour Statistics, *Handbook of Labour Statistics,* Washington 1989).
4. Norberto Bobbio, "The Upturned Utopia," *New Left Review* 177, September-October 1989, 38-39.
5. Elster, John. *Making Sense of Marx.* Cambridge: Cambridge University Press, 1985.
6. See e.g. Sarah Benton, "The Decline of the Party" in S. Hall and M. Jacques, eds., *New Times,* Lawrence and Wishart, London 1989, 333-46.
7. Raymond Williams, "Towards Many Socialisms," in Milós Nicolié. *Socialism on the Threshold of the Twenty-first Century.* London: Verso, 1985. pp. 294-311.
8. Op.cit., 152.
9. Stuart Hall, "The Meaning of New Times," in Hall and Jacques, op. cit., 128.
10. Frank Mort, "The Politics of Consumption," in Hall and Jacques, op. cit., 128.
11. "Feminism and postmodernism," *New Left Review* 178, November-December 1989, 12.
12. *The Great Transformation,* 129.
13. Quoted in Milton Singer, "The Concept of Culture," in *International Encyclopedia of the Social Sciences,* Vol. 3, 527.
14. Kroeber and Kluckhohn, quoted in Singer, loc. cit., 528.
15. Ibid., 530.
16. Polanyi, op.cit., 159.
17. Singer, loc.cit., 533.
18. Singer, loc.cit., 534.
19. Marx and Engels, *The German Ideology,* International Publishers, New York 1947, 18.
20. Derek Sayer, *The Violence of Abstraction,* Blackwell, Oxford 1987, Chs. 1 and 4.
21. For an excellent exposition of the implications of the "Saussurean" revolution in linguistics see Catherine Belsey, *Critical Practice.* London: Methuen, 1980. It should be noted that the epistemological position resulting from this line of thought does not entail the view that there is no such thing as a "reality out there," nor the view that the "fit" between a system of signs composing a particular discourse, such as an economic theory, and the reality experienced by people in their daily lives, is of no consequence. It does, however, imply that reality is "compatible" with many different, mutually incompatible discourses; and that what counts as "compatible" is also given by a discourse.
22. On the necessity of "causal" thinking for political action, and the implications for this of a poststructuralist position, see the exchange between John Dunn and Gayatri Spivak in Spivak, G.C. "The Post-modern Condition: The End of Politics?," *The Postcolonial Critics.* S. Havasym (ed) New York: Routledge, 1990. pp. 17-34, especially 22-23.
23. See especially Ernesto Laclau and Chantal Mouffe, *Hegemony and Socialist Strategy,* Verso, London 1985, and John Keane, *Democracy and Civil Society,* Verso, London 1988.
24. Kroeber and Kluckhohn, quoted in Singer, loc. cit., 528.
25. Claus Offe, "New Social Movements: Challenging the Boundaries of Institutional Politics," *Social Research* Vol. 52, No. 4, Winter 1985, 817-68.
26. Ibid., 826.
27. Ibid., 838.
28. Ibid., 831.
29. Ibid., 851.
30. Ibid., 865-66.
31. Ibid., 866-67.
32. Lash, S and J. Urry, *Disorganised Capitalism.* Cambridge: Polity Press, 1987. p. 219.

33.   David Plotke, "What's So New About New Social Movements?," *Socialist Review* No. 1, 1990, 81-102.
34.   Loc. cit., 101.
35.   Ibid.

REFERENCES

Belsey, Catherine. *Critical Practice*. London: Methuen, 1980.

Benton, Sarah. "The Decline of the Party" in S. Hall and M. Jacques, eds. *New Times*. London: Lawrence and Wishart, 1989.

Claus Offe. "New Social Movements: Challenging the Boundaries of Institutional Politics," *Social Research*. Vol. 52, No. 4, Winter 1985.

David Plotke. "What's So New About New Social Movements?", *Socialist Review*. No. 1, 1990.

Economic Council of Canada. *Good Jobs, Bad Jobs: Employment in the Service Economy*. Ottawa 1990.

Elster, John. *Making Sense of Marx*. Cambridge: Cambridge University Press, 1985.

Keane, John. *Democracy and Civil Society*. London: Verso, 1988.

Laclau, Ernesto and Chantal Mouffe. *Hegemony and Socialist Strategy*. London: Verso, 1985.

Lash, S and J. Urry. *Disorganised Capitalism*. Cambridge: Polity Press, 1987.

Lovibond, Sabina. "Feminism and Postmodernism," *New Left Review* 178, November-December 1989, 12.

Marx, K and F. Engels. *The German Ideology*. New York: International Publishers, 1947.

Norberto Bobbio, "The Upturned Utopia," *New Left Review*. 177, September-October 1989.

Polanyi, Karl. *The Great Transformation*. Boston: Beacon Press, 1944.

Sayer, Derek. *The Violence of Abstraction*. Oxford: Blackwell, 1987.

Singer, Milton. "The Concept of Culture," *International Encyclopedia of the Social Sciences*. Vol. 3.

Spivak, G.C. "The Post-modern Condition: The End of Politics?," *The Postcolonial Critics*. S. Havasym (ed) New York: Routledge, 1990.

Tylor, Edward B. *Primitive Culture*. Gloucester, Mass.,: Smith, 1958.

US Department of Labor, Bureau of Labor Statistics. *Handbook of Labor Statistics*. Washington 1989.

Williams, Raymond. "Towards Many Socialisms," in Milós Nicolic. *Socialism on the Threshold of the Twenty-first Century*. London: Verso, 1985.

Chapter 1

Colin Leys

MARXISM AND SOCIALISM AT THE END OF THE TWENTIETH CENTURY

It is often remarked that Marxism has been in a state of crisis since at least the death of Engels, when Edward Bernstein first declared that it had become necessary to separate what was scientifically valid in Marx's work from what was not.[1] Among Marxists it has generally been agreed that Rosa Luxemburg was an easy victor in her debate with Bernstein over his theses. She certainly was philosophically nimbler, as well as more imaginative, closer to the spirit of Marx's militancy, and a much better rhetorician. She was also right on many points where Bernstein was wrong. But taken as a whole, her polemical response was a defence of orthodoxy, as those German social democrats, who cynically embraced her stance while privately agreeing with Bernstein, fully appreciated. As capitalism undergoes another great mutation and renewal, analogous to the transition to monopoly capitalism that marked the end of the Great Depression of 1873-1895, and which precipitated Bernstein's request for a revision of Marxism, it is his call for scientificity, rather than Luxemburg's defence of faith, that deserves attention.[2]

History has exacted a heavy price for the failure to revise Marxism, for treating it as a corpus of more or less sacred texts, in which the truth can always be found, provided one has the right interpretive keys. Marxism has never had less credibility, among either intellectuals or the working class, East or West, than it has today; yet, it is precisely now, when capitalism is in the process of finally subordinating the entire world to its logic, that Marx's understanding of it is most needed. The defences that were erected, at the cost of so much suffering, against the ravages of the self-regulating market, are being dismantled; we are being asked to accept, once again, that there is no better alternative to a world driven by the needs of capital. At the same time, we are informed that a growing proportion of the population — already some ten percent — are permanently surplus to the needs of the economy in the advanced industrial countries (not to mention the rest of the world). In addition, there is every prospect that the "two-thirds society" (in which one third of the people are in one way or another condemned to insecurity and poverty) can look forward only to becoming a "one-half society," and then a "one-third society," as it is steadily exposed to the logic of competition with countries that have much lower real wage levels, and little or no welfare provision, labour rights, or political freedom. The extraordinary current dominance of capitalist ideology in the face of capitalism's growing inability to maintain real wages, employment, social services, or even the basic infrastructure in the countries where it is most advanced, let alone to offer hope of a better future, owes a great deal to Marxism's self-inflicted wounds.

THE "DESACRALISATION" OF MARXISM

History has at length accomplished what Bernstein could not: it has "desacralised" Marxism in two senses. First, the chief bastions of orthodoxy have collapsed in the USSR and Eastern Europe. Second, world history has pronounced definitive verdicts against some of Marx's central claims. In the early 1890s, when Marx had been dead for little more than a decade and Engels was still alive, it was reasonable to think that changes in world capitalism might be giving Marxism a new lease of life, while still disproving Marx's claims. Therefore, the theoretical task was only to identify the new *forms* which the struggle of the proletariat must take in order to overthrow the bourgeoisie and undertake the transition to communism.

Today, however, this response is only possible for a dwindling band of believers, not for practical people who would like to act on the world in order to change it. It is not that the contradictions of capitalism have disappeared, or the need to transcend capitalist society has diminished. It is rather that no amount of reinterpretation or qualification of Marx's texts, or infinitely ingenious resorts to "higher" modes of understanding (dialectics, structural causality, etc.) can any longer deflect the common-sense perception that a large number of Marx's central hypotheses have been disconfirmed. The social structure created by capitalism in the advanced capitalist countries has not been simplified; society has not been divided up more and more into two great opposing "camps," as Marx wrote, and several generations of activists believed. The working classes have not been absolutely immiserated in these countries but on the contrary have, in the majority, greatly increased their real incomes during capitalism's first two hundred years. Correspondingly, the workers in these countries have not been radicalised, nor have class conflicts displaced non-class conflicts. Crises of accumulation have not become more frequent and more severe, and proletarian revolution in these countries looks ever less likely than it did in Bernstein's time. Each of these propositions can be "explained away" as being inessential to the overall structure of Marx's thought, but taken together, these and many other failed predictions, which are rightly thought to be among the central tenets of Marxism, can no longer be *believed* as they once were.

Besides the verdict of history, contemporary followers of Bernstein's revisionist project have taken a hard look at the logical and theoretical weaknesses of Marx's work. I am referring particularly to the so-called "analytical" Marxists — Cohen, Elster, Roemer, Przeworski, Brenner and others.[3] Although their work suffers from academicism, and sometimes arrogance, as well as specific shortcomings of argument, it is hard to deny that they have conclusively shown some major problems at the heart of Marx's work, which they take to be his scientific analysis of social change. Of course, it must be remembered that there are other ways to consider Marx. As Michael Walzer rightly remarked, in a review of Elster, Marx carried forward the great emancipatory project of the Enlightenment in the name of the new wage-earning masses.[4] It was a gospel of hope and a programme of political mobilization and it has profoundly marked the modern world; its capacity to do so depended on its apparent "fit" with nineteenth century experience, and once that fit no longer existed, its ability to move men and women dwindled steadily. Its weakness as a social science therefore needs to be confronted, which is why the analytical Marxists have something important to offer, in spite of their defects.

The analytical Marxists have brought forward several important observations concerning the materialist interpretation of history in general. They have shown that:

(1) If Marx proposed a general theory of history (as most people, including most Marxists, have always supposed), it involves either (a) a functional explanation, in which new relations of production are brought into being as forms of development required by the productive forces (the position taken by G.A. Cohen in what is really the founding text of this school. It is problematic, because Marx does not show *how* class struggles work reliably to ensure that this happens). Or (b), it involves a causal explanation, in which the productive forces develop as they do because of the periodic reconstruction of the relations of production to permit this (the position taken by Robert Brenner; and this too is problematic, because — once again — nothing seems to assure that such reconstructions must occur.)[5]

(2) The concept of "fettering" the forces of production by the relations of production is ambiguous. Marx says it is the *development* of the forces of production that is fettered, necessitating a revolution in the relations of production. But as Cohen, Elster and Przeworski have argued, the motivation needed for making a revolution depends, in Marx's political analyses, on the suffering that is due to the *use made of* the existing forces of production (inequality, unemployment, etc.), not on the wish to see them expanded.[6] *Ex post* it may be argued that revolutions made from this motive have the function of clearing the way for a new development of the forces of production, even if this was not what was in the minds of the revolutionaries. But, this does not appear at all believable in relation to most workers in today's advanced capitalist countries. Przeworski has also argued plausibly that the costs which capitalists will be sure to impose on any working class that makes a revolution against them are such that it is likely to be preferable to live with both the level of the forces of production

created by capitalism, and the use to which they are put.[7] The upshot is that Marx does not provide a convincing theoretical link between the motivation for revolution, and the historical progress of technology and productivity.

(3) The statement that "all history is the history of class struggles" is not substantiated in Marx's and Engels's writing and is not plausible. For example, it is not clear that the transitions from one precapitalist epoch to another can be understood in terms of class struggles. Whatever plausibility there may be in the idea that capitalism will be replaced by socialism through the struggle of the proletariat against the bourgeoisie is not to be sought in this law-like claim.

The analytical Marxists have also come up with several important observations concerning capitalism alone. They have shown that:

(1) Some of Marx's reasoning in relation to a certain number of the central ideas about capitalism on which revolutionary activists have relied is unsound (e.g. the theory concerning the tendency of the rate of profit to fall, the theory of capitalist crises).

(2) Marx does not show that social classes must be the central political actors in advanced capitalism. No good arguments have demonstrated either that non-class actors such as the "new social movements" (or old social movements like religion or national movements) cannot be central, or even that they cannot bring about the sort of epochal changes that Marx said were always the work of classes. Marx also refrained from showing that classes can and must make such changes.[8]

(3) Marx in general failed to provide "micro-foundations" for his social theory. This is an overall weakness, not resolvable by appeal to esoteric methodological principles. For instance, in relation to class formation and the development of class consciousness Marx often took for granted determinants of behaviour and ideas that, in retrospect, often seem contingent and far from universal. An example of this is the homogenisation and immiseration of the whole (European) working class. It may be that in different circumstances and times other working classes may also be able to be mobilised politically, and to struggle for socialism, but the analysis of the possibilities of this always needs to be undertaken afresh.

The analytical Marxists have been criticised for applying to Marx's work canons of scientificity (especially "methodological individualism," the principle that explanations of social phenomena "must only involve individuals — their properties, their beliefs and their actions") which Marx, according to their critics, explicitly rejected. But if Marx rejected methodological individualism, it is a defect, in their eyes, in so far as it led him to rely on methodological principles which are obscure (such as dialectics), and on which we rarely if ever rely in any other sphere of experience which is important to us. In spite of the obloquy they have experienced at the hands of orthodox Marxists, and the (partly correct) charge from Marxologists that they are trying to make Marxism into something different from what Marx intended, the interesting point about the analytical Marxists is that they are genuinely sympathetic to Marx's values and hopes, and would like to see them realised. Like Bernstein, however, they argue that for this it is necessary to get rid of the Hegelian, metaphysical elements in his thought, and build on the rest, genuinely treating it as science, not religion. It is not necessary to agree with all their claims, or their proposed revisions, in order to accept the timeliness of this stance.

A further contribution to the desacralisation of Marxism comes from both Marxist and non-Marxist philosophers who have shown that ethics were central to Marx's thought. It would seem paradoxical to call this desacralisation, were it not for the mystical or religious aspect of the assertion, adhered to by many if not most orthodox Marxists until quite recently, that ethics had no place in revolutionary socialism. Norman Geras and Steven Lukes, in particular, have convincingly shown that on the contrary, Marx had strong moral commitments, and even a theory of human nature; that no one can reasonably be asked to support any projected social change that is not based on these; and that, to the extent that Marxism's ethics are confused, leading to bad (undemocratic or illusional) politics, it is essential for anyone who shares Marx's values to clarify and argue for them.[9] (Although it is not idealistic to assert this, it would be to assert that his values could be realised through clarification and argumentation alone.)

THE NEED FOR A REVISED MARXISM AND ITS MAIN COMPONENTS

Faced with so many problems, such as the adverse verdicts of history, the logical and theoretical shortcomings, and the large and difficult ethical task to be undertaken, many Marxists have abandoned the whole legacy and have sought to start afresh (to go "beyond Marxism" to "post-Marxism," as Laclau and Mouffe have put it), while others have abandoned even the ideal of socialism.[10] In general, the current aversion to grand narratives, especially those which purport to explain absolutely everything, is a reasonable one. But, if we do not think that capitalism as it now exists is likely to yield a desirable or even a tolerable life for most of the world's population, or even for our own children and grandchildren in today's advanced industrial countries, we need a general theory of contemporary capitalism and the possibilities of social change, linked to a practical project for such change, however difficult it may be to formulate one. As for a possible basis for such a project, there is still no theory which even distantly rivals Marx's analysis of capitalism. In spite of its defects and limitations, it is still *marxisme faute de mieux*.

We need therefore, to establish what is valid, clear, usable and suggestive in Marx's analysis of capitalism. First of all, we can dispense with his general theory of history, and, for the purpose of trying to change the contemporary world, dominated by the capitalist mode of production, it is not necessary to be convinced that there is any general pattern, spanning all epochs, to which such world-changes must conform. My confidence in the prospects for a transition to socialism (whatever "socialism" is now going to mean) is not going to be increased by being persuaded of the validity of the kind of abstract "law" that would cover both this transition, and all the earlier transitions (from slavery to feudalism and feudalism to capitalism, etc.). In general, I think the debate about the nature of the transition from feudalism to capitalism, which has exercised Marxist historians so much, is a *scholastic* question, as Marx himself said about the debate concerning the truth value of abstract thought. Although scholastic debates are often interesting and sometimes valuable, we do not need to resolve this one in order to make use of Marx's analysis of capitalism and its contradictions, and their implications for the prospects of socialism.

Secondly, with regard to capitalism as it actually exists today, we need a theory *of the type Marx proposed*, which sought to combine (a) a social ideal — democratic, equal, humanistic, creative social relations; (b) an understanding of the dynamics of the "self-regulating market" under capitalist relations of production; (c) an understanding of the social forces generated by, and acting on, those dynamics (equivalent to Marx's theory of classes and class struggle, the State, and the possibility of the dictatorship of the proletariat); and (d) a political project based on (a), (b) and (c).[11] To say we need a theory of this type may seem a truism but it does rule out quite a lot, from purely idealist projects (such as the New International Economic Order) to deterministic projects such as those of many Leninist and Trotskyist groups. In fact, most modern projects for social change have been more or less influenced by Marx's political economy of capitalism. There is really little alternative to trying to revise it.

The demand for (a), a social ideal, reflects our need for a convincing utopia, and a developed ethical case for it. Engels's famous attack on "utopian socialism," coupled with Marx's aphorisms about the working class having no ready-made utopias to introduce by popular decree, have been a severely disabling legacy for the socialist movement, and should be firmly rejected. It is one thing to say that sketching utopias, however attractive, is of no use if the conditions could *never* exist for them to be realised; or to criticise over-elaborate models of alternative social forms because these may give rise to the illusion that they can be realised in all their speculative detail.[12] But, it is absurd to suppose that a popular movement for social change can be mobilised unless people have some vision of the alternative society they are being asked to make sacrifices to achieve. In reality, Marx and Engels subscribed, tacitly, to a utopia which already had wide currency in Europe, a utopia of plenty in which everyone would get what they needed, at least in the way of essentials, and in return would be glad to give of their best to the rest of society. Marx's and Engels's rejection of detailed blueprints for this utopia allowed them to avoid facing up to some critical weaknesses in it, such as the fatally contradictory idea of absolute abundance, or the idea that problems will be solved by changes in human nature. Utopias are needed, not only to give us concrete dreams to fight for, but also to allow us to test the mutual compatibility of our various dreams. (Examples of the former use of utopias are the feminist utopias of Marge Piercy and Ursula Le Guin, while Alec Nove's sketch of market socialism is an example of the second).[13]

An exploration of (b), understanding the dynamics of the "self-regulating market" under capitalist relations of production, reveals that the classical Marxist agenda has simply become more vast and more complex. The only comfort to be had is that it is a task to be pursued collectively, and that it is not a question of getting it "right." Abandoning struggles over who is "correct" is one immediate gain from the abandonment of a religious attitude to Marxism, and it should be possible to make headway by devoting saved energy to the task of trying to figure out what is going on, free from the burden of always having to make it appear to be in conformity with some tenet or other of Marx's.

Moreover, although the task of analysis has become so much more daunting with the accelerating integration of global capitalism, including many developments that Marx could not anticipate, the central dynamic of capitalism that he identified and analyzed is as palpable as ever. As we move into the second decade of neoconservatism, we can see that the social democratic era was produced by highly specific circumstances which are not likely to return. So long as productive capital was concentrated in the countries where technology was most developed, national-level social-democratic politics expressed the contradiction between capital and labour in a powerful form. Eventually, however, the power of social democracy to enforce near-full employment through electoral pressure led to a strengthening of labour to the point where it threatened the profitability of capital and even the control of production by the owners of capital. But the growing international mobility of capital, organised in multinational firms, combined with the rise of new centres of accumulation (Japan, the NICs) meant that the crisis of 1967-82 led to a new offensive by capital to break the social-democratic consensus, an offensive which has been increasingly successful. The protections gained by labour in the west are being gradually eroded by neoconservative governments with electoral majorities under the slogan of "enabling national economic survival"; once again, we begin to see the social costs of subordinating society to the market in the way that Marx, and later Polanyi, understood. The process still has some way to go before capitalist governments in the industrialised countries say frankly to the workers that their living standards must be reduced to those of the poorest and most defenceless workers in the countries whose exports they must compete with. However, it is hard to detect, as yet, a growing popular apprehension of the long-run implications of the logic that has been so effectively reasserted from the early 1980s onwards. At some point, in some form or other, it is not hard to predict that a new form of the socialist ideal will become widely shared again. In relation to this, a revised and unmystical Marxism has a vital role to play.

We have arrived at the third component of the required theory: (c), the analysis of the social forces generated by the dynamics of contemporary capitalism, and the way they act on those dynamics. Speaking generally, it is easy to see that capital has developed the institutional capacity to operate on a world scale — the MNC, the IMF/World Bank, GATT, "rapid deployment" military forces, etc.; while labour not only has not done so, but will have extreme difficulty in doing so, given the very different national and regional interests at stake, the distances and costs, etc. It is also easy to see that capitalism does not automatically "form the proletariat into a (single, unified) class," even in countries where proletarianization is most complete. Other classes persist, non-class social forces are also generated (e.g. the "new social movements") which pose demands that have no necessary coincidence with interests defined in class terms. Also, in the so-called periphery countries, the impact of capitalism on social and political consciousness is often very different from the optimistic scenario of Marx's political writings.

It is necessary to acknowledge and to try to analyze all of these observations if a new socialist project — the fourth intellectual prerequisite mentioned above — is to be formulated; and given the difficulty of developing effective political communities even on the national plane, the task of trying to develop a socialist project that corresponds to the global reality of capitalism seems almost too daunting to contemplate. Presumably it will be accomplished in the end piecemeal, sometimes accidentally, often indirectly, as a product of the interactions of innumerable lesser, more imaginable projects, that nonetheless increasingly do reflect the global changes that must occur if the human race is to survive, let alone realise its humanity and diversity.

* * *

Although Marxism has not become superfluous, Marxism-as-religion has. The latter is a Marxism defended against revision, since revision is the means by which any attempt to understand the world can be kept objective, scientific, and useful: "hitherto most Marxists have only interpreted Marxism, in various ways: the point, however, is to change it."[14]

NOTES

1. E. Bernstein, *Evolutionary Socialism*, Schocken, New York, 1961.
2. Cf. Lucio Colletti, *From Rousseau to Lenin*, New Left Books, London 1972, at pp. 59-72.
3. See especially Jon Elster. *Making Sense of Marx*. Cambridge University Press, Cambridge 1985, and J. Roemer (ed.) *Analytical Marxism*. Cambridge University Press, Cambridge 1986. I prefer the label "analytical Marxism" to "rational choice Marxism" (the term adopted by Alan Carling in "Rational Choice Marxism," *New Left Review* 160, 1986, pp.24-62) because their analytical method for identifying and clarifying problems within Marx's work seems to me much more valuable than

their use of rational-choice-based theorisations to solve them. Ellen Meiksens Wood's critique of the latter in "Rational Choice Marxism. Is the Game Worth the Candle?" in *New Left Review* 177, 1989, is excellent in many ways but does not do justice to the seriousness of the problems which these writers' probings (and especially Elster's) reveal in Marx.

4. Walzer, Michael. John Elster. *Making Sense of Marx*. New York Review Books. November 21, 1985.

5. In response to this critique Derek Sayer has argued very persuasively that Marx did not propose a general theory of all history in the sense of a proposed explanation of all epochs of history in terms of a single dynamic mechanism. He thus rescues Marx from this particular set of problems at the price of greatly lowering the claims attributable to this theory, which in Sayer's hands becomes essentially a heuristic method. I prefer this strain in Marx's thought, but I am not convinced that the one more usually attributed to him is not also to be found in his work.

   G.A. Cohen, *Karl Marx's Theory of History: A Defence*, Oxford University Press, Oxford 1978: Robert Brenner, "Bourgeois Revolution and Transition to Capitalism," in A.L. Beier et al., eds., *The First Modern Society*, Cambridge University Press, Cambridge 1989, pp. 271-304, and "The Social Basis of Development" in J. Roemer (ed), *Analytical Marxism*, Cambridge University Press, Cambridge. 1986, pp. 23-53. Also see Derek Sayer: *The Violence of Abstraction: The Analytical Foundations of Historical Materialism*, Blackwell, Oxford 1987.

6. Cf. G.A.Cohen, "Forces and Relations of Production", in B. Mathews, ed., *Marx: 100 Years On*, Lawrence and Wishart, London 1983. pp. 111-134.

7. A. Przeworski, "Material Interests, Class Compromise, and the Transition to Socialism," in Roemer, *Analytical Marxism*, pp. 162-88.

8. Cf. Elster, *Making Sense of Marx*, ch.6, esp. pp 390-94.

9. See N. Geras, *Marx and Human Nature: Refutation of a Legend*, Verso, London 1983; S. Lukes, *Marxism and Morality*, Oxford University Press, Oxford 1985. For an important though sympathetic critique of Lukes see K. Soper, "Marxism and Morality," *New Left Review* 163, pp. 101-13.

10. E. Laclau and C. Mouffe, "Post-Marxism Without Apologies," *New Left Review* 169, pp. 34-62.

11. This is very close to the position taken by Ronald Aronson in "Historical Materialism, Answer to Marxism's Crisis," *New Left Review* 152, 1985, pp. 74-94.

12. Marx's "anti-utopian utopianism" is excellently discussed in Lukes, *Marxism and Morality*, pp. 36-46. Useful critiques of Marx's utopianism are offered in Elster, *Making Sense of Marx*, pp. 522-27, and in A. Nove, *The Economics of Feasible Socialism*, Allen and Unwin, Boston 1983, Part I.

13. Cf. Marge Piercy, *Woman on the Edge of Time*, Knopf, New York 1976; Ursula Le Guin, *The Dispossessed*, Harper and Row, New York 1974; Alec Nove, *The Economics of Feasible Socialism*, Part V.

14. Alec Nove was perhaps the first to adapt Marx's famous eleventh "thesis" on Feuerbach in this sense, on p. 60 of *The Economics of Feasible Socialism*, Allen and Unwin, Boston 1983, Part I.

REFERENCES

Aronson, Ronald. "Historical Materialism, Answer to Marxism's Crisis," *New Left Review*. 152, 1985. pp. 74-94.

Beier, A.L. et al., eds., *The First Modern Society*. Cambridge University Press, Cambridge 1989.

Bernstein, E., *Evolutionary Socialism*. Schocken, New York 1961.

Carling, Alan. "Rational Choice Marxism," *New Left Review*. 160, 1986. pp.24-62

Cohen, G.A. *Karl Marx's Theory of History: A Defence*. Oxford University Press, Oxford 1978.

Colletti, Lucio. *From Rousseau to Lenin*. New Left Books, London 1972.

Elster, Jon. *Making Sense of Marx*. Cambridge University Press, Cambridge 1985.

Geras, N. *Marx and Human Nature: Refutation of a Legend*. Verso, London, 1983.

Laclau, E. and C. Mouffe, "Post-Marxism Without Apologies," *New Left Review*. 169, pp. 34-62.

Lukes, S. *Marxism and Morality*. Oxford University Press, Oxford 1985.

Mathews, B. ed., *Marx: 100 Years On*. Lawrence and Wishart, London 1983.

Meiksens Wood, Ellen. "Rational Choice Marxism. Is the Game Worth the Candle?," *New Left Review* 177, 1989.

Nove, Alec. *The Economics of Feasible Socialism*, Allen and Unwin, Boston 1983. Part I.

Piercy, Marge. *Woman on the Edge of Time*. Knopf, New York 1976.

Le Guin, Ursula. *The Dispossessed*. Harper and Row, New York 1974.

Roemer, J. (ed) *Analytical Marxism*. Cambridge University Press, Cambridge. 1986.

Sayer, Derek. *The Violence of Abstraction: The Analytical Foundations of Historical Materialism*. Blackwell, Oxford 1987.

Soper, K. "Marxism and Morality." *New Left Review*. 163. pp. 101-13.

Walzer, Michael. John Elster. "Making Sense of Marx," *New York Review of Books*. November 21, 1985.

Chapter 2

Jean-Pierre Deslauriers

THE RELEVANCE OF ANARCHISM*

After having been presented as the alternative to the capitalist system, "actually existing" socialism has ended in spectacular bankruptcy. For its part, capitalism has been waving its flag and dancing up and down as it contemplates the good times heralded by the new world order. Yet not every alternative is dead. As we go back through the history and the practice of social change we meet the anarchist current, whose fortunes have varied but which continues to offer an alternative solution. The purpose of this chapter is to briefly outline this political current, and to show its value for Canada and Québec.

WHAT IS ANARCHISM?

Murray Bookchin defines anarchism as follows:

> Viewed from a broad historical perspective, anarchism is a libidinal upsurge of the people, a striving social unconsciousness that reaches back, under different names, to the earliest struggles of humanity against domination and authority.[1]

We can, of course, go back to Antiquity to rediscover theorists who opposed the authority of the State, or collectivities which fought to maintain a more decentralized political organization. However, the movement as we know it today dates from the last century. In the French tradition, the name comes from Pierre-Joseph Proudhon, who gave it a political meaning. Proudhon loved shocking expressions, and he liked to shock. He dedicated his book to the leading men of Besançon who had awarded him a scholarship to study in Paris. There was nothing extraordinary in this, except that he then posed the question: "What is property?," to which he responded: "theft." Needless to say his scholarship was not renewed. Proudhon had tried to give a positive content to the word anarchism; from his point of view, anarchism was not chaos, but a higher level of order,

---

* This article was translated by Rev. George Topp, S.J.

in which people can live in freedom, without constraints and without any hierarchy. However, this word "anarchism" was already loaded with the pejorative content that we are all familiar with, and it is never easy to give a different meaning to a word drawn from current usage. It seems that Proudhon was ready to abandon it shortly after he had launched it. Some twenty years ago, Yvon Bourdet suggested a different term which did not enjoy much popularity, but was a better expression of Proudhon's idea: the concept of autarcky, which means "the self-initiative of a group or a social body...,"[2] "free association, the free coordination of self-managed groups,"[3] and "the social self-creation of an organization which makes freedoms 'co-possible' [possible together]."[4] Although the concept of autarcky is more accurate than the word anarchism, which is loaded with ambiguities, emotions and prejudices, the word anarchism has won out, despite its inaccuracies, and we continue to use it.

ANARCHISM: THE PROVOCATIVE FACE OF CHANGE

Recent events in Eastern Europe clearly show that the socialist move-ment has leaden wings. For Touraine, socialism is dead, not only because it has lost the battle at the hands of capitalism, but also because the condi-tions which witnessed its birth are now rapidly changing.

> A movement in decline, socialism is now nothing but an ideology which is delaying the understanding of the society which is being born under our own eyes. From class-action, it has become a discourse of intellectuals: of those who refuse to look at the facts, trying to protect the role of the scribblers and controllers which socialist ideology gave them.[5]

Castoriadis expresses the same view, claiming that the word socialism is as empty of meaning as the word "church," which at the beginning, meant assembly of the people, but today represents a powerful institution far removed from its popular origins. However, the disgrace into which socialism has fallen at present should not make us forget that for a time it represented the hopes of the peoples for a more just and egalitarian social organization and for a better life.

In the past century, the labour movement had to take a political position to confront the emerging liberal State, democracy and universal suffrage. Even many of those whose final goal was anarchism accepted the idea that it was necessary to get there through a period of transition. This strategy rested on two pillars: the union and the party. Trade unionism as a means of workers' actions was at first a powerful opposition movement which waged heroic battles for better working conditions. However, it soon became centralized and far removed from social conditions in general, to the point where it seemed like an instrument whose capacity for renewal decreased in proportion to the deepening of the crisis. We must also not forget that while the trade unions did succeed in organizing the employees of large enterprises, they did not enjoy the same success with employees in general, including those in small firms. To be sure, the activities of employer organizations has had something to do with this, but we must also recognize the union's failure to adapt to new social conditions.

Moreover, preoccupations have changed. Although work was, and remains, of primary importance for the population, especially in this period of increasing poverty and massive unemployment, the accelerated deterioration of society has put living conditions back into the forefront of concerns; whatever affects health, housing, personal safety and personal services arouses the interest of the new generation. By paying too much attention to working conditions, trade unions have seen themselves overtaken on the left by a large number of community groups. Although there is certainly some affinity between the two, it must not be exaggerated: the sense of difference remains.

The same remark applies to the workers' party. In the Communist Manifesto Marx claimed that the first objective of the party should be the conquest of democracy. But in light of experience, while the goal seems as noble as ever, the party has not proved to be the best means of attaining it. It has become an instrument of control over its own members, a means of ideological manipulation and the guardian of orthodoxy. In comparison with organic communities, Bookchin offers this assessment of the party:

> ...the party was simply a mirror-image of the nation-state, and its fortunes were completely tied to the state's development. The party was meant to be very large, often embracing sizable masses of people who were knitted together bureaucratically in depersonalized, centralized organs.[6]

In Europe, links still exist between trade unions and parties, but the same tendency is not present in Canada and the United States. There is mutual sympathy, but it is rather cautiously expressed, as in the kind of support that Canadian unions give to the New Democratic Party and that the Fédération des travailleurs et travailleuses du Québec gives to the Parti Québecois.

As a general rule, the labour movement was drawn to State socialism: it made the conquest of State power the centre of society and the key to social change[7]. However, the failure of Statism is bringing back onto centre stage the current of thought which opposes Statism in the most vigorous fashion, namely anarchism. Contrary to the sort of "reasonable" socialism which foresaw a period of transition from a capitalist society to a socialist society, anarchism suggests that it is possible for a society to change rapidly and that the period of transition, far from being necessary, only allows time for another elite to establish itself. Anarchism put forward a different strategy.

Its first element consists in being opposed to every form of hierarchy and all ruler-ruled relationships in all the spheres of social life. Anarchism seeks to establish equality as a means of change, not just as its goal; the means used must prefigure the desired end. The State is certainly the place where inegalitarian power appears in all its splendour, but it is not the only place; there is also the family, the school, leisure activities, the hospital, the workplace. These are all places where the psychology and personality of individuals are fashioned sites for apprenticeship in democratization.

Anarchism is opposed to the State because in it the power of society takes on a separate life of its own, becoming a power which turns against its source. Every society is endowed with power; it is the essential muscle, the energy which it needs to act. When the State assumes the power of society, it prevents it from being self-administering; it draws a sort of surplus-value from the power of society and uses it not just to administer society but also to keep it on a leash, to control it, robbing it of its freedom. It is this transfer of power to the State that anarchism opposes.

To attain the goal of equality, anarchism takes its stand, firstly, on the liberty and autonomy of human beings. "By basing itself on freedom, unity is inevitably achieved; but through unity it is difficult if not impossible to attain freedom."[8] This freedom does not develop in a vacuum, but in contexts in which people can act; this is what anarchists have called direct action. The term means that individuals become aware of their power by acting, without waiting for the dictates of parties or any other centralized organization. Through direct action individuals launch projects, become familiar with management and act on their own. That is what the community movements in the course of the last fifteen years have been about: when a social problem arises, they are no longer content to ask the State to take care of it but set up organizations themselves that are more efficient than the State bureaucracy.

A second key idea of anarchism is decentralization: in whatever sphere it is implanted the State centralizes, whereas anarchism seeks to decentralize. Decentralization is not merely a technical question, it is first and foremost a political question. Decentralization does not exclude larger groupings; on the contrary, Bakunine, Kropotkin and Proudhon were the first to talk about federalism as the form which future society must adopt. However, in this case, it is not a question of two levels of State oppression, but of the organization and coordination of different collectivities and societies, on a voluntary basis and in the mutual interest of the parties involved.

The last powerful idea of anarchism is spontaneity. In political circles people scoff at it and, in fact, the idea does have a certain lack of precision. Understood in an anarchist sense, spontaneity means that people can behave freely and effectively, without having to follow a pre-established plan in order to succeed. Spontaneity does not exclude organization or structures; on the contrary, it usually engenders forms of organization that are egalitarian, non-hierarchical and voluntary. It is opposed to every form of hierarchical and authoritarian organization.

> Spontaneity is a way of behaving, feeling and thinking that is freed from all external constraint and restrictions imposed from without. It is a way of behaving, in which feelings and thinking are self-directed, directed from within, and not an unbridled excess of passion and activity. From the point of view of liberal communism, spontaneity consists in the capacity of the individual to impose upon himself a self-discipline, and to formulate in an intelligent way, the principles which guide his activity in society. Whenever an individual has eliminated all the shackles through which domination was stifling his autonomous activity, that individual acts, feels and thinks in a spontaneous fashion.[9]

Contrary to what some people may say, anarchism is not just another political ideology; in it lies all the great social movements of our time. The anarchists were at the heart of the Paris Commune of 1871, of the Russian revolution of 1917, of the German revolution of 1921 and of the great Spanish revolution of 1936. It inspired the fantastic upset which shook the Western societies in the sixties, and anarchist principles of organization have links with the feminist, the ecological and community movements of the seventies and eighties.

Spontaneity is thus opposed to strategies determined in high places, and is based instead on direct action and equality of persons. That is why we see it as the provocative face of change. For the right, anarchism represents chaos and disorganization, in short everything that happens when people are left to themselves. As for the left, even though some of its representatives claim to be in agreement with the ultimate goal of anarchism, which is an egalitarian society, it retains a great deal of confidence in State power and its institutions. Basically, both the left and the right are incapable of conceiving another social order whose destiny they would not be able to control. But when we contemplate the chaos we have been led into by those who were supposed to be enlightened leaders, it is clear that they have lost control of events, and that they are more concerned with the preservation of their privileges than with the fate of ordinary mortals.

ANARCHISM AS UTOPIA

Anarchism presents itself as a concrete utopia. In the past century, one branch of the movement for social reconstruction conducted practical experiments which were labelled utopian. The utopian vision certainly did not originate at the end of the nineteenth century; we find traces of it in Antiquity in Homer, Plato and Ovid. Later, utopian thought was taken over by Catholicism and it was not until the end of the Middle Ages that more secular utopias appeared, like those of Erasmus of Campanella, and above all, Thomas More, whose book *Utopia* gave this current of thought its name. Defined briefly, utopia consists in proposing a vision of society radically different from the one we are familiar with, while still anchored in reality.

> The power of utopian thinking, properly conceived as a vision of a society which questions all the presuppositions of the present-day society, is in its inherent ability to see the future in terms of radically new forms and values. By 'new', I do not merely mean 'change' — 'change' that can be merely quantitative, inertial, physical. I mean 'new' in terms of development and processes, rather than 'motion' and 'displacement'. The latter are just logistical phenomena; they are changes of places and quantity, as distinguished from a development that is qualitative. Hence, under the rubric of 'utopia', I place only consistently revolutionary visions of a future that is emergent, the result of deep-seated processes that involve the radical reconstruction of personality, sensibility, sexuality, social management, technics, human relations and humanity's relationship with nature. The time lapse that turns present into future is not merely quantitative; it is change in development, form and quality.[10]

The utopian current, therefore, draws our attention to new ways of approaching reality and the future, to possibilities that now lie fallow. It helps us to liberate ourselves from the weight of history and the inertia of the present, and forces us to be creative. This is why the extension of the State, and the problems which it entails, has put the anti-Statist utopia, which is anarchism, back on the agenda.

Like anarchism, the word utopia has acquired a pejorative connotation, and its detractors have not always been wrong; many utopias have had more to do with science fiction than with any insight into society. Following Henri Desroche, we must distinguish between chimerical utopias, which are nothing but pure speculation, and practical utopias, which advance plans for action and are plausible ideas for dealing with reality. It is to this second category that anarchism belongs; it suggests avenues of activity, concrete solutions and forms of organization. We can, however, retain from the utopian tradition its concern to take advantage of radically new possibilities offered by new circumstances, and the need to read the future in the present.

THE CURRENT SOCIAL CRISIS

Our era is marked by a twofold movement of social disintegration whose elements are closely related. On the one hand, it is a question of social decomposition: institutions, norms, values and conventional life-styles are being abandoned by people of different social classes. The inability of the economics of Canada and Québec to absorb the young work force is producing people who have no social class; university graduates find themselves in jobs well below their abilities, and the middle class is undergoing profound changes. On the other hand, this social decomposition is accompanied by a disintegration of the social and individual personality. Personality is affected by the influences that are prevalent in any given society: hierarchy moulds the psyche, emotions and feelings. On the other hand, the disturbances in this same hierarchical system are giving rise to new forms of behaviour which no longer respect established norms. The breakdown of traditional family life, the collapse of the work-ethic, and the questioning of patriarchy are fostering a new sensitivity.

In response to this process of decomposition, a counter-process of recomposition of the social fabric is occurring. This current is certainly very fragile and is up against formidable pressures from social disintegration caused by the increasing poverty of rural areas, the homogenization of urban districts, and the restructuring of regional economies. Still, there has been a new flowering of community experiments over a thirty years period which stems from the utopian current and direct action. What is most striking, however, when one compares these current experiments with those of the last century, is the moderate character:

> ...[this] second flowering of the community manifests more moderation; there were few associations that were tainted with the folly of greatness. Their avowed reasons were more modest: they fled from urban, technocratic and statist constraints; they struggled against proletarian insecurity; urban collectivities, refuge-communities, these ectoplasms with fleeting and disparate forms defy any attempt at synthesis; nevertheless, these projects almost always revolved around a rediscovery of subjectivity, the social bond and the ecology.[11]

These experiments do not always claim to be anarchist, even though they often share anarchism's characteristics, such as equality between the participants and direct action self-management. The organizations involved have emerged especially in the service sector and have acquired an important role in the domains of mental health, youth and women. They have even forced the State to recognize them, since the State is very interested in passing on to them the cost of social policies but cannot, at the same time, compete with them in terms of efficiency and service delivery. In Québec, this recognition was established in the report of the Commission d'enquête sur les services de santé et les services sociaux (1988). Also, in the recent reform of health services, the State of Québec has undertaken to subsidize community groups, not because it wants to but because it cannot do otherwise; in the face of popular pressure and the successful experiments and proven efficiency of small organizations. It is this that leads some authors to take the view that community groups are in the process of communalizing State services, and that the privatization preached by neoliberalism is unrealisable.

ANARCHISM AND CANADIAN AND QUÉBEC SOCIETY

What can Canadian and Québec societies learn from anarchism? It is not easy to say, stuck as we are in the constitutional rut. One thing is certain: Canadian society is undergoing profound transformations and we must be prepared for changes that will go far beyond repatriation of the Constitution, the Charter of Rights or the establishment of official bilingualism.

First of all, the role of government is undergoing profound modification. The federal government is deeply in debt, more deeply than any of the provinces. It can no longer meet the needs of Canadian citizens, since it is incapable of reducing its annual deficit or even of beginning to pay off its debt. Indebted as it is, it is quite possible that the central government will find it difficult to impose national norms which it will no longer be capable of enforcing; it will probably find itself unable to launch major programmes in the course of the next few years.

Because of the financial difficulties of the State, social policies are in danger. However, a qualification is needed here: the main social policies are insurance schemes which the tax payers pay for, not a gift from the State. This is the distinctive characteristic of the social welfare system of Canada in which Québec also participates. We have seen that the government has withdrawn from the financing of unemployment insurance, leaving it up to employees and to employers, but the programme continues to function. As far as health insurance is concerned, the contribution of the federal government is decreasing from year to year, so much so that its contribution assigned to Québec should be close to zero about the year 2000. From the moment that the central State is no longer able to contribute its share, it will find it difficult to impose any national norms: that is when citizens will discover that they are more independent than they thought.

We usually say that the indebtedness of the State comes from its social policies and from the transfer of revenues to the citizens. However, we need to know exactly how much the operation of the State itself is costing. The indignation of the Auditor General merely calls attention to the most glaring accounting errors; it does not question the increase in military spending, or tax shelters, or disguised subsidies to companies under the form of research and training. If we make this kind of calculation, we discover immense costs from which citizens do not benefit at all. Far from being the guarantor of social justice, the State is at best a very bad administrator.

René Lévèsque used to say, from a Statist point of view: "Canada's problem is that, to survive, Canada must centralize, and for the same reason so must Québec." Today, however, desire for autonomy is no longer limited to Québec. For example, the existence and success of the Bloc québécois is paralleled by that of the Confederation of Regions. Despite their conservative aspects, such developments show the need to take account of regional needs and sensibilities.

The power of the central government is being questioned at a time when it is at its weakest. During the seventies and eighties federalism was seen as advantageous for everyone; that was the wonderful time when the federal government could spend beyond its means, so that everyone could have a share, even if the provinces were eating their seed corn. It is no longer the case today.

As for the rebuilding of Canada, the dialogue is not advancing very quickly and we have been treated to a spectacle of great imaginative exercise. The two Germanies reunited and quickly attacked the complex problems involved in reunification. During the same period, in Canada, people were still asking what the expression "distinct society" really meant for Québec, or whether we should elect our senators.

In the process of social reconstruction, Canadians and Québecers would do well to profit from the lessons of our aboriginal societies. Different nations coexisted here for a long time. Their experience, of course, cannot be applied directly to our situation. Big urban and industrial societies like our own do not correspond very well to small rural ones. Be that as it may, it would be worth conducting a deeper study of their models of social organization; we are still far from doing so. In the fall of 1991, representatives of the First Nations of the three Americas met in Ottawa to discuss their situation. Despite the unique character of the event, the newspapers and television hardly made any mention of it. This silence testifies to our ethnocentricity and to our resistance to undertaking the study of difference. The constitutional crisis has, however, changed this. Aboriginal peoples have become political actors, whom we will have to hear, willy nilly.

CONCLUSION

The coming years will demand great imagination and creativity; they will, at the same time, demand tolerance of differences, more openness, and the need to accept a political realignment which may turn out to be radical and profound. In these conditions, anarchism offers a project and a practice from which we can draw inspiration. Will we be able to draw some lessons from the community activities which have developed during the last thirty years? It is difficult to say. For, even though these groups have acquired a great deal of political maturity, they do not yet seem ready to consider reconstructing society as a task that they can handle; so far, no matter how effective their activity has been, these social movements tend to be confined to rather narrow sectors.

Still, bearing in mind the distinction proposed by Boudert, we must be careful not to confuse the impossible with the extraordinary. The impossible refers to the impracticability of an idea or a theory which has no application; the extraordinary designates a reality which we do not know, but which might appear ordinary in another context. As long as we do not rub shoulders with it in our daily life, or do not recognize it in its microscopic manifestations, we declare it to be impossible. In a Statist and hierarchical society, an egalitarian society seems impossible because it is extraordinary. This leads us to exclude what is possible from what we have inherited from the past and which arbitrarily set limits to our actions. Nevertheless, a good idea keeps making headway; it only needs the right circumstances for it to be quickly applied. This will be true of anarchism as well.

NOTES

1. Bookchin, Murray. *Pour une société écologique.* Paris: Bourgois, 1976. p.19.
2. Bourdet, Yvon. "Automation et autorité, autogestion et autarchisme," *Participation and Self-Management.* Première conférence sociologique internationale sur l'auto-gestion et la participation, Zabreb, vol. 2. p. 13.
3. Ibid., p. 14.
4. Ibid., p. 15.
5. Touraine, Alain. *L'après-socialisme.* Paris: Grasset, 1980. p.67.
6. Bookchin, Murray. *The Ecology of Freedom.* Palo Alto: Cheshire, 1982. p. 189.
7. Rosanvallon, Pierre and Patrick Viveret. *Pour une nouvelle culture politique.* Paris, Seuil, 1977.
8. Leval, Gaston. *La pensée constructive de Bakounine.* Paris: Spartacus, 1976. p.58.
9. Bookchin, Murray, 1976. p. 54.
10. Bookchin, Murray. *Toward an Ecological Society.* Montréal: Black Rose Books, 1980. p.281.
11. Creagh, Ronald. *Laboratorires de l'utopie: les communautés libertaires aux Etats-Unis.* Paris: Payot, 1983. p.11.

REFERENCES

Bookchin, Murray. *Pour une société écologique.* Paris: Bourgois, 1976.
Bookchin, Murray. *Toward an Ecological Society.* Montréal: Black Rose Books, 1980.
Bookchin, Murray. *The Ecology of Freedom.* Palo Alto: Cheshire, 1982.
Bourdet, Yvon. "Automation et autorité, autogestion et autarchisme," *Participation and Self-Management.* Première conférence sociologique internationale sur l'autogestion et la participation, Zabreb, vol. 2, pages 5-21.
Commission d'enquête sur les services de santé et les services sociaux. Rapport. Québec: Les Publication du Québec, 1988.
Creagh, Ronald. *Laboratorires de l'utopie: les communautés libertaires aux Etats-Unis.* Paris: Payot, 1983.
Desroche, Henri. "Panorama de l'utopie," *Encyclopaedia Universalis,* pp. 557-559.
Leval, Gaston. *La pensée constructive de Bakounine.* Paris: Spartacus, 1976.
Robert, Lionel. "Le partenariat entre le réseau institutionnel et la communanté: un paradigme à définir," *Nouvelles practique sociales.* vol. 2, no. 1 pp. 37-53.
Rosanvallon, Pierre and Patrick Viveret. *Pour une nouvelles culture politique.* Paris: Seuil, 1977.
Touraine, Alain. *L'après-socialisme.* Paris: Grassey, 1980.

Chapter 3

Gregor Murray

UNION CULTURE AND ORGANIZATIONAL CHANGE IN ONTARIO AND QUÉBEC

The labour movements of Ontario and Québec provide a wealth of information concerning the interplay between cultural and organizational change. The information required to investigate this interplay stems from a study of the response of a number of large Canadian trade union organizations to market changes since the recession of the early 1980s.[1] The particular focus is on the experience of Ontario and Québec sections of selected Canadian Labour Congress (CLC) affiliates. The intent is to ascertain how larger market changes are transforming union organizational structures, practices and strategic orientations, and to explore the cultural implications of these changes. It is argued that internal union cultures necessarily play a role in the ability to react to and act on these larger environmental changes; they generate new forms of solidarity and of identity with other workers, and they establish linkages with some of the newer social movements, such as those concerned with gender, ecology, or ethnic, regional or national identities.

The comparison of union movements in Ontario and Québec is the focus of the conferences from which this book has emerged, and provides a platform from which we can gain an understanding of changes in the larger Canadian labour movement. The two union movements are of a roughly comparable size and they both operate in advanced capitalist economies with similar, though not identical, industrial structures. However, they have developed in somewhat different ways over the past decade, reflecting their different market situations and political environments, as well as differences in their overall orientations. The similarities in the strategies of the two labour movements are certainly more striking than the differences, possibly because so much of the underlying political economy of change would appear to be the same in the two provinces. There are also interesting divergences, however, which the analysis will attempt to take into account.[2]

The particular methodological interest of this chapter is its case study approach to the same "national" unions in both provinces, thus placing in sharp relief comparable organizational arrangements and different cultural dispositions. The field research was conducted at the level of selected affiliates of the Fédération des travailleurs et travailleuses du Québec (FTQ), and of the Ontario Federation of Labour (OFL). The high degree of decentralization which characterizes unionism in Canada means that many of the current organizational and strategic adjustments are concentrated, at least in the case of the CLC, within labour central affiliates, such as in national and international unions and their different regional components. As a result, this study is focused specifically on that level of action. Unfortunately, many of the rich contrasts between different labour centrals in Québec, such as between the FTQ and the Confédération des syndicats nationaux (CSN), not to mention between Québec and Ontario, fall outside the scope of this chapter, though some effort will be made to draw attention to these differences where appropriate.[3]

The first of the five sections which make up this chapter considers some of the linkages between social change, organizational structures and cultures in the context of the contemporary evolution of union organizations. This is followed by a look at the underlying dynamics of change confronting the Ontario and Québec labour movements over the past decade. The third section examines some of the similarities and differences in the composition, representativeness and structures of union organizations in Ontario and Québec, while the fourth focuses on the different organizational and cultural initiatives currently pursued by the two labour movements. The final section returns to some of the broader themes underlying this volume to look at the relationships between new union cultures, organizational structures and social change.

STRUCTURES, CULTURES AND SOCIAL CHANGE

The decline of the labour movement as a focus for industrial citizenship, a source of mass identity and a force for epochal social change has, of course, been much heralded.[4] From the decade of the 1970s with the double oil shock, and throughout the recession and continuing economic adjustments of the 1980s, unions have represented a diminishing proportion of the labour force in a number of the industrialized Western economies.[5] Their capacity to maintain, yet alone expand, their membership base and to represent effectively those members, has increasingly been under challenge. A range of environmental changes have affected union organizations and their relations with their members, and these changes bring about further transformations in the composition of the labour movement in its relative representativeness and in its basic structures. Thus, the organizational structures and the cultures that were forged in previous periods of economic and social transformation, whether prior to World War II or in the long years of economic expansion in the post-war period, are now being altered by larger market changes. The time is therefore ripe to consider some of the interrelations between the organizational structures and cultures of unions, and the larger social and economic changes taking place.

Generalizations about these current organizational and cultural adaptations are complicated by the highly differentiated nature of both union organizations and the impact of the new environmental pressures by sector, by organization and by cluster of skills. Although there is a common set of environmental pressures pushing unions in Canada towards multiform organizational adaptations, not all organizations appear as open to change. Unions are most frequently intermediaries in the social structures of production; they organize and mobilize the identities and capacities of workers in specific industries, first around their contracts of employment and, then, beyond. They are necessarily driven by changes in the marketplace and, if they are to be relevant for the people that they ostensibly represent, they have to react to them and provide explanations for them. At the same time, unions draw upon traditions and values of collective activity which tend to differentiate them from a simple pursuit of market logic. It is the search for fundamental human freedoms and the extension of certain types of social solidarity within and beyond the marketplace that have rendered them the vehicles for social change.

Union responses to current changes are thus profoundly cultural and must be understood as such — cultural in the sense of a critical capacity, an interpretive filter through which these changes are understood, and also in the sense that culture provides a way of understanding the articulations between different values and visions of a society or of an organisation within a given context.[6] Union actions necessarily spring from a cultural foundation; these actions are themselves an articulation between the specific organizational cultures of particular workplaces, unions and larger societal cultures. The particular organizational culture of a union melds larger political and labour movement cultures with specific organizational sub-cultures, based on more specific ethnic, gender or professional identities. Such cultures promote certain types of solidarity at the expense of others; they are learned and, indeed, particular notions of solidarity will evolve over time. The articulation between these different components of an organizational culture holds particular significance in connection with the mobilization of identities, the propensity towards certain types of strategies or collective actions, and the willingness of groups of workers to take action in particular contexts. An understanding of union organizations in periods of economic and social change must necessarily draw on the relationship between culture, organizational change and larger socio-economic transformations. It is to the analysis of the larger political economy of change, and to its impact on union organizations and culture in Ontario and Québec that we now turn.

CHANGING POLITICAL ECONOMY OF TRADE UNIONISM

This section briefly considers some of the principal changes acting on the Canadian labour movement. The exposition is greatly simplified in order that we might better identify their impact on union structures and practices. Of particular interest is the way in which various contradictory pressures have challenged long standing union structures and practices; not only in terms of collective bargaining, but also in terms of the values and structures around which unionists have mobilised to attain their objectives.

The first major source of change in the labour movement is undoubtedly the restructuring and relocation of capital on a global scale which, in turn, profoundly affects the labour markets in which unions operate.[7] Unions have, of course, had to adjust to the rise of the transnational enterprise, but the last decade has seen an acceleration in the internationalization of production, which has implications for the transfer of technology and production across national frontiers as well as between production units. Workers have been subjected to increased competition between production units with all of the attendant consequences for the negotiation of wages and working practices, as unions are asked to participate in a kind of competitive tendering to maintain their jobs.

For traditional union culture, one of the most striking features of this new environment is the loss of confidence in the "golden" productivity formula according to which economic growth meant job and income security for workers in core industrial sectors.[8] The shift to a more competitive corporate paradigm opens up at least some questions about the traditional operative assumptions of North American business unionism. However, we shall see that it is quite another question to ask whether this challenge is resolved in terms of a more critical stance or a closer integration into the competitive constraints of individual firms (a kind of enterprise unionism).

The liberalization of trading arrangements is another dimension of the globalization of capital as the dismantling of traditional protective mechanisms accelerates economic restructuring, challenges existing modes of regulation, and opens new areas of economic insecurity for workers and their unions. One important difference here between Ontario and Québec appears to be their different types of articulation with the international and, notably, with the American economies. While both provinces continue to depend heavily on branch plant manufacturing for the domestic economy, the manufacturing sector in Québec appears to be somewhat weaker than that of Ontario. In terms of overall employment, manufacturing employment in Québec represented 19.9% of the active labour force in 1986 as opposed to 21.5% in Ontario.[9] Moreover, the Québec economy, as opposed to that of Ontario, was characterized by a greater concentration of low value-added manufacturing activity.[10] In this sense, the economy of Québec relies more on the export of natural resources and their primary transformation as well as on light industry.

Other manifestations of the restructuring of capital are the shifts in industrial structure, particularly those which move away from manufacturing and into private services. Between 1967 and 1988, employment growth in the goods sector of the Canadian economy (primary, manufacturing and construction) was limited to 0.9% per annum, whereas service sector growth (both public and private) was 3.2% annually.[11] As we shall see below, although union growth has largely kept pace with the growth in public service employment, this is not the case with private services; this is of particular importance as public service employment growth stagnates while private services continue to expand. Moreover, all of these changes in employment structure have had a profound effect on traditional union jurisdictions.

A second source of environmental change for the labour movement can be seen in the shifts in corporate strategy and organization. The origin of this is the social reorganization of production at the workplace which is particularly evident in the implantation of new production systems and the re-organization of internal labour markets in the firm. The result is what might be seen as a dual, and sometimes contradictory, process of integration and differentiation. By integration, we refer to the ideological reconstruction of the workplace around new production systems and management techniques, which seek to mobilize employee enthusiasm and know-how and therefore to achieve greater productivity and competitiveness.[12] At one end of the spectrum, this might be perceived as yet another management mode in a never-ending cycle of participative initiatives. However, it might also be seen as an entire reconstruction of the social system of the enterprise,[13] and it can, indeed, seek to integrate (or exclude) certain forms of participation and workers' representative mechanisms in the very culture of the firm. This can involve a range of new managerial practices: total quality management, quality circles, different modes of remuneration, new forms of participation in the firm, etc. Whatever its orientation, and it surely varies greatly from one firm to another, this integrative process opens up a range of strategic questions for union organizations which we will soon address.

Often within the very same firms, however, there is also a process of differentiation whereby firms seek to attain new levels of "flexibility" by transforming traditional full-time, secure jobs into other categories of employment, be they part-time, contractual, temporary, sub-contracted, different profit-centres, or other. They also try to reach this goal by re-organizing production and services either into smaller, more highly differentiated units or by foregoing employment relations altogether in favour of outside contractors.[14]

Another aspect of differentiation is the creation of new specialist categories of employees outside traditional orbits of promotion and wage systems. This multiplication of internal labour markets cuts across traditional lines of union solidarity as relationships between workers, their wages and conditions are entirely redefined. Some employers in particular, have sought to disconnect or reorganize traditional wage comparisons between firms and units through this same philosophy of differentiation. In the retail food sector, for example, there have been numerous franchising activities which result either in de-unionization or increased differentiation between contracts. Moreover, this is far from a private sector phenomenon as public agencies have sought to emulate differentiation strategies both in terms of the organization of services and the wages and conditions of their direct employees or their contracted workers. Integration and differentiation thus shift the very basis of traditional union structures and practices, thereby opening up a range of questions for union organizations about the nature and extent of internal and external solidarities.

The dual internal labour market process is reflected in the increasing bifurcation of the external labour market — a third source of change in the political economy of Canadian trade unionism. On the one hand, there seems to be greater scope for an aspiration to some kind of professional status at work whereby the "profession" acts as a profound source of identity and belonging in work.[15] On the other hand, another part of the labour market is increasingly characterized by unemployment, underemployment or precarious employment. Part of the expansion in the service sector would appear to be fuelled by the availability of low-wage and often part-time employment, particularly of women and the young, but also, increasingly of older workers; this polarisation of employment status also spills over into worker income.[16] The problems that arise for union strategy within firms are thus posed in an even more acute way in the larger labour market. In essence, the labour movement is obliged to internalize the very contradictions of the labour market and, somehow, to produce solidarity strategies in the face of these increasing inequalities when its own internal structures and operative assumptions are often based on these very contradictions — seniority, skills, professional identities, etc. Thus, the labour movement is subject to increasing tensions between micro-corporatist and/or professional types of strategies and identities, and more generally, labour market strategies, possibly relying on the political regulation of the most disadvantaged in the labour market.

Albeit, this is scarcely a new dynamic; we need only think of the traditional divisions between craft and general or industrial unionism and their relationship with different visions of political action in the old industrialized economies. The labour market changes of the past two decades, however, re-open some of the traditional solutions and compromises between different visions of how to assure a degree of worker security and to promote the improvement of working conditions in the labour market. They also raise questions about the limits of collective bargaining strategies in dealing with these issues.

A fourth area of change arises from the entry of "new" groups in the labour market, such as women and visible minorities, as well as the departure of other groups such as older workers. The sea-change is, of course, the participation of women in paid employment. Between the 1961 and the 1986 censuses, the profile of the typical family was completely reversed as the two-income family became the norm.[17] This change was further reflected in the composition of family income where real revenue stagnated unless it was increased by greater family working time in the wage economy, such as women's paid work outside the home.[18] This massive entry of women into the labour market has stimulated a range of debates within trade unions about women's work and the role of women in general.[19] The emergence of women's committees and networks has arguably been an important source of democratization within unions and has challenged, not always successfully, a whole range of patriarchal practices.[20]

Other "new" entrants into the labour market are the different ethnic groups and particularly visible minorities. While immigration is hardly a new phenomenon, roughly half of the immigrants entering Canada between 1976 and 1986 were visible minorities.[21] Youth were not a new group in the labour market, but continued high unemployment among youth means that their attachment to work is often precarious which clearly has an effect on their opportunity to join unions. By the same token, the older worker, particularly males over the age of fifty-five, has increasingly withdrawn from the active labour force,[22] and thus, has had an increasingly tenuous attachment to the paid labour market.

All of these changes raise questions about the capacities of union organizations to integrate women, young people, visible minorities and even the elderly, into the ranks in an effective way, while genuinely espousing their identities and aspirations in order to promote them. In this sense, women's struggle for a greater voice within workers' organizations has possibly served as a model for other groups aspiring to some degree of recognition, particularly the widespread implantation of womens' committees at various levels of unions' organizational structures.

A fifth area of change in the political economy of trade unionism is related to the role of the State, particularly the common pressures to reduce its protective and providential roles in favour of a "free market" approach, be it in terms of tariff protection, fiscal policy, social programmes, or industrial policy. This has been particularly evident in the management of public services where cutbacks, privatization, contracting-out and commercialisation have been some of the common themes of public sector industrial relations throughout the last decade. While there have been considerable pressures to move towards an overall decrease in employee protection, the Ontario and Québec labour movements have, at the level of provincial States at least, proved relatively successful in defending many of the gains of the 1960s and 1970s. In addition, through their links with particular political parties, the New Democratic Party and the Parti Québecois respectively, actually made some legislative gains in collective labour rights. In particular, because of the force of women's and other minority rights groups, there has been a notable expansion of employment rights in the areas of pay equity and equal access provisions. While the effectiveness of these measures is certainly open to question, it does demonstrate the permeability of the State to popular political pressures. This has, to a much lessor degree, been evident in the defense of some public services such as resistance to the erosion of the principle of universality in social programs. The defence of collective bargaining rights in the public sector, however, has proved much more problematic.[23]

Changes in both State policy and the State sector have highlighted the need for union political strategies, and have often led to quite different visions about appropriate forms of union political action. Moreover, the State in both provinces has continued to be a site of union political activity in attempts to ensure a relative degree of employment protection in the face of larger changes in the international political economy. Again, both the Ontario and Québec States have proved susceptible to union political pressures on these issues. In particular, when threatened with popular political pressures, the Québec State has, through its different investment agencies, such as the Caisse de dépôt et placement du Québec, often in close collaboration with the FTQ's investment fund, taken a number of exceptional measures to protect employment and to ensure indigenous ownership in the face of movements in international and even, in the case of the Steinbergs grocery chain, anglo-Canadian capital.[24]

Recent evidence from Ontario, notably in the cases of Algoma Steel and DeHavilland Aircraft, suggest that the Ontario State, particularly an NDP government, is likely to prove as susceptible to pressures to protect employment. Moreover, such preoccupations are at the heart of recent moves in both provinces to promote various sectoral forums on issues such as training, competitiveness and industrial restructuring.

Finally, a sixth area of change arises from the penetration of market relations into all social relations. In the context of dramatic political changes between East and West, the market has been declared the ultimate arbiter of all social relations. This can been seen in the commodification of services, both formal and informal, in spheres of production and social reproduction. Rampant consumerism is, of course, the most blatant example as we see the simultaneous increases in family debt and the proliferation of consumer temples. At the same time, there exists a kind of counter-reaction in the environmental movement. This presents new problems for labour unions as they seek to come to grips with the relationship between production issues and the environment. Unions operate most naturally on the terrain of the wage relationship. Although there are some examples of workers' organizations addressing issues such as the social ends of the production in which they are engaged, it often appears to be difficult territory on which to mobilize their members.[25] Where concerns about health or environmental and community issues stem directly from the point of production, there is clearly growing scope for union intervention. This area of change then, has both cultural and strategic implications for the labour movement, particularly in terms of the relative capacity of union organizations to articulate and join the concerns of their members with those in some of the newer social movements, often outside of traditional collective bargaining channels.

STRUCTURE AND REPRESENTATIVENESS

These economic and social changes have profound implications for union organizations. The patterns of representation established in the post-war period are subject to change at several levels: in terms of the numerical representativeness of the labour movement in each province, of the distribution of sectoral and professional jurisdictions between and within union organizations, of the integration of new workers in the labour market, and, more globally, of the capacity of labour organizations to act as effective advocates of social transformations and new collective identities. Labour market change thus confronts the labour movement with questions about its representativeness and, ultimately, about its legitimacy. Moreover, this is scarcely a phenomenon which is confined to Ontario and Québec as different national labour movements have similarly sought to come to terms with a common set of market pressures, albeit in different institutional settings.[26]

How then do these larger trends translate into the actual membership representativeness, the composition of the labour movement and its structures?[27] Trade union membership has been expanding in the two provinces at roughly comparable rates over the past two decades. Thus, union membership in Québec expanded by 64.2% from 1967 to 1987 and by 73% in Ontario over the same period. The marked difference between the two provinces really comes in the 1962 to 1967 period during which time union membership grew by 4.3% annually in Ontario (roughly comparable with the overall growth profile) whereas the Québec labour movement enjoyed a tremendous surge of growth, 15.6% annually. The latter results from the earlier growth of public sector unionism in Québec; Ontario would experience similar public sector growth, but much more gradually and never to the same degree.

The relative significance of this absolute growth in union membership in the two provinces is, however, quite different when looked at as a measure of union density or as a percentage of paid workers.[28] Whereas Québec union growth has translated into increasing union density throughout the 1962 to 1987 period, increasing from 25.8% in 1962 to 36.7% in 1972, and to 40.7% in 1987, the Ontario labour market has expanded much more rapidly. Thus, the Ontario labour movement's expansion has not kept pace with changes in the labour force relative to Québec, which explains the relative stability in union density in Ontario. Over the same period in fact, the level of union density in Ontario declined slightly, from 32.7% in 1962 and 32.9% in 1972 to 31.9% in 1987. Thus, while it might be argued that the Québec union movement has been increasingly representative of the labour force, the Ontario labour movement has remained relatively stable despite the underlying absolute growth in the number of actual union members.

In terms of their relative sectoral composition, both labour movements are characterized by the relative importance of the public sector with respect to the overall composition of those covered by a collective agreement. Public services, particularly health and education, account for more than 40% of the labour movement in each case (42.7% in Ontario and 45.1% in Québec).[29] What distinguishes the two union movements is the greater importance of manufacturing in Ontario compared to the relatively greater importance of private services as a component of the Québec labour movement. Whereas the most important non-public service sectors of the Ontario labour movement are to be found in the manufacturing sector (primarily the automobile and steel industries — 8.2% and 5.7% of workers are covered by a collective agreement respectively), in Québec we can note the relative importance of private services such as retail and wholesale trade (8.6% and 4.6%), and hotel and catering (5.8%). This is due, in part, to the traditional weakness of the manufacturing sector in Québec as manufacturing is a highly unionized sector in both provinces.[30] However, it also suggests that the Québec labour movement has gone further than its Ontario counterpart in establishing a presence in the private service sector.[31]

Such an interpretation is reinforced when considering relative collective bargaining coverage by sectors in the two provinces. In December 1986, Québec had a higher percentage of workers covered in all major sectors: the discrepancy between the two varied from a low of 3.5% in manufacturing (46.8% coverage in Québec as opposed to 43.3% in Ontario) to a high of 27.2% in construction, where a public regime of compulsory union membership ensured a higher rate of coverage in Québec. Marked differences also existed in both the private services and the public services, where the more centralized bargaining system in Québec has presumably worked in favour of first establishing and then maintaining higher union membership.[32] Although the reason for the discrepancy in private services is more open to speculation, the reconstruction of unionization in that sector lies outside the scope of this particular project.[33] However, it is clear that the main thrust of recent union recruitment activity in Québec has been in this sector. This is partly due to the relative saturation achieved in public services as well as the weak prospects in manufacturing where the size effect, for example, the difficulty of unionizing smaller establishments, would appear to be a limiting factor.

The Québec labour movement appears to have been relatively more successful than its Ontario counterpart in attaining a presence in the sector which is most associated with employment growth. There are a number of other indicators which are consistent with such an interpretation. Recent discussions about the possible reform of the Ontario Labour Code tend to refer to provisions in Québec's Code du travail.[34] Similarly, union recruitment strategies in chain establishments in private sector services have tended to target the Québec establishments of these chains.[35] We might also note the greater success of Québec unions in establishing a presence in smaller firms.[36]

Another dimension of these changes in the political economy of trade unionism is their impact on union structure. In terms of affiliations, the 1980s have witnessed the continuing proliferation of labour centrals with the creation of new centres of affiliation such as the Canadian Federation of Labour and the continued growth of unaffiliated unions. Another important trend has been the relative decline in the importance of international or American unionism. In the latter case, we might note the weaker presence of international unionism in Québec. For instance, in 1988, roughly 25.4% of union members belonged to international unions in Québec as opposed to 40.7% in Ontario.[37]

The changing organization of the firm and larger trends in the labour market have also had a marked, if highly differential, impact on the structures and strategies of local unions. Most notably, the declining size of existing bargaining units and the small size of many new certifications in both Québec and Ontario have prompted some unions to amalgamate different certifications into larger, composite locals.[38] This is particularly evident in many of the older unions which are characterized by a craft structure, such as the United Food and Commercial Workers' Union, which have traditionally organized a multiplicity of units within a single local and built their servicing structures around this type of arrangement. The local structures of "industrial model" unions, such as the United Steelworkers of America, are also undergoing significant change. Perhaps because of its location in a weaker industrial sector, but also because of the infusion of new private service sector certification units, the Steelworkers Union in Québec (les Métallos) has altered its local structures much more rapidly than its counterpart in Ontario. While the average size of a Steelworker local actually declined from 217 members to 202 members in Ontario over the period from 1978 to 1987, that of a Québec Steelworker local increased from 203 members to 283 members with the average number of certifications per local also increasing from 1.7 per local to 3.2. By contrast, the average number of certifications per local in Ontario increased from 1.4 to 1.7 over this same period.[39] This represented a conscious organizing and servicing strategy in Québec designed to better meet the needs of new membership groups in both the service sector and in small manufacturing units. Indeed, it aimed to create union locals which are better able to adjust to the small size of new units typically being organized during this period. It also sought to achieve a viable servicing strategy in terms of the relative cost of reaching a multiplicity of small units and providing access to basic services, sometimes assured by newly trained full-time lay representatives rather than by professional business agents or servicing staff.

ORGANIZATIONAL AND CULTURAL CHANGES

The changes in the political economy of Canadian unionism challenge national union organizations in a number of important ways. For instance, economic restructuring in both Ontario and Québec has challenged the representativeness of the labour movement, and unions have had to invest heavily in new organizing initiatives both to enhance their legitimacy as socio-political actors in a changing economy as well as, in many cases, to stave off organizational decline. Union leaderships are re-assessing where, how and whom they organize. This has immediate internal cultural implications where existing union cultures play a critical role in facilitating or hindering the integration of new groups into larger notions of solidarity. There is, for example, a continuing debate about whether organizing is to be accomplished by specialists or generalists. Activist education on organizing strategies and techniques has also become a component of union educational offerings in both Ontario and Québec, though some unions in Québec appear to have evolved more rapidly in this direction, possibly because the weaker industrial structure meant that there was less scope for organizing in manufacturing. Union leaderships, such as in the Steelworkers, are increasingly confronted with the cultural implications of the changing composition of their union's membership, in order to avoid potential backlash from traditional sectors of the union where there may be some nostalgia for an older industrial structure.

The national union organizations are also challenged by the number of common internal structural adjustments that reflect the changes in membership composition, the movements in corporate structure, the rise of new identities at work and the real problems of organizing new groups of workers into unions. In particular, at the local level, we have mentioned the rise of the composite or amalgamated local, particularly in Québec where both the dispersion of manufacturing activities and the existence of multiple union centrals have contributed to the rise of this form among FTQ affiliates. By contrast, the CSN remains constitutionally tied to an organizational form in which a single certification constitutes a local.[40] At other levels, there is the question of how to achieve effective coordinating mechanisms in an effort to organize the new groups into viable structures and to make links between core and peripheral workers.

Although this is an enduring problem in a large number of unions in both provinces, it is doubtlessly exacerbated in Québec where disaffected groups within unions can generally seek to affiliate with another labour central — an option which is not readily available in Ontario.[41] This is particularly evident before each round of public sector negotiations in Québec. Indeed, there has been considerable movement by different groups of public sector "professionals" attempting to enhance the representation of their specific identities. The challenge of fostering participation and giving a sense of ownership in their organizations is, of course, a major preoccupation behind attempts to achieve structural adjustments at different levels of union organizations, especially for the newer groups of workers in the labour market, such as women and immigrants, who have traditionally been excluded from such a sense of belonging.

Another change that is challenging national union organizations includes the various new strategies emerging which concern negotiating structures and strategies. In structural terms, this entails some attempt to link new representational structures with bargaining structures, or to create such bargaining structures in order to obtain greater bargaining power and viable servicing structures. There are a number of important examples in the Québec service sector, such as in the case of security guards and garage employees, where the regional collective agreement decree system has been used as the basis of some forms of wider-based bargaining structures. Similarly, in Ontario's para-public and privatized public service sectors, the Ontario Public Service Employees Union (OPSEU) has sought to achieve increased coordination among multiple employers. With respect to the bargaining agenda, in addition to the traditional and ever present concern with job security and remuneration, there has been some effort, albeit quite differentially, to expand bargaining strategies to reflect the changed political economy and the preoccupations of the new groups on the labour market. The Canadian Autoworkers Council structure, which brings together local union activists on a quarterly basis, is an innovative model inasmuch as it facilitates the transmission of such bargaining concerns between different units, and thereby contributes to the building of a larger union culture about how to tackle the "new times."

The unprecedented demand for more sophisticated union services and the decreased capacity to pay for them also challenges national union organizations. In particular, structural changes in the labour market have resulted in reduced real dues income per member as overall income has remained stable with new members often either working part-time or earning less in the general service occupations. This has increased the pressure on union services and has led to a certain re-thinking of the role of full-time staff in some unions, particularly as regards the relative division of labour between staff and activists and the role of education and self-empowerment in the provision of services by activists. Once again, there are potential profound cultural ramifications for the way that people think about their organizations, although it is altogether less clear that widespread changes have actually taken place. Indeed, there would appear to be some scope for a larger debate about the nature of union democracy and how this is to be reflected in the creation of new structures and the provision of services.

An additional challenge concerns solidarity and political action: unions have been faced with the question of how to reflect the new labour market developments and the preoccupations of their new membership into the larger sets of political and social action. In both Ontario and Québec, there is considerable evidence of union attempts to effect broader coalitions with other social groups, be it in terms of free trade, ecology, international solidarity, human rights and, most recently, political sovereignty and constitution-building.

Finally, in terms of overall strategizing, it needs to be asked in what ways a union's endeavours in each of these areas can be linked with a longer-term analysis of the changes that it is experiencing and how to respond to them. This would seem to be particularly critical, both techni- cally and politically, especially in terms of the development of a galvaniz- ing force to lift the morale of activists and staff, and to develop a robust political culture around the future of the union. It is at this juncture that organizational culture, interacting with union leadership, plays a critical role in the way in which older solidarities are reinforced and the possibility of new solidarities are opened up. The move to either "enterprise" unionism with a predominant micro-corporatist perspective, or to a kind of general "social" unionism both imply cultural shifts which have a filtering impact on the way that other changes in the labour market are perceived.

NEW UNION CULTURES, ORGANIZATIONAL STRUCTURES AND SOCIAL CHANGE

This chapter has sought to portray some of the links between the environmental changes which make up the landscape for the social move- ments of the late twentieth century and the labour movement, certainly the most traditional of the social movements. Despite accusations that the labour movement is hidebound in its conservatism and its inability to change, we have tried to establish that there has emerged a new "common sense" to the effect that union organizations are obliged to come to terms with market changes, even if the extent and the direction of adaptation is quite different from one union to another.

These changes are remarkable in at least two respects. First, they presage a change in model to new union forms which take account of the broader changes in labour and product markets. Just as we can now look back on the decline of craft unionism as the passing of an inclusive and effective organizational form for the mobilization of collective iden- tities, so too, can we increasingly discern the limits of the industrial union model. This latter model was closely associated with the creation of the Congress of Industrial Organizations (CIO) in the United States in the 1930s and was widely diffused in Canada in the years of post-war industrial expansion. The model was premised on the protection of its particular membership, primarily male, mass-production workers, through the elaboration of unit or company level collective agreements regulating in detail most aspects of the job. Its jurisdiction was restricted to particular industries and its organizational form was focused on particular units, generally one agreement per local, with external solidarities being extended as far as pattern bargaining required some kind of articulation with other units. Both the changes in union member- ship and practices, and the mutation of previous organizational forms, appear to point in the direction of the emergence of new or modified forms of union organization.[42]

Secondly, it should be appreciated that these changes have been made in a context of relative success, a kind of Canadian "exceptionalism" during this period.[43] Not only has union membership continued to increase in Canada in almost every year since the 1960s,[44] but the labour movement has sought, however imperfectly, to adapt to the major environmental changes of the 1980s: integration of part-time workers, integration of women, changing structural dynamics of the labour movement and the articulation of the identities of at least some of the new labour market groups.

The main characteristic regarding the nature of change in both labour markets and the union responses to them therefore, is convergence. Indeed, the differences between individual unions are probably greater than the differences between provinces. There are a number of factors fuelling this reality such as, as we have argued above, the common set of pressures in the two provinces. Notions of solidarity are constructed around cultural values. From there, structures are created which institutionalize and reproduce at least some of these solidarities. While the exact mechanics may sometimes be different, the direction is by and large a common one.

There is also, in some unions at least, a strong intra-organizational emulation effect. New union policies and approaches are frequently transmitted institutionally as the same organizations adopt common policies or learn from comparable experiences across the Québec-Ontario border. This has certainly been the case of both the Steelworkers and the Autoworkers, the former developing new approaches first in Québec and the latter importing many of the innovations first discussed in Ontario.

Moreover, a generational factor also exists in which a new union generation of union leaders, many of whom have had experience in other social movements, has both been obliged and sought to differentiate its practices from a previous generation focused more exclusively on the demands of the collective agreement and its renegotiation.

An additional factor not to be forgotten concerns the inter-organizational emulation effect. The impetus for change is so great that all union leaders seem compelled to jump on the "bandwagon," whatever the degree of commitment to real change. No organization can afford to be without a women's officer, a health and safety specialist, a "visible minority" relations committee, etc. This tendency is, of course, fuelled by the collapse of inter-union jurisdictions and the increased competition for the recruitment of new members.

Finally, there are comparable temptations and real limits as regards the diffusion of the "new" cooperative union strategies which focus almost exclusively within the firm to the detriment of larger labour market solidarities. Some unions, be they at local, provincial, or sectoral levels, are, by the nature of their own histories and the product markets of the firms in which they are present, clearly tempted by the appeal of enduring, cooperative, strife-free relationships with their employers — a kind of new "enterprise" unionism currently being promoted in a number of countries.[45] Moreover, the threat to employment in an era of economic restructuring pushes many local and national union leaders towards more collaborative relationships with their employers. However, the real vulnerability of the Canadian economy and the inability of firms to provide a satisfactory explanation of some of the more blatant contradictions of the new social enterprise means that the promise of this type of unionism often does not endure. This applies both at the level of the enterprise where performance does not always meet promise, but also outside the immediate universe of the firm where a growing group of workers are defined by their "exclusion from" rather than by their "inclusion in" such a cooperative paradigm.

It is by no means impossible, however, to construct different forms of "partnership" to protect employment on a company-by-company and, occasionally, even on a sectoral basis, although such agreements often entail a significant narrowing of the scope for or interest in larger solidarities on the part of the local union. Moreover, there are currently many examples of such attempts in both Ontario and Québec, although — for reasons to which we shall return below — the ideological thrust in this direction would appear to be much stronger in Québec.

When we move from organizational cultures to societal cultures, how then do we disentangle the relative impact of markets, State regulation, cultural differences between Ontario and Québec, and the very different organizational cultures of the various unions under investigation? There is certainly no simple response to this question. What is required is a more satisfactory account of the differential developments of the Ontario and Québec States and their different articulations with the labour movements of the two provinces. Several factors need be considered in such an account.

Firstly, there is the question of how regional or community cultures vary and shape attitudes towards market relations and State regulation, and how this accounts for a whole variety of differences in union strategies.

Secondly, there is the role of State modernization and the relative incorporation of the labour movement in that project. This is, for instance, much more clearly the case with the Québec labour movement than with that of Ontario where, until quite recently, through their historic identification with the NDP, the major labour unions have maintained a distance with regards to the various projects of the Ontario State and vice versa. By contrast, various organizations in the Québec labour movement have at different times experienced close relationships with the Québec State on certain issues since the "Quiet Revolution" of the late 1950s and early 1960s. This was the case with the CSN in the 1960s and that of the FTQ during the tenure of the Parti Québécois through the late 1970s and early 1980s. By contrast, such engagements are a more recent evolution in the case of Ontario. The long ruling Conservative Party and the labour movement were both somewhat reluctant to engage in significant consultative exercises. This attitude appears, however, to have dissipated in recent years first, under the influence of the NDP during the lib-lab coalition, then, more directly, during the second Peterson government, particularly given that both the Peterson Government and the labour movement were advancing similar sets of arguments about the dangers of free trade and the importance of structural adjustments in the economy. This trend has clearly accelerated with the election of an NDP government in Ontario.

A third factor to be considered involves the question of the role of nationalism as regards the presence or absence of a critical stance on the part of the labour movement towards capital. While nationalism has played an important role in both Ontario and Québec, the Ontario labour movement has arguably been more frequently anti-capitalist than its Québec counter-part — perhaps because the Québec labour movement has more strongly identified with a nationalist struggle which clearly crossed class lines in the face of both Anglo-Canadian and American capital. This somewhat more positive opening to the exigencies of capital accumulation has probably been exacerbated by Québec's weaker industrial structure and recent efforts, in the context of endemically higher levels of unemployment in Québec, to maintain a viable manufacturing sector and a degree of indigenous leverage in key sectors of the economy. This can be seen, for instance, in the role played by the Québec pension fund investment agency, La Caisse de dépôt et placement, and the symbolic union participation in the management of this agency. Thus, while the history of both the Québec and Ontario labour movements has been marked by various epic struggles with foreign capital, the leadership of the Ontario labour movement might be seen as more marked by a certain critical culture regarding the "market" than by the "national" struggles which have typified the Québec labour movement (at least in the private sector.)

The definitive study of the fascinating differences in the articulation between Ontario and Québec labour movements and their respective States remains to be completed.[46] An important difference can be seen in the creation of the Solidarity Fund, put in place by the FTQ in 1983 as a risk investment fund to safeguard and promote employment in Québec firms.[47] By contrast, in Ontario, there has been a continuing debate about the merits of such an intiative. It is important to note, moreover, that many of the differences between Ontario and Québec on this point are just as contentious between unions within each of the provinces, especially on issues such as workplace re-organization and union advocacy of various new human resource management strategies.[48]

An additional factor to be considered is that the relative fragmentation of union structures in Québec has meant that many strategic differences have more traditionally been in evidence between labour centrals — even though there would currently appear to be an important degree of convergence. The pursuit of a degree of market differentiation in the evolution of the positions of the Québec labour centrals vis-à-vis the State has been a powerful motive in the development of different union positions in Québec. For example, the FTQ has sought to occupy a pre-eminent place within Québec State consultative bodies, while the CEQ and the CSN have only more recently sought to re-activate their presence in these bodies.[49] There is a particular irony in this as the CSN initially used its pre-eminent position in the Québec Cultural Revolution to occupy a privileged place in these types of bodies.

There is a compelling argument to be made for a comparative political economy of trade union culture in the two provinces, although much remains to be done before we arrive at a satisfactory set of explanations of the dynamics of the similarities and differences between the two.

A final question, and one of a different order, concerns the degree to which the labour movement, among the various social movements, is able to provide a culture, that critical facility for the interpretation of larger changes, which is challenging and which raises questions and makes people the subjects of their own histories. There is evidence that real efforts to pursue at least part of that critical project have been made, although these vary greatly from organization to the next. Moreover, they encounter several obstacles which appear to be inscribed in the structural location of the labour movement itself. There are, for example, difficulties in "subordinating" a larger range of market changes to trade union identity. By the same token, however, the very location of the union organization in the employment relationship is an obvious source of strength inasmuch as wages and work are still powerful generators of social identity in a structural and organizational way with collective institutions and traditions that can protect and foster those identities. The labour movement thus enjoys powerful advantages not available to many other social movements. It is also that very strength that makes it the object of external groups who seek to integrate its institutions, be it within the firm or the State. The very strength of identities founded on the wage relationship also facilitates the worst bureaucratic reflexes of labour leaders who seek to control or stifle other social identities rather than learning to work with them and to build upon them.

This chapter has sought to depict the common and convergent tendencies of the Québec and Ontario union organizations to adjust their own cultures and structures in response to larger socio-economic changes over the last decade. This can be seen in the efforts to achieve greater representativeness and legitimacy; to develop new structures which take account of the larger changes in the labour market; to better integrate new groups of workers and new poles of identity in the labour market; to articulate and address the real problems of workplaces and work; to make better links with other social movements; and to construct a more socially oriented and robust union project. In a context in which older institutional forms are being transformed, it is scarcely surprising that the "old" union actor should be subject to tough scrutiny and considerable scepticism. But in these avenues of strategic renewal, there are many signs of a new critical culture which is seeking, however unevenly, however imperfectly, to invent its own future.

NOTES

1. This study has benefited from the financial support of the Social Science and Humanities Research Council of Canada. The author wishes to thank the many trade unionists who have assisted in the gathering and the interpretation of the data and without whom this study would not have been possible. Thanks are also due to Luc Cloutier, Jean-Pierre Gilbert and Julien Larouche for their research assistance on particular aspects of the data presented here.
2. Much of this analysis applies more generally to the Canadian labour movement. However, the focus of the field research was generally in Ontario and Québec and no attempt is made here to account for the similarities and differences in the western and maritime provinces.
3. Among recent efforts to explore some of these differences, see Verge and Murray (1991) and Lipsig-Mummé (1991).
4. See, for example, Touraine *et. al.* (1984) and Rosanvallon (1988).
5. See, for example, Kane and Marsden (1988) and Vesser (1989).
6. Sainsaulieu (1987: 142) writes that culture "apparaît comme le réservoir intériorisé, transmis et soigneusement élaboré par l'histoire d'un ensemble de valeurs, de règles et de représentations collectives qui fonctionnent au plus profond des rapports humains."
7. See, for example, Kolko (1988) and Holmes and Leys (1987).
8. Variously referred to as the "glorious" thirty years, Fordism, or simply as the post-war economic expansion, a variety of authors have discerned a common set of factors characterizing these years. See, for instance, from a political economy perspective, Boyer (1986), Jenson (1989), Piore and Sabel (1984), Boismenu and Drache (1990). See also Kochan, Katz and McKersie, 1986, for a comparable industrial relations explanation of the advent of a period of concessionary bargaining.
9. See Tremblay and Van Schendel (1991: 286-287).
10. Ibid., 179-218.
11. Economic Council of Canada (1990). Ontario and Québec have both experienced a comparable decline in the percentage share of employment in the goods sector. In Ontario the relative share fell from 32.0% in 1971 to 28.0% in 1986. In Québec it declined from 30.9% to 27.1% over the same period. Calculated from Tremblay and Van Schendel (1990: 286-287), Table 9.1.
12. See, for example, Wells (1987 and 1991) and Ferland and Bellemarre (1988).
13. On this point more generally, see Mona-Josée Gagnon's text in this volume; also Sainsaulieu (1990), Leuthold *et. al.* (1988), and Saint-Pierre (1990).
14. See, for example, Laflamme *et. al.* (1989).
15. Moreover, such aspirations can be encouraged by shifts in managerial policies, for instance from wage to salary model payment systems. See, for example, Osterman (1989).
16. This process is well documented in a recent Economic Council of Canada (1990) document which is aptly titled *Good Jobs, Bad Jobs*. See also Myles *et. al.* (1988).
17. Statistics Canada (1961 and 1986).
18. See *Globe & Mail* (1989) and le *Soleil* (1989).
19. See the chapter by Warskett in this volume.
20. See, for example, Briskin and Yanz (1983) and Leah (1990).
21. See Balakrishnan (1988). In 1986, 15.6% of the Canadian population was born outside of the country and roughly half of all new immigrants in the previous

decade were visible minorities. There were clearly pronounced differences, however, in settlement patterns. While 15.9% of Montréal's population was born outside of Canada, the comparable figure was 36.3% in Toronto.

22. From 1975 to 1987, for instance, the participation rate of older male workers in Canada declined from 50.5% to 39.2% (Statistique Canada, 1975 and 1987).

23. See, for example, Panitch and Swartz (1988).

24. On the extensive network of union participation in State consultative and administrative bodies in Québec, see Verge and Murray (1991: 240-243 and 330-334). On the FTQ's investment fund, le Fonds de solidarité, see Fournier (1987). The purpose of the fund is to invest a part of worker Registered Retirement Savings contributions in Québec based firms, often on a risk or equity capital basis, in order to safeguard and promote employment.

25. See Wainwright and Elliott (1982).

26. See, for instance, Kane and Marsden (1988).

27. Statistics on the labour movement in Canada can be obtained from a variety of sources and these invariably present problems. This section uses a variety of those sources and there can, as a result, be discrepancies in the information presented because not all of the data sources are strictly comparable. The focus here is on the comparative picture of the union movements in Ontario and Québec, regardless of source. It is however important to note, and it is always specified, that at some points we refer to actual union members, as derived from labour union reporting under federal legislative requirements. At other times, we refer to collective bargaining coverage which can either be derived from Labour Ministry data banks or from labour market survey evidence. For a fuller discussion of the strengths and weaknesses of these different sources, see Coates et. al. (1989).

28. Union density is here defined as the percentage of paid non-agricultural workers who are union members. The union density figures are derived from Coates et. al. (1989: Table 15); the union membership figures from CALURA (1989).

29. This data comes from the Labour Market Activity Survey of December 1986 from which, inter alia, it is possible to link sectoral location and collective bargaining coverage in the two provinces.

30. As a percentage of the active labour force, the importance of employment in the manufacturing sector in Québec has declined continuously from 26.4% in 1961 to 19.9% in 1986. Over this same period, the importance of this sector has declined from 26.9% to 21.5%. See Trembly and Van Schendel (1991: 286-287).

31. In December 1986, private services accounted for 24.9% of collective bargaining coverage in Québec as opposed to 20.2% in Ontario.

32. The split between public and private services can only be very approximate at best. We have counted the following sectoral groupings as broadly constituting public services: utilities, education, social and medical services, and federal, provincial and municipal levels of government. The other sectors in the tertiary sector are counted as private services. This leaves considerable scope for overlap, but gives an approximate idea of the different collective bargaining profiles of private and public services as derived from the Labour Market Activity Survey.

33. It would be of particular interest to chart the evolution of relative union density in private services, as opposed to other sectors, between Ontario and Québec over the past several decades. Unfortunately, there is a real dearth of reliable sectoral data as regards union density prior to the first Labour Market Activity Survey in 1986. A study of certification data provides another potential source of comparison as regards the sectoral location of new organizing activity but the differences in the methods of data collection and publication between the provincial labour boards or their equivalent in Quebec presents complex problems for any systematic comparison.

34. See Allen (1991).

35. See McKenna (1991).

36. Again, drawing on data from the 1986 Labour Market Activity Survey, the rate of unionization in firms employing less than twenty persons in Québec was 16.2%, as

opposed to a rate of 8.5% in Ontario. Similarly, in medium-size firms, employing between 20 and 99 persons, it was 37.8% in Québec and 21.6% in Ontario.

37. CALURA (1988). Calculated from Appendix 1.4, p.49.
38. See Murray (forthcoming).
39. These averages are calculated from data reported by individual unions by province in CALURA (1978). The 1987 data is derived from a special compilation.
40. See Verge and Murray (1991: 66-71).
41. It might also be noted that despite its very weak formal powers over its affiliates, and undoubtedly because of the threat of competition between competing labour centrals, the FTQ leadership has a tradition of interventionism to achieve greater coordination within its affiliates than is evident with the O.F.L. in Ontario.
42. See Murray (forthcoming).
43. See Murray (1991).
44. Overall membership in Canadian unions increased in every year from 1962 to 1988, except for very slight declines from 1981 to 1982 and 1983 to 1984. See CALURA (1964-1988).
45. See, for example, Heckscher (1988) or Reynaud (1991).
46. A particularly interesting avenue of inquiry in this respect concerns the different attitudes in the two provinces to a free trade agreement with the United States. Both labour movements were clearly opposed to free trade in principle although a number of individual FTQ affiliates were studiously ambiguous on this question given the support of the Parti Québécois for such a trade arrangement. This illustrates both commonalities and differences, both in terms of the different industrial structures of the two provinces and their anticipated adjustment problems and in terms of the different articulations of nationalism to class politics in Ontario and Québec.
47. On the creation of the Solidarity Fund, see Fournier (1987).
48. Note the differences, for example, in the positions of the Canadian Autoworkers and the Communications Workers Unions on workplace re-organization and new managerial strategies.
49. See Verge and Murray, 1991.

REFERENCES

Allen, Gene. 1991. "Ontario Ministry Calling for Ban on Strikebreakers," *Globe and Mail*, 4 September, A1.

Balakrishnan, T.R. 1988. "Immigration and the Changing Ethnic Mosaic of Canadian Cities," *The Review of Demography and Its Implications for Economic and Social Policy*, Winter. Ottawa: Government of Canada.

Boismenu, Gérard and Daniel Drache (eds.). 1990. *Politique et régulation*. Montréal: Éditions du Méridien.

Boyer, Robert (ed.). 1986. *La flexibilité du travail en Europe*, Paris: Editions La Découverte.

Briskin, Linda and Lynda Yanz. 1983. *Union Sisters: Women in the Labour Movement*. Toronto: Women's Press.

CALURA various years. *Annual Report of the Minister of Industry, Science and Technology under the Corporations and Labour Unions Returns Act Part II — Labour Unions*. Ottawa: Minister of Supply and Services Canada.

Coates, Mary-Lou; David Arrowsmith and Melanie Courchene. 1989. *The Labour Movement and Trade Unionism Reference Tables*. Kingston: Queen's University Industrial Relations Centre.

Economic Council of Canada. 1990. *Goods Jobs, Bad Jobs*. Ottawa: 1990.

Ferland, Gilles and Guy Bellemarre. 1988. "Nouvelles stratégies patronales de gestion et leurs impacts possibles sur les conditions de travail," *Pour aller plus loin: Les actes du colloque CSN sur les relations du travail*. Montreal: Confédération des Syndicats Nationaux, 45-92.

Fournier, Louis. 1987. "Le fonds de solidarité (FTQ): une petite révolution syndicale," *Interventions économiques*, no.17, 39-46.

Globe and Mail. 1989. "Average Families Real Incomes Remain Unchanged in 1988 from 1980," 5 December.

Heckscher, Charles C. 1988. *The New Unionism*. New York: Basic Books.

Holmes, John and Colin Leys (eds.). 1987. *Frontyard Backyard*. Toronto: Between the Lines.

Jenson, Jane. 1989. "'Different' but not 'exceptional': Canada's Permeable Fordism," *Canadian Review of Sociology and Anthropology*, vol.26, February, 69-94.

Kane, E.M. and D. Marsden. 1988. "L'avenir du syndicalisme dans les pays industrialisés à économie du marché," *Travail et société* vol. 13, no.2, 113-130.

Kochan, Thomas A.; Harry C. Katz, and Robert B. McKersie. 1986. *The Transformation of American Industrial Relations*. New York: Basic, 1986.

Kolko, Joyce. 1988. *Restructuring the World Economy*. New York: Pantheon.

Laflamme, Gilles; Gregor Murray, Jacques Bélanger and Gilles Ferland. 1989. *Flexibility and Labour Markets in Canada and the United States*. Geneva: International Institute of Labour Studies.

Leah, Ronnie. 1990. "Linking the Struggles: Racism, Feminism and the Union Movement," *Reprint Series*, no. 93, Industrial Relations Centre, Queen's University at Kingston, 1-30.

Létourneau, Jocelyn. 1987. "L'économie politique des trente glorieuses. Apport et originalité des analyses en terme de régulation." *Historical Reflections/Réflexions historiques*, vol. 14, no. 2, 345-379.

Leuthold, Patrice; Yves Lichtenberger, Dominique Martin, Denis Segrestin et Pierre-Eric Tixier. 1988. *L'entreprise et le syndicalisme*. Paris: Travaux sociologiques du L.S.C.I. no.7, CNRS-IRESCO.

Lipsig-Mummé, Carla. 1991. "Wars of Position: Fragmentation and Realignment in the Québec Labour Movement," *Queen's Papers in Industrial Relations*, 1990-11. Kingston: Queen's University Industrial Relations Centre.

McKenna, Barrie. 1991. "Union Targets Québec Bay Stores," *Globe and Mail*, 25 September, B6.

Murray, Gregor. 1991. "Exceptionalisme canadien? L'évolution récente du syndicalisme au Canada," *Revue de l'I.R.E.S.*, no. 7, automne, 1-25.

Murray, Gregor. forthcoming. "The Political Economy of Organizational Adjustment in National Trade Unions" in *The Political Economy of Canadian Industrial Relations*, Anthony Giles and Gregor Murray (eds.).

Myles, John; Garnett Picot and Ted Wannell. 1988. *Wages and Jobs in the 1980s: Changing Youth Wages and the Declining Middle*. Ottawa: Statistics Canada.

Osterman, Paul. 1989. "Employment Systems in the United States: Competing Models and Contingent Employment," *The International Journal of Comparative Labour Law and Industrial Relations*, vol. 5, no.1, 17-48.

Panitch, Leo and Donald Swartz. 1988. *The Assault on Trade Union Freedoms*. Toronto: Garamond Press.

Piore, Michael J. and Charles F. Sabel. 1984. *The Second Industrial Divide*. New York: Basic Books.

Reynaud, Emmanuèle. 1991. *Le pouvoir de dire non*. Paris: Éditions l'Harmattan.

Rosanvallon, Pierre. 1988. *La question syndicale*. Paris: Calmann-Lévy.

Sainsaulieu, Renaud. 1987. *Sociologie de l'organisation et de l'entreprise*. Paris: Presses de la Fondation Nationale des Sciences Politiques et Dalloz.

Sainsaulieu, Renaud (ed.). 1990. *L'entreprise: une affaire de société*. Paris: Presses de la Fondation Nationale des Sciences Politiques.

Saint-Pierre, Céline. 1990. "Transformations du monde du travail" in *La société québécoise après 30 ans de changements*, Fernand Dumont (ed.). Québec: Institut québécois de recherche sur la culture, 67-80.

Soleil, le. 1989. "Le revenu familial moyen plafonne depuis 10 ans," le 5 décembre.

Statistics Canada. 1961 and 1986. *Census*. Ottawa: Information Canada and Ministry of Supply and Services.

Statistics Canada. 1975 and 1987. *La population active.* Ottawa: Ministre des approvisionne-
ments et services Canada.

Touraine, Alain; Michel Wieviorka and François Dubet. 1984. *Le mouvement ouvrier.* Paris:
Fayard, 1984.

Tremblay, Diane Gabrielle and Vincent Van Schendel. 1991. *Economie du Québec et de ses
régions.* Sainte-Foy: Téléuniversité et Editions Saint-Martin.

Verge, Pierre and Gregor Murray. 1991. *Le droit et les syndicats.* Sainte-Foy: Les presses de
l'Université Laval.

Wainwright, Hilary and Dave Elliott. 1982. *The Lucas Plan: A New Trade Unionism in the
Making.* London: Allison & Busby.

Wells, D.M. 1987. *Empty Promises: Quality of Working Life Programs and the Labour Movement.*
New York: Monthly Review Press.

Wells, D.M. 1991. "What Kind of Unionism is Consistent with the New Model of Human
Resource Management," *Queen's Papers in Industrial Relations* 1991-9, 1-33.

Vesser, Jelle. 1989. *European Trade Unions in Figures.* Deventer, Netherlands: Kluwer.

Chapter 4

Mona-Josée Gagnon

TRADE UNIONS IN QUÉBEC: NEW STAKES*

The official view regarding the trade union movement in both Québec and English Canada is that it is not in a state of crisis; a constant or even slightly increasing membership supplies the proof for such a claim. This conclusion, which is based solely on statistical analysis, reflects today's preoccupation with numbers: that which is not quantifiable has no credibility. Unfortunately, it is this over-confidence in statistics which has concealed major problems with trade unions to be overlooked.

Trade unions are indeed in a state of crisis, and the nature of their situation can be examined by focusing on culture and ideology. The problem facing trade unions is the possible conflict between culture and ideology and class relations in which trade unions are "still" engaged, and more specifically in the capacity of the workers to form new collective identities. The best method of illustrating this is to look alternatively at changes in society and in the workplace.

The 1980's will be remembered as the decade of the economy, of the rehabilitation of profit and entrepreneurship, and of a decline in ethical values. The elevation of the firm and the entrepreneurial class to the status of representing the general well-being of society goes, however, well beyond the economic sphere. Although it could be read as the ideological and cultural triumph of employer's practices and discourses, such a novel interpretation may well undermine the very foundations of the trade union movement.

In addition, we may also cite the numerous studies in the field of sociology of work which, while remaining critical, have nonetheless moved away from a strictly materialistic interpretation to emphasize the importance of cultural factors in the social relations of work, and in the formation of collective identities. The sociology of the "new social movements" has, in a sense, completed this process by considering these movements as new collective identities and endowing them with the capacity to

---

*This chapter was translated by Rev. George Topp, S.J.

generate social change. Writers such as Alain Touraine and Claus Offe, for example, have gone so far as to declare the workers' movement, and even its very manifestation in the form of trade unions, to be sociologically obsolete.

The observations which follow are based on research and on participation in the trade union movement in Québec. A deliberate decision has been taken however, to avoid any systematic presentation of research data in order to write freely without, hopefully, weakening the argument.

UNDERSTANDING TRADE UNIONISM

A short detour helps to define the approach which underlies these observations. In order to understand the trade union movement, we begin by examining the socio-political function it performs. This function, which is of course defined very subjectively, appears to be twofold, each element dialectically involved with the other. Whether at the level of the enterprise or at a societal level, the role of trade unions is both to regulate social relations (the institutional function), and to make demands on behalf of their members (the representative function) (M.J. Gagnon, 1989). Alain Touraine, as is well known, distinguished between the "institutional" and "social movement" aspects of unionism, concluding that the second aspect disappears, a phenomenon which is inevitable in all movements. But we do not believe that the trade union movement can be understood exclusively in terms of its institutional function and its regulatory role. Although it is indeed, an institution which is necessarily concerned with its own self-preservation, the union movement must be representative of workers and also be able to make claims on their behalf, at the risk of otherwise losing its legitimacy. The current threat to the movement, in our opinion, is rather that this representative function is becoming increasingly hollow; it has progressively lost the capacity to generate counter-identities, counter-projects or counter-values, and has reduced itself to making purely instrumental claims. The problem is not that any specific claim may have failed, but that these claims are elaborated without any coherent conception of an identity-creating or oppositional role.

Our approach excludes any attempt to understand the trade union movement through a systematic analysis of its discourse or its practice. This discourse is in fact, a complex political product, rather than a reflection of a coherent ideology. Moreover, it is poorly linked with practice, which is itself difficult to follow because of its inherent discontinuities. There are no single reference points from which to understand trade unionism; they are multiple, volatile and changing. Trade unionism is discourse and practice, appeasement and upheaval, splintering and fusion, uncertainty and contradiction, image and reality. Any attempt to define it with precision can hardly have a positivist character.

THE RETURN OF THE ENTREPRENEUR: THE CREATION OF CONSENSUS

In Québec as elsewhere, the economic crisis of the sixties and eighties, especially the reconstructing of all economic parameters by the new world order that has yet to take shape, has focused attention exclusively on capital. Capital must be protected, valorized and respected; social and cultural problems are increasingly treated as mere economic data. As always, in times of international conflict, national solidarity is a predictable reflex. What we are speaking of here, is economic warfare: our national economy must survive and be able to compete internationally. Firms, together with their entrepreneurs (a term that has resurfaced in all its glory — the new heroes, if not media stars), have become the outposts of our national strategy.

> Twenty years ago, managers and businessmen were either the subject of mimicry or associated with power-game dramas. Now, they occupy a central role in images of modernity, and the leaders of business have become super-heroes.[1]

The firm has been rehabilitated; profit is a necessity that no longer causes one to blush. Daring heads of industry, whose Québec prototype is Bernard Lemaire of Cascades, have even become familiar subjects for television dramas. At the beginning of the 1990's, Québec, which perpetually hesitates to declare itself politically as it awaits more support, looked to "its" businessmen, those who have proven their ability to balance the books, to manage and to invest under foreign skies. And how has the union movement in Québec responded? The CSN (Conféderation des Syndicats Nationaux) and the CEQ (Centrale de l'enseignements du Québec) have adopted the social democratic flag long displayed by the FTQ (Federation des travailleurs et travailleuses du Québec). The crisis of Marxism, and of the left in general, has led to this.

Modern social democracy was originally conceived as an alternative to the violent upheaval of the established order, as much as to a capitalism without ethics. Keynesianism provided the rationale for the social democratic project and its generous ideals of social justice and solidarity (A. Przeworski, 1985), thereby not only providing the project with an identity but also assuring its legitimacy. The problem is that the current crisis is also a crisis of Keynesian economic principles and their application; the globalization of the economy and movements for continental integration are undermining national economic strategies. As the French socialists have discovered, "left" policies have fared no better.

As a result, we have a trade union movement whose socio-political project demonstrates no specificity nor any effective oppositional capacity, but which has nevertheless achieved a previously unknown level of institutionalisation. Union officials and representatives hold key positions on all advisory groups, committees and government task forces of any political significance. State funding for certain union activities is diverse and unquestioned; the State apparatus absorbs a great number of labour union veterans. The "concertationist" period in Québec (1979-1985) now continues in only a minor key, but Québec's political dynamic, the interaction between State, unions and business, has retained some of the fundamental features of this period.

Consensus has become a value in itself as well as a way of life; it is celebrated and eagerly sought with open arms and declarations of shared interests. Everything which stands for good intentions in Québec is symbolized in the recent creation of the gigantic and hybrid Forum for Jobs (the 1989 Forum pour l'emploi), to promote a social and economic project stripped of all "class" friction: employment — "full employment" for the most daring — is consensus raised to the level of fantasy, the marriage of Québec nationalism and social democracy, and one of the manifestations of the current decay in political debate.

> From the possibility of a political agreement that is so desirable among groups with divergent social and economic interests, we then advance to the miracle of consensus. The political function is necessarily diminished, since it consists, among other things, in managing the disagreements without, however, denying their existence. Henceforth, can we still speak of *political choice*, or is it not rather a question, in certain cases, of a *consensual* reflex, obliterating the problems and the solutions at one and the same time? (Author's emphasis)[2]

Having fallen into the net of "institutionalisation," the union movement has become non-utopian, focusing instead on realizable objectives and producing analyses based on data perceived as representing reality. Union creativity is now directed towards practical projects with an immediate purpose, thereby further institutionalizing the movement. Still, trade unionism, wherever it exists, and no matter what organizational form it takes, continues to function "ideologically." The current impression that it has lost its ideological character stems perhaps from a confusion: it is not lacking an ideology, it has simply lost touch with its ideals.

Ideological crossbreeding, does however, still characterize the trade union organizations of Québec, more so than in societies where labour relations are very centralized. By separating the different levels of intervention, and by adapting to diverse kinds of membership, Québec's labour unions are able to manage their own internal contradictions. The question is whether the union movement can define itself as such within the confining social framework of its recently adopted said democratic reformism. Although its regulation and management roles continue to increase, the question is whether unionism, in fact, requires conflict, even contradiction, to gain support.

Is the trade union movement therefore, not heading towards destruction, if it allows itself to be entirely engulfed in a project that is partly defined by others, and for that reason, fundamentally ambiguous? Is it enough for it to proclaim, when convenient, an immanent, quasi-ontological "difference," which most of the time is used only as a rallying-cry ?

THE FIRM AS A SOCIOLOGICAL CATEGORY

The firm has now become a *"creative social site"*(R. Sainsaulieu and D. Segrestin, 1986). Formerly situated at the heart of class antagonisms which it nourished and embodied, the firm now appears as a *site for consensus building*, and as the basis for workers' self-identification. Previously an institution of an economic nature devoted to the valorisation of capital and to the search for profits, the firm has suddenly become both a space for creating social relationships and an organic element in a society where it pretends to play a positive role. Recent literature on business management (e.g.: Peters and Waterman, W. Ouchi) emphasises both the internal and the public image of the enterprise. For example, workers will be proud to work at enterprise Z if the latter contributes to charities and demonstrates ecological awareness.

This Durkheimian vision of the firm has generated a great deal of literature on how to achieve this corporate change. Organizational culture occupies a central place in these writings: it has become an incantation, a magical recipe, as if firms had special vocations and distinct social objectives. The nature of the goods and services produced by firms no longer matters. What does matter is the culture of the enterprise itself. Firms which have no culture are compared to uncultivated land: others simply have "bad" cultures, and finally there are the winners; their achievements are celebrated in all these writings.

If we take a look at the corporate texts which one of the promoters of enterprise culture offers us (W. Ouchi, 1982) in order to illustrate what a "good" entrepreneurial culture is, we find a great number of commonplaces, clichés and empty words which poorly mask the promotional aspect of the contents:

> The culture of an enterprise consists of a group of symbols, ceremonies and myths which permit the *transmission* to the employees of the intrinsic values and convictions of the enterprise (Our emphasis).[3]

In fact, there are no theoretical differences in this literature on corporate culture. It is concerned primarily with promoting a humanized management, one that is apparently democratic and egalitarian, and with developing the flexibility and responsibility of the individual and of the group. With this common emphasis, each author then proceeds to focus on one aspect. Whatever new "concepts" are added by individual writers, they are of little use to the now exhausted managers whose role it has become to build and to promote this enterprise culture. A recently acclaimed work in the managerial literature summed up the whole problem with the expression "cynical enterprise," the evil of the century, on which the good manager must now declare war (D. Kanter, 1989). Even writers who do not reject the notion of enterprise culture are annoyed by the naïveté and trendiness of this massive literature. (e.g., O. Aktouf, 1988).

What, in fact, is happening in Québec firms? To tell the truth, no one really knows. Sociological research is no longer interested in social relations *in* the firm; it has been replaced by research *for* the firm, which is not at all the same thing. Official speeches by employers, their numerous publications of the kind produced for the "general public," the popularization of a few judiciously chosen success stories, a few scattered monographs — these do not reveal the extent to which the incantations in favour of the promotion of a democratic entrepreneurial culture are realities. But this emphasis on culture and ideology is in itself significant, not as an account of the changes in the management of labour, but rather because it indicates a change in the political-ideological strategy of the managerial world and the current elites. It is difficult to doubt, or even to express scepticism, in the face of this tidal wave of good intentions. Although it remains to be proven that management is engaged in an irreversible process of change, the burden of proof is upon those who question this process.

NEW MANAGERIAL APPROACHES

Exploratory research conducted in 1987 with labour union militants and representatives on behalf of the Québec Federation of Labour (FTQ) has led us to propose a twofold hypothesis. On the one hand, traditional management (Taylorism, authoritarianism, nit-picking control) is still alive and well. On the other hand, wherever management is modernised in the sense described above, it is a question of the superimposition of new managerial practices on earlier ones, rather than any real reversal. The modes of social control and where and how power is manifested may have undergone some modifications, but this does not alter the fact that everywhere there remains those who exercise control and make decisions, and those who submit. However, it is certainly true that present day managerial experiments are disturbing the dynamic of social relations in the firm.

An illustration of this involves reviewing three well known models of managerial control none of which is, however, exclusive. To distinguish between them, we will adopt the notion of *the mode of creation of the collective worker*,[4] a criterion which then enables us to reflect on the central problem of worker-identity.

In the first case, the Taylorist model, strict workers' compliance is expected. Taylorism is founded on the belief that a work effort characterised by obedience and intensity will be profitable for both the worker and the firm. The examples given by F.W. Taylor (1957) have, in fact, less to do with persuasion than with Pavlovian conditioning. The inherent authoritarianism in Taylorism stifles any personal or social aspirations on the part of the worker; the social existence of a work group is acknowledged only to be discredited. Taylorism is an attempt to "deconstruct" the work group, the collectivist outlook of the workers and autonomous social relations which, by their nature, conflict with the management of the enterprise. Any social or intellectual legitimacy of the work group is denied; *it exists only on a technical level.* Yet the very violence implicit in the Taylorist project provides a common ground on which workers can mobilize.

The human relations school has proposed an alternative model founded on the existence of the informal group: it begins with *the social construction of the collective worker.* In this approach, informal social relations play an indispensable role in the cohesion, and in the search for a collective identity, of the work-group. However, these social relations may be channelled in very different directions: towards the consolidation of a workers opposition, as much as towards serving the overall objectives of the firm. Despite the growing awareness of sociological phenomena in the work place and the growing concern for the feelings of workers associated with this "human relations" approach, the great challenge for managers, according to this school of thought, is to transform *individual feelings* with regard to work and the firm into social relations within the group which will promote an active loyalty to the interests of the firm. While the human relations approach sets as its objectives the happiness of workers, and a portrayal of the firm as an environment of consensus and harmony, it does not seek conscious, thoughtful support on the part of the workers for any particular "cultural" model. On the contrary, it tries to promote an almost automatic compliance by applying different psycho-sociological techniques, or by means of a more "human" kind of personnel management. Both the worker and the work-group become raw material to be moulded, rather than minds to be convinced. The human relations approach is, in the end, based on the extensive manipulation of workers, not on any a battle of ideas. The most obvious result, not surprisingly, has been the development of more sophisticated practices of personnel management.

Although management practices popularized in the 1980's are not inconsistent with the human relations' approach (G. Salaman, 1986), they do go much further. The disenchantment of workers has been a matter of great concern for a long time, but the new international conditions of competition are such that simple lamentations are not enough. Productivity and quality have become indispensable. This requires a qualitative reversal of orientation, aimed at the cultural and ideological construction of the collective worker. As Michel Crozier (1977) emphasized, we have become aware that the worker is not merely hands and heart, but intellect as well.

The worker whose support is now being sought, is no longer the Taylorist robot nor the simpleton of human relations; he or she is someone endowed with intelligence and with a capacity for reflection, with professional and intellectual aspirations, not merely economic. To be sure, the manipulation involved is pregnant with implications. All the discourses on the development of a "good" enterprise culture imply that such an approach is productive, and therefore that workers can be manipulated. Besides, what is presented to the individual and to the worker collective is a cultural model which is coherent and which rests on an attractive and logical vision of the firm and of society. In a way, it is fair play, and one may contrast this new approach favourably with the underhanded tactics of the "human relations" approach.

The new managers have added a certain amount of sociological shrewdness to their skills in social engineering and in psychology. The more "primitive" strategies persist for sure, but the general climate has changed. Workers are more and more approached in all their identities; they are even offered help in developing bases for these identities.

(a) Working men and women are designated as social beings who feel the need to belong and to conform. These needs are all the more intense when social and traditional networks are being shattered. The firm is presented as a family of equals, as a life environment, as the first source of identity.

(b) Working men and women are also appealed to in their private lives, since the firm now aspires to become the channel for the solution of all problems. Personalized management of human resources, programs to help employees, the organization of leisure... — all reflect this drive to provide individualized attention.

(c) Working men and women are also perceived as legitimately ambitious, capable of self-improvement and of learning. Possibilities for professional advancement are emphasized; professional training is presented as a vehicle for individual promotion. Even when the deskilling of labour precludes professional training, there is always the possibility of acquiring psycho-social skills (initiation into group work, methods of problem-solving, participation in committees, etc.)

In this model, it is through various mechanisms associated with "participative management" that the changes most directly impact on workers. Quality circles, semi-autonomous management and team work are just attempts to "constitute" a collective work based on the labour process. These experiences are widespread, but difficult to quantify. Management discourse stresses making workers responsible, and these reforms are associated with a significant reduction in supervision.

The constitution of the group, however imperfect it may be, changes the social relations among employees (P. E. Tixier, 1986). Norms of production are internalised and the group becomes a site for the implementation of a new mechanism of control; despite itself, it becomes involved in competition with other groups. The firm, on the other hand, is presented as a unifying force that is capable of reconciling competing individuals and groups. It functions in a hostile economic environment; any mistake may well prove to be fatal for all concerned. Since the entire enterprise is at risk, everyone must work together to avoid failure. We are confronted here with a novel marriage of constraint and consent which is built on a perpetually unstable economic environment and an employer strategy centred on workers' identities.

UNION IDENTITIES

Historically, unionism has always been the principal element in structuring the identities of working men and women. As C. Offe and H. Wisenthal (1980) have noted, even here the union's organizing role is derivative, since it is really capital — or the public employer — that determines both quantitatively and qualitatively the types of workers to be brought together. In any case, material organization does not necessarily lead to the construction of an identity and the formation of a community, in the sense of one capable of mobilizing for the defense of its own interests (D. Segrestin, 1981). The construction of an identity is neither an inevitable nor an incidental consequence of the formation of groups: it is the result of a process begun successfully by the union movement in the past, but one which was never fully articulated or reflected upon. This failure was aggravated by the fact that "identity creation" was for so long the union's exclusive prerogative thanks to the inertia of management in this regard. Certain features of the North American legal system, which, for better or for worse, recognize the union as the exclusive representative of its members, also reinforced its monopoly character.

We should avoid the kind of nostalgia for the past which attributes to the labour unions of yesteryears exaggerated virtues of unity, of homogeneity, or of combativeness, which, in the homeopathic doses they so often come in, give contemporary unions a more negative image than they deserve. Equally, however, we must not underestimate the significance of the cultural changes which are currently taking place in the workplace.

The two dominant union models in Québec as elsewhere, were the craft union and the industrial union, both of which were represented by specific structures at the level of the firm. These models reflected two worlds: the historian M. Perrot (1984) drew sharp distinctions between the strikes of skilled and unskilled workers at the end of the 19th century. These continue to exist as two different worlds even today; two ways of constructing collective identities. Traditional craft unionism is disappearing in Québec; it survives only in certain construction unions. The printers' unions, — especially the typographers, the proud and powerful archetypes of craft unionism — have suffered a decrease in numbers, have undergone changes in the labour process and have been forced to accept union mergers, all of which has stripped them of their original identity.

In Québec, traditional craft unions, often victims of bad press, have long been associated with a Gompers-style corporatism. But as D. Segrestin mentions in his work on the French craft unions, belonging to a labour union, which is implicitly organized to protect a craft and to serve as a symbolic representation of professional pride, can also provide a link with the wider working class as easily as it can prevent one. It seems that craft unions fulfil their identity-creating function in the most natural way possible, which is very important when the moment comes to confront the employer. The near-disappearance of craft unions is, therefore, a significant threat to the identity-creating function of labour unions; in fact, one could speculate that the new management identity strategies would run into a brick wall if they were aimed at workers in the traditional crafts. Previously one was considered a "typographer"; today, one is considered to be working at a specific firm.

The other form of union organisation, the industrial unions, developed in North America largely in opposition to the craft unions, were indifferent to the large segments of the population undergoing the process of being proletarianised. For several decades now, their organizational strategy has dominated the union movement; even the earlier craft unions have adopted their structural approach. Industrial unions organize working men and women, regardless of status, function or income, into "natural" subgroups which correspond to the legally defined accreditation units: blue-collar, and white-collar, with or without semi-professional or professional employees. Since its membership is heterogeneous, this kind of union is more sheltered from corporatist tendencies. In practice, however, workers with higher skills and qualifications are generally not the spearhead of the union movement (L. Sayles, 1958). On the contrary, they are careful always to keep out of trouble and to protect their comparative advantages.

Therefore, it is not the worker's qualifications which are the source for identity building within the industrial union; qualifications are fragmented, often dramatically absent, and, in all cases, elaborated and defined by the employer. Our hypothesis is that identity building within industrial unions is founded on opposition, and defined in terms of status within the enterprise. On the one hand, there are those who make the decisions, or who share in the decision making process; those who have knowledge and who are arrogant. On the other hand, there are those who submit, those whose views are of no significance. It is this common attribute from which identity is woven, and which at the appropriate moment, imposes solidarity. This brings us to the second source of the crisis in the identity-creating function of trade unionism caused by the new management approaches.

THE CHALLENGE TO THE UNIONS

We have deliberately directed our analysis to those organizations we are most familiar with, which represent traditionally unionized, semi or non-professional workers. But we cannot ignore the fact that, following the massive unionisation of labour in the 1960's and 1970's in the public and para-public sectors, the Québec labour unions have distanced themselves greatly from their worker roots, and that they now constitute a mixed ensemble. Two phenomena are apparent here: on the one hand, pluralistic organizations (e.g. the CSN and the FTQ) have experienced difficulties, diverse but very significant, in maintaining some cohesion between the different fractions of their membership. On the other hand, several professional groups, or groups with some autonomous power, have decided to go it alone and are doing very well. And, as we know, the public sector unions no longer constitute a common front. One labour union out of four is not affiliated with any labour central and the centrals themselves engage in a cyclical wrangle over the allegiance of the remaining three-quarters.

One is forced to conclude that, on the collective union front, there has been a serious identity crisis, to the extent that the capacity of the trade union movement to found collective identities which are not based on job classifications seems threatened — a minimal capacity without which we cannot expect it to constitute any strong opposition at any level whatsoever. Whether at the societal level or at the level of the firm, the union movement is continually being invited to assume more responsibility, to be more open, and to accept a partnership. In this end-of-the-century mood of economic panic, is there no other choice but to declare oneself effectively open and responsible, and to fully perform a primarily regulatory function which the political and economic powers that be are not slow to take advantage of?

Must we therefore agree with the sociologists of the new social movements, that trade unionism must now be consigned to the status of walk-on parts in period films? To be convinced of that, one would have to assume that the tidal wave of consensus and the net of institutionalization have not also affected the new social movements. We know that it is not only the trade union movement which has undergone an upheaval. Besides, the union movement will continue to be the most accessible and the most widespread means of organization; its ascendency within the work environment, where class contradictions are still notably manifested, makes it necessary to preserve it, at least potentially, its central role.

The fact remains however, that in Québec as elsewhere, trade unionism does not seem at present, for the reasons given in this chapter, equal to becoming the central means for building a collective identity and offering an effective opposition to the powers that be and their hegemonic discourse. The experience of the last few decades has encouraged within the trade union movement a tendency to assign itself a "universalising" role, which is more the result of the growing recognition it has received from the political and economic powers that be, than from any real articulation of its discourse and practices with other progressive forces. Still, we are among those who feel that the universalising claim made by the trade union movement — that it has a unique capacity to represent the broad interests of the working class — retains some legitimacy. Certainly, this claim is not likely to be realised under current conditions, which have produced a weakened and divided trade unionism, but which have also paradoxically strengthened it in those aspects which separate it most from the "historic mission" we still assign to it.

As this book goes to press, it is impossible not to comment on the impact of the national question on the current position of the labour movement in Québec. The three large labour centrals have gone all out to support Québec sovereignty; the "minimalist" sovereignty platform of the *Forum pour l'emploi* has united employers associations with a large portion of the economic elite. In the current "last round" of constitutional negotiations, there is no room for internal struggles. Even if the economic paralysis in Québec provides the justification for the frenetic call for "concertation" between labour, government and business, only the naive would miss the underlying unifying nationalist sentiment. It is difficult to predict when or, indeed, if the trade union movement can reclaim an independent political project in this atmosphere of political and economic turmoil.

NOTES

1. Wood, Stephen J. "New Wave Management?," *Work, Employment and Society.* September 1989, Vol.3, no.3. p. 379.
2. Olender, Maurice. *Le consensus, nouvel opium?* Coll. Le genre humain, Paris, Seuil, 1990. p.i.
3. Ouchi, W. Théorie Z. *Faire face au défi japonais*, Interéditions, 1982. p. 52.
4. Marx conceived of all those whose work goes into the production of a product under capitalism, from managers, through designers, engineers, supervisors, workers, cleaners, etc, as composing a single, complex, many-skilled "collective worker.

REFERENCES

Aktouf, Omar. "La communauté de vision au sein de l'entreprise," in Symons, G. (ed.) *La Culture des organisations.* Institut québécois de recherche sur la culture, 1988. pp. 71-98.

Crozier, Michel and E. Friedberg. *L'acteur et le système.* Paris: Seuil, 1977.

Gagnon, Mona Josée (ed.) *Les nouuvelles stratégies patronales.* FTQ, Montréal, 1987.

Gagnon, Mona Josée. *Théories du syndicalisme et rapport syndicats-État.* (Doctoral Thesis: Université de Montréal, 1989).

Kanter, D. and P.H. Mervis. *The Cynical American. Living and Working in An Age of Discontinued Illusion.* London: Unwin Hyman, 1989.

Offe, C. and H. Wiesenthal. "Two Logics of Collective Action: Theoretical Notes on Social Class and Organizational Form," *Political Power and Social Theory.* Vol.7, 1980.

Olender, Maurice. Le consensus, nouvel opium? Coll. *Le genre humain,* Paris, Seuil, 1990.

Ouchi, W. Théorie Z. *Faire face au défi japonais*, Interéditions, 1982.

Perrot, M. *Jeunesse de la grève.* France 1871-1890. Paris: Seuil, 1984.

Peters, T. and R.H. Waterman. *In Search of Excellence.* New York: Harper & Row, 1982.

Przeworski, Adam. *Capitalism and Social Democracy.* Cambridge: Cambridge University Press, Paris: Maison des sciences de l'homme, 1985.

Sainsaulieu, R. and D. Segrestin. "Vers une théorie sociologique de l'entreprise," *Sociologie du travail*, 3-86. pp. 335-352.

Salaman, Graeme. *Working*. Ellis Horwood Ltd., 1986.

Sayles, Leonard R. *Behaviour of Industrial Work Groups*. New York: John Wiley and Sons, 1958.

Segrestin, Denis (ed.) *Les communautés pertinentes de l'action collective*. Laboratoire de sociologie et des relations professionnelles (C.N.A.M.), 1981.

Segrestin, Denis. *Le phénomène corporatiste*. Paris: Fayard, 1985.

Taylor, F.W. *La direction scientifique des entreprises*. Éd. Gérard & Cie, Marabout Service, 1957-1967.

Tixier, Pierre-Eric. "Management participatif et syndicalisme," *Sociologie du travail*, 3-86. pp. 353-372.

Touraine, Alain et al. *Le mouvement ouvrier*, Paris: Fayard, 1984.

Wood, Stephen J. "New Wave Management?," *Work, Employment and Society*. September 1989, Vol.3, no.3. pp. 379-402.

Chapter 5

Laurie E. Adkin

ECOLOGY AND LABOUR: TOWARDS A NEW SOCIETAL PARADIGM[1]

A radical critique of past socialist theory and practice is now widely recognized to be a necessary precondition for a convergence between socialists and the new social movements [NSMs]. In fact, the "ideal revision" required is really so profound that it amounts to the construction of a new societal paradigm. A new synthesis is required that would consist of the insights introduced by socialism's critique of capitalism and by the new social movements and their theorists. "Socialism" has not succeeded in encompassing diverse forms of domination and oppression, which have become increasingly "politicized," or conflictualised, in the post-World War II era. Moreover, the term has such deeply-rooted associations with the anti-democratic, the environmentally disastrous and other negative aspects of "formerly existing socialism," that it may be a politically bankrupt label.

As a result, "eco-socialism" does not adequately describe the societal project envisioned as a "new paradigm," and neither does "post-socialism" because we cannot ignore the continuing existence of capitalism. So what will we call this "new synthesis"? We find ourselves, like the members of the former Italian Communist Party, searching in the rubble of toppled symbols and overturned assumptions for the elements of a new discourse.

Current paradigmatic shifts reflect not only a changing reality and the resulting crisis of our analytical frameworks, but also the arrival of a new generation of theorists. Attachment to a widely shared left culture and ideology — to la gauche fordiste — (whose negative aspects included productivism, technocratic positivism, and an inadequate concern with democratic questions) and to its political organizations, is more characteristic of left intellectuals who are now in their late forties or older, than it is among those who were born after 1960 (Mushaben, 1983). For the emerging generation of social theorists, it has been movements concerning women, the environment, peace, civil liberties and other alternative movements,[2] rather than the unions or traditional political parties, which have fundamentally challenged societal values and the model of development. While for many of us, this reality may mean rethinking old assumptions about the agents of radical social change, for a younger generation this may seem a very arcane debate indeed.

Although "social agency" tends to be the focal point of debates about the NSMs, what is at stake is not a simple "transfer" of importance from the labour movement as "revolutionary subject" to other actors, such as the anti-nuclear movement, as Touraine's group suggested in the early 1980s. I agree with Chantal Mouffe and Ernesto Laclau (1985) that social actors must be understood in terms of multiple, interacting subject positions. We cannot separate, as discrete "social agents," "workers" from "women" from "immigrants;" these identities and others are embodied, in various permutations, within each of us. What is at stake, therefore, is a reconceptualisation of the entire project — the common threads that link the experiences of oppression and the struggles for emancipation which are associated with these identities, or subject positions.

THEORETICAL QUESTIONS

What are the cultural values and goals of the alternative movements, particularly the environmental movement, and the unions? How do these values and goals underly their respective strategies of social action, and what are their implications for 1) the relations between the two actors, and 2) our understanding of the forces propelling social change?

First, I think we should view the struggles of the alternative movements as evidence of a transition to what Claus Offe has called a "new political paradigm" (1985), in which fundamental social conflicts are defined both in "broader" and in "deeper" terms than was possible within classical Marxist theory. A growing number of theorists (including Jurgen Habermas, Michel Foucault, Chantal Mouffe, Ernesto Laclau, Joachim Hirsch, Jean Cohen, Alain Touraine and Raymond Williams) argue that relations of conflict have proliferated, and that the widespread mobilizations for peace, ecology, women's emancipation, and other goals contain the elements of what, in Gramscian terms, we might call a new counter-hegemonic project.

There is a broad consensus about the roots of the NSMs in the contradictions created by the maturing and internationalization of Fordism, and the development of the welfare State. Some theorists, including Alain Touraine, have associated the NSMs with "post-industrial" society. What this means, roughly, is that while the labour movement contested the terms of capitalist industrialisation, it did not profoundly challenge its legitimacy as a model of social development. With advanced capitalism, the forms and loci of social struggles have proliferated beyond questions of ownership and distribution of wealth, to control over technology and information. The NSMs challenge the neutrality, the authority and the rationality of bureaucratic and technocratic decision-making, as in the case of the anti-nuclear movement in France. Touraine argues that they are engaged in a struggle for control over "historicity and of the action of society upon itself."[3]

Joachim Hirsch, using the analytical framework of the French regulation school, is one of a number of theorists who have drawn attention to the declining relevance of "class" identity for millions of workers in the developed capitalist countries. The conflicts produced by the commodification of social relations, and of human needs, are now so diffuse that they "no longer manifest themselves along traditional class lines and in traditional political forms."[4] The working class cultural and political associations rooted in the era of industrialization have been dissolved in a myriad of identities — some derived from positions in the relations of production, many not. As Touraine's group said in 1980,

> "social domination embraces much more than work, extending to almost every domain of social activity, so that it is no longer possible to appeal to tradition, to a local or professional culture, or to a specific community, as the artisans were able to do, or the miners, the steelworkers, or the fishermen, living in a working-class environment that was both homogeneous and isolated from the rest of society."[5]

The consequences of this are, first, that it has become increasingly difficult, if not impossible, to build a mass movement around a "core" *working class* identity: the exploitation of wage-labour is no longer a sufficiently homogeneous experience of oppression for enough people. Capital-labour struggle around the appropriation of surplus-value is not a broad enough definition of social conflict to encompass such struggles as women's emancipation, or citizens' mobilisations against private corporate or State investment decisions. It cannot, therefore, in itself constitute a fundamental organising principle for a broadly-based "historical bloc." A more encompassing definition of social conflict is, on the other hand, suggested by the central themes of the alternative movements and the more radical elements within the trade unions: democratization of decision-making, individual autonomy, and the creation of new solidarities.

The politics of the new social movements do not compel us to "bury" class, or Marxist theory, but they do demand that we develop a more inclusive and holistic analysis of the determinants of social change (in which the working class loses its former "privileged" role). Age, generation, gender, sexual orientation and race, among other factors, impart to individuals and groups specific identities and values whose importance in determining social or political behaviour becomes evident when one studies social movements. Take, for example, the category of "youth." Youths today, in most of the advanced capitalist countries, are relatively unwilling to join traditional political organizations, although they are greatly affected by the social and economic crisis (unemployment, a shrinking social security net), lack of adequate housing, restriction of women's reproductive rights and other freedoms, and racism. They have been born into a world threatened with environmental degradation and even destruction, and in an era when parliamentary-institutional paths of change seem to be too little, too late. For many, the future looks so bleak that the only options are despair or direct action. As Joyce Mushaben points out, these young persons are not "post-materialists;" affluence and security are experiences that their parents' generation may have known, but which they probably never will. The point is that these identities/experiences are just as important as the identity/experience of wage labour if we are trying to explain why individuals or groups participate in social action and what kind of social changes they seek.

This broad interpretation of the significance of the alternative movements also draws on the work of the Italian theorist, Alberto Melucci, of Habermas, and of Foucault. Melucci, like Touraine, emphasises the production of cultural identities and images, control over information, fragmentation of individual identity and experience, and the "artificiality of life" to explain the alienation of people from power, which he sees as the common root of the alternative movements. These movements are, he argues, about "making power visible" by challenging "the logic governing production and appropriation of social resources." They "present to the rationalizing apparatuses questions which are not allowed."[6] Claus Offe summarizes the explanations of Habermas and Foucault as, respectively, the theses of "broadening" and "deepening" (of conflicts and deprivations). Habermas has argued that "the work role is neither the exclusive nor the basic focus of the experience of deprivation, an experience which equally affects the roles of the citizens, the client of administrative decisions, and the consumer."[7] Foucault emphasised the enormous capacity of modern political economies and technology to displace conflict, and the increasing scope and costs of the system's failures.[8]

The alternative movements reflect a cultural resistance to the further penetration of commodity relations into every aspect of human existence and the natural environment, entailing the loss of both individual autonomy and belonging, deprivation of a social and spiritual nature, and escalating fear in response to capitalism's "death wish" (nuclear weapons, toxic chemical pollution, radioactivity, environmental destruction, resource depletion, and the devastation of third world wars). They offer resistance, as well, to homogenisation and conformity, and validate the diversity of experiences and needs integral to individual development. The ecology and feminist discourses, for example, criticize what Ursula Franklin (1990) calls "prescriptive technologies" for creating a "culture of compliance" and for depriving people of holistic experiences of creativity and production. The alternative movements also share a goal of self-determination, or autonomy, which can be achieved only through decentralization and democratization of the State and the economy. They therefore represent both a "brake" on the old model of development — their anti-productivist, needs-oriented aspects — and the elements of a new order. In *La Voix et le Regard* (1978/1981), Touraine argued that the central theme of these movements was the demand for auto-gestion, or self-management.

Claus Offe has conceptualised the alternative movements as modern critics concerned with the internal contradictions in the value system of modern culture. With Jean Cohen (1983), he sees these movements not as a premodern, romantic, or traditional petit bourgeois reaction to modernity, but as a predominantly rational response to certain negative aspects of modernity, which at the same time offers a vision of the future (rather than a nostalgic appeal to the past). Offe argues that the values of the alternative movements (dignity and autonomy of the individual, the integrity of the physical condition of life, equality and participation, peaceful and solidaristic forms of social organization) are not new, but rather are rooted in modern political philosophies and inherited from the progressive movements of both the bourgeoisie and the working class. The novel component is the belief that these values cannot be satisfied within the dominant institutions (property, market, parliamentary democracy, nuclear family, mass culture and media) or within the dominant political paradigms (liberalism, statist socialism, social democracy).

Zsuzsa Hegedus extends the idea that NSMs are about empowerment and democratization, in an era when human and planetary survival are at stake, and the old model of industrial society and its ideologies have been radically undermined. She argues that:

> A social movement is a very complex process — with a multiple time/space perspective — of empowerment and alternative problem-solving which assigns the finality of maximising the possibility of choices on all levels and in every aspect of social life, and creates this possibility by its capacity to engender new (multiple) options....
>
> In other words, what is at stake in self-creative society, characterised here by the permanent invention of new possibilities and the realisation of possible futures, is not 'the' power but empowerment: the capacity of people to intervene directly in problems they are concerned with and to 'control' the choices of their own futures; that is, to decide their collective and individual destiny or, simply, the choices concerning different aspects of their own lives. [9]

The activists of the NSMs are drawn predominantly from the so-called "new middle class," especially people who work in the human service professions and/or the public sector, and are relatively educated. As a result, these activists directly experience and critically analyse issues of control over decision-making (at the level of the State and the economy), of social priorities, and of the rationality of the system. They also tend to be young, and to have higher female participation than the activist bases or official ranks of political parties and many unions. Another important component of the NSMs is made up of what Offe calls "decommodified groups" — people who are outside the labour market, such as unemployed workers, students, housewives and retired persons. Marc Lesage, a Québecois sociologist, has observed that the regular, permanent worker is being succeeded by a "multitude of new faces": part-time workers, temporary or casual workers, volunteer labour, illegal labour, and involuntary household workers, in addition to the unemployed, the socially assisted, and those getting money by some other means (scholarship, grants, self-employment) (1986). Current trends suggest that these strata will continue to grow. The unions — managed by officials whose mandate is derived from the security interests of the permanently employed — are finding it hard to respond to, let alone to integrate, the interests of this "new proletariat." There is, on the other hand, potential for their interests (in autonomy, liberation from work, in finding new solidarities and meanings) to be associated with the organizational forms and agendas of the NSMs.

At certain conjunctures — particularly in environmental struggles — the issues of the alternative movements have attracted support from the traditional middle class (farmers, shop owners, artisans-producers) whose interests are threatened by proposed developments. The one group the alternative movements have typically not included is the primarily male, industrial workforce: the traditional working class. Some theorists, such as André Gorz and Touraine, have gone so far as to argue that there is an objective, historical conflict of interests between this class, which is deeply committed to the institutional rules and ethics of the industrial capitalist era, and the interests represented by the alternative movements. Others, like Offe, have stopped short of such a claim, while pointing out that "the classes, strata, and groups that are penetrated least easily by the concerns, demands, and forms of action of the 'new' paradigm are exactly the 'principal' classes of capitalist societies, namely, the industrial working class and the holders and agents of economic and administrative power."[10]

Relations between industrial and resource-sector workers and environmentalists, given the "jobs-versus-the environment" construction of trade-offs in a capitalist economy, are most often conflictual. Short-term material security is also typically pitted against occupational or public health and safety concerns. There are numerous examples of such conflicts in Canada and elsewhere.[11] At the same time, it is evident that these conflicts stem from a particular construction of the choices available to citizens-as-workers, one which imposes the costs of harmful industrial practices on wage-earners either in the form of economic deprivation and insecurity, or in the form of the degradation of health and the quality of life. This trade-off, although experienced by many as "a fact of life," is the conjunctural outcome of existing relationships of power. Objectively, it is workers in the most polluting industries who have most to gain from the success of environmental demands. Thus, rather than posit an objective or historical conflict between certain strata of workers and the alternative movements, it is more useful to examine the factors which allow these trade-offs to be reproduced, and which prevent alternatives from being considered.

Among these factors is the question of union leadership. Classical Marxists, including Gramsci, advanced various explanations of what they viewed as the bureaucratic conservatism of the trade unions.[12] My view is that union leaderships may not be characterized as invariably conservative, but that there do exist certain institutional limits to the potential of union organizations to become counter-hegemonic actors. Radicalization of union structures, priorities, and tactics, will occur only in the context of an external social mobilization, such as when a tidal change appears to be occurring which could oblige employers and the State to make significant concessions to the new consensus. Moreover, a study regarding the strategic responses of the Canadian Auto Workers and Energy and Chemical Workers' unions to environmental issues (Adkin, 1989) supports the view that the unions which will take the lead in making alliances with the alternative movements depends on a complex inter-play of factors, including the political economy of various sectors, State policies, and the cultural-ideological perspectives of union leaders and rank-and-file members.

The above thesis has been put forward at a highly general level, with a view to showing that the alternative movements herald the end of one era and the beginning of another, in which the central social conflict will be defined no longer in terms of class struggle but in terms of struggles for democratization and self-determination. We dwell, however, in a period of international capitalist restructuring, of the decline of traditional identities and movements, and of the still amorphous and contradictory forms of the new ones. As soon as we undertake the task of research, we find an immense diversity of phenomena. Empirical research yields evidence of certain trends, or tendencies, but their potential development remains a question of prediction, and of present practice.

THE CANADIAN CASE

There is insufficient space here to provide a detailed analysis of the discourses which I have identified in the Canadian environmental movement,[13] and which may be labelled as follows: 1) eco-capitalist; 2) popular-democratic; 3) social-democratic; 4) fundamentalist; and 5) eco-socialist. Setting aside, for the moment, the "eco-capitalist" discourse, one finds in the environmental movement a number of counter-hegemonic themes. These include critiques of patriarchy, andro-centrism, productivism and the logic of capitalist accumulation. On one hand, the popular-democratic discourse of the citizens' groups defends "popular" interests against corporate, technocratic, and bureaucratic interests, involving a conflict between social conceptions of property, of access to resources, and of the rights of future generations; on the other hand, it defends the prerogatives of private ownership and appropriation of (social) resources and (socially-produced) wealth. "Popular interests" also refers to a fairly widespread critique among the citizens' groups of science and scientists, and of "experts," as agents of corporate and technocratic interests. The concerns of the citizens' groups give rise to demands for the democratization of institutions, the political system and economic decision-making.

A "fundamentalist" tendency, often associated with the environmental movement's "vanguard," expresses ecological and humanist ethics which (re)validate our relationships to our bodies, to nature and to other species.[14] It affirms the desirability and possibility of non-exploitative and non-violent relationships both among humans and between humans and nature, a vision shared by many feminists. Derived from these ethics is opposition to growth for the sake of growth (viewed as a non-optimal and unsustainable path of development), and a vision of society tending toward equilibrium — not to be equated with stagnation. In this model the criteria for the production of goods and services include meeting needs in an egalitarian manner, maximizing leisure, autonomy and creativity, and minimizing harmful effects on the natural environment, resource depletion, and mentally and physically oppressive working and living conditions. This vision, however, may be only very vaguely attached to a theory of social change (the processes and actors which can bring it into being), or may be linked to pessimistic (apocalyptic) ideas.

Eco-socialists do attempt to provide a theory of social change which identifies the objective and subjective bases for alliances among social actors. Without convincing alternatives to the eco-capitalist project, the environmental movement cannot attract the support of people whose livelihoods are presently dependent on the growth of what Vaclac Havel has called "some monstrously huge, noisy, and stinking machine, whose real meaning is not clear to anyone" (1990). The priority for eco-socialists, is to link the alternative movements to the traditional social movement (organized labour) by way of a renewed socialist theory and practice.

What is the likelihood that the democratisation, feminist, ecologist, and socialist discourses will be "synthesized" in the form of a "new-paradigm," and that such a convergence will find significant political expression in Canada? Many observers have dismissed the NSMs as single-issue-oriented, apolitical, scatterings of groups, with no direct interests in the concerns of citizens-as-workers or conflicts with capital (Wood, 1986). This perception arises from what Alain Touraine's group described ten years ago — with respect to the French anti-nuclear movement — as a "state of equilibrium between a cultural refusal that [the movement] has already gone beyond and a political influence that it [does] not yet have." The uneven ideological development of the environmental movement has resulted in an inconsistent and only partially conscious linking of its democratic demands and ecological-humanist ethics to an analysis of the State and the economy. The cases of the Green movement in Germany, where there is a tradition of socialist discourse, and of the environmental movement in the United States, which has evolved within a "populist" (Boggs: 1986) and liberal tradition, suggest that interaction with socialist discourse is a key factor in explaining the extent to which alternative movements have succeeded in becoming transformative social movements. However, this thesis refers both to the ways in which socialist theory has informed the critique of ecologists, Greens, feminists, and others, and to the rejection of certain aspects of socialist theory and practice by these new actors. Thus it bears emphasising that the issue is not an "amalgamation" of areas such as socialism and ecology, but a new synthesis founded upon a critical re-examination of both.

Given the relative weakness of a culturally-rooted socialist tradition in Canada, which forms of discourse and which social actors may we look to for a radical critique of the model of development? As I have argued elsewhere (Adkin: 1992a), elements of a radical critique are found in the developing agendas of many of the citizens' initiatives. Groups organised around problems of toxic chemical pollution, for example, generally form in response to threats regarding community health or quality of life, but over time become "politicised" and radicalised by their experiences of confronting corporate, bureaucratic and technocratic interests.[15] The struggles of these groups lead them towards a greater understanding of systemic biases which prevent certain alternatives from being considered, and towards demands for the democratisation of decision-making. In Canada, these demands have been largely directed towards governments.[16]

The citizens' groups which form the grass-roots base of the environmental, peace, international solidarity, urban quality of life, anti-poverty, anti-free trade and other networks, are, in a sense, the "laboratories" of the radical democratic project. They are the sites of intense conflict among competing discourses, which seek to interpret, politically, the particular issues and values espoused by the members of these groups. The issues they confront create problems for the relationship between subordination and domination. Questions are raised which (often unconsciously) challenge the traditional prerogatives of capitalists to control economic development, or of bureaucrats and technocrats to make decisions affecting various excluded collectivities. Questions about the purpose and the meaning of the model of development suggest there are alternatives. In this sense I view alternative movements (or at least, certain elements within them), as posing more radical challenges to the entire post-war Fordist model of development, its values and its institutions, than the labour movement or traditional political parties. The radical elements within the alternative movements have allowed the posing of questions and the contemplating of alternatives to constitute their raison d'être, whereas in the case of the unions, challenging the institutional rules or the logic of growth have not been priorities, not even part of the conceptualisation of their role. In addition, liberals, conservatives, social democrats and the "Fordist left" regard such issues as being, at best, utopian.

This is not to say, of course, that because the alternative movements place questions on the political agenda which "are not allowed," a radical discourse has achieved predominant influence within these movements. For the most part, the grass-roots base of the environmental movement, like the labour movement, continues to have faith in social-democratic solutions to the environmental and economic crises. Nor would I argue, with regard to the Canadian environmental movement, that the "fundamentalist" and "socialist" elements have transcended the "green versus red" debate[17] sufficiently to articulate a "radical and pluralist democratic" discourse, the term used by Chantal Mouffe and Ernesto Laclau describing a project to create links among multiple struggles against subordination and domination. In this conception of hegemonic struggle — of politics — no one subject position, be it defined by class, race, gender, or other relation, creates a "centre" which gives to all other forms of oppression their essential meaning. Subject positions are constructed by practices of articulation, as are the relations of equivalence or difference among them. "Radical and pluralist democracy," therefore, expresses a project which is capable of articulating to one another the themes and struggles of the alternative movements and the workers' movement without insisting on the "privileging" of one identity or struggle over the other. It is such a privileging which the term "eco-socialist" suggests, and which is at the centre of the debate between "ecologists" and "socialists."

THE UNIONS

The positions of the more progressive unions are similar to the popular-social-democratic discourse and agenda of the Canadian environmental movement. While certain rank-and-file militants have espoused radical, eco-socialist views,[18] union organisations have not taken the lead in posing the "questions which are not allowed." For instance, questions about the purpose and nature of production and growth, about the meaning of work, self-development and autogestion, and about decentralisation of planning and decision-making, continue to be raised primarily by radical ecologists, feminists, and libertarian or "new left" socialists.

How have union structures sought to transform cultural values and to create solidarities? With regard to an earlier era, one thinks of such collective and individual identities as "the ordinary guy," "the little guy," "the working man," which convey the ideas of subordination, maleness, and a certain nobility stemming from sacrifice and "honest labour." These identities strike fewer and fewer chords in the majority of the work forces of the advanced capitalist countries, following the growth of non-manual occupations, the entry of women into the work force, and the less rigid hierarchies which characterise management-worker relations in many white-collar work places (but not gender or racial relations within these organisations). They are, moreover, not free of associations with an age of deference, and of class position experienced as a natural and inevitable ordering of a hierarchical society. Struggles for workers' rights have often been defended ideologically in terms of respect for the contributions of workers to society, or for the dignity of the "working man," or of the defence of the traditional family, whose preservation depends upon the secure employment of a male breadwinner. (This kind of discourse has long characterised the struggles of steel plant workers in Cape Breton, and is still quite rooted among predominantly male industrial work forces and their communities.) In other words, it is often the terms (even the perpetuation), rather than the elimination, of relations of subordination-domination which are considered to be the stakes of the struggle.

Clearly, the politicization of many relationships between subordination and oppression, particularly by the women's movement, but increasingly by other political subjects as well, has helped cause labour organisations to broaden the scope of their discourse and to make references to forms of domination which criss-cross the identity of "worker." However, insofar as it is preoccupied with the creation of a collective identity, the union is primarily concerned to raise consciousness and to define what is specific or unique about the experience of wage-labour. With respect to the conditions for the creation of a counter-hegemonic project, the problem is not the function of the union in defining a unique, or different subject position, but the way in which the relationships among this subject position and others are understood. The subject position of "worker" (articulated in terms of exploitation and subordination) may be privileged (as in Marxist discourse) as the central axis of social conflict, in which case other subject positions are necessarily of secondary, tangential, or tactical importance. This interpretation, when couched in terms of a radical (transformative) political project, means that the labour movement must be "hegemonic" vis-à-vis its allies, and that the capital-labour conflict must have strategic priority.

The subject position of "worker" may also be privileged, however, within a social democratic discourse whose aim is primarily to "manage" the existing institutions of a capitalist and productivist society. This is the predominant ideological discourse of those who lead the Canadian labour movement. It is interesting that the "privileging" of the identity and interests of the "worker" (what union officials often describe as their "bottom line") is increasingly challenged by the identities and interests defended by the alternative movements. Union officials try to avoid "choosing sides" in conflicts which pit their members' job security against the environment, health, gender or racial equality, peace, or the aspirations of "third world" peoples. They may do this by down-playing or minimizing the costs to "the other side" of an outcome which favours the immediate interests of profit and job security (a position taken by the Energy and Chemical Workers with regard to toxic chemical pollution problems in the Chemical Valley, leaded gasoline, and other issues, and by the United Steelworkers' local in Sydney, Nova Scotia, with regard to pollution from the Sydney Steel Corporation coke ovens, until the ovens were finally closed by Environment Canada). They thereby attempt to ward off accusations of having narrowly and short-sightedly defined the interests of their members, or of having "sacrificed" the interests of other social groups.

However, the above response is usually adopted only when an appeal for the State to intervene in a conflict between the interests of workers' economic security, environmental protection or health, and the conditions of profitability for corporations, has failed, and the union believes itself to be in too weak a position to confront employers in the sphere of collective bargaining. Many union leaders and members view the appropriate role of the State as being to facilitate both economic growth and the fulfilment of an array of other goals, such as the redistribution of wealth, environmental protection, and the safeguarding of civil and political rights. Since it is the social democratic party — in Canada, the New Democratic Party [NDP] — whose election is viewed as necessary to secure these State functions and to "resolve" these kinds of conflicts, much of the "political" strategy and resources of the Canadian labour movement is directed toward support for the NDP.

Another important aspect of the social democratic orientation of union leadership is that the articulation of the "equivalences" among social movements (among subject positions) is seen to be primarily a responsibility of the political party — the NDP. Apart from large unions, which have considerable financial resources, most labour organisations function as "service agents," assisting members in the interpretation of legal rights, mediating during collective bargaining and monitoring agreements. Rank-and-file education and grass-roots coalition-building are activities outside these institutional priorities. The bureaucratic organisation created to carry out these functions is characterized by hierarchical and representative, rather than inclusive and participatory structures. "Mobilisation" increasingly comes to refer to recruiting picketers during strikes, rather than to an ongoing process of education, skill-development, analysis and empowerment.

There are limits to the challenges facing capital that unions can pose within the framework of collective bargaining — hence the division of labour with a social democratic political party. The current direction of capitalist restructuring (greater freedom/mobility for multinational capital, structural unemployment, erosion of social security, etc.) further constricts the gains that can be made through collective bargaining. Even the relatively progressive leadership of the CAW — which implemented an environmental policy in 1986, and has developed committees and policies dealing with women's issues and racism — and the dedicated rank and file activists who share the vision of the radical currents of the alternative movements, are constrained by the union's institutional role within the existing constellation of State and economic structures, and by the need to avoid political isolation.

The CAW may be considered the "strong case" of social unionism in the industrial sector.[19] A study of the implementation, between 1986 and

1989, of environmental committees in six CAW locals, showed that there was potential for two different political-strategic conceptions of a labour-environment alliance to develop (Adkin, 1989). A "social democratic/institutional" orientation was supported by existing union structures and practices, as well as by the local executive officials. This approach is characterised by:

1) Alliances at the level of organizational elites (with environmental organisations). Joint activities consist mainly of co-signed statements or briefs to government bodies, or endorsements, rather than educational and cultural events organised for rank-and-file union members and environmental activists. This kind of relationship maintains the ability of executive officials to control the nature and extent of contact with their own base by "outside" groups, while allowing them to claim that they are fulfilling the policy objectives of the national leadership. It does not necessitate internal changes in union practices or priorities.

2) Participation in citizens' campaigns whose demands do not necessitate risk-taking in the sphere of collective bargaining or job security (which indeed, may strengthen the position of the work force vis-à-vis employers), but which are directed towards governments (such as incentives or penalties affecting production practices or investment). The union typically uses such campaigns to argue that an NDP government would resolve conflicts in favour of public and workers' interests.

3) Environment committee functions which centre around lobbying for legislative reforms, instructing stewards in interpretation of legislation, and monitoring workplace observance of legislation. By 1989 it appeared that the environment committees would be modelled closely on the functions of the occupational health and safety committees.

A "convergence/transformative" tendency, on the other hand, was manifested in the views of some of the rank-and-file activists (who were nevertheless expressing conflicting views about these two directions), as well as in the choices expressed by a significant minority of workers in a rank-and-file survey. Environment committee members tended to be partially seduced by the greater freedoms of action bestowed by holding official union positions, and by the sense of influence attached to representative roles. At the same time, they were conscious of the real limitations of these roles, and sympathetic to the more radical goals of the environmental movement. A survey of rank-and-file workers showed that there was very substantial support for a more "pro-active" or "pre-emptive" union strategy,[20] especially in the areas of research and educational opportunities.

A "transformative" direction for the environment committees would be characterised by:

1) Emphasis on organising joint actions and events for members of the environmental groups and the union's rank-and-file, to eventually build links among subject positions.

2) A conception of political work centred not around electoral support for the NDP, but around the articulation of a discourse which links the experiences of workers' subordination with other forms of oppression, and which seeks to define the "frontiers" of political conflict, or of counter-hegemonic struggle.[21]

3) A refusal of a "representative" role based on little meaningful direction from the rank-and-file, but which is really one of transmitting or implementing campaigns that emanate from the national executive and must have approval from national and local executives. Instead, the environment committees would seek ways to democratise union structures, and to increase participation, with the goal of empowering members.

4) A formulation of campaigns in such as way as to pose questions about the meaning and the purpose of production, of work, and of the control of economic decision-making, and also to allow consideration of radical alternatives. For example, in the case of the auto workers, questions could be raised about the need for automobiles, urban transportation alternatives, plant conversion, and strategies for reducing work time and unemployment.

5) The incorporation of environmental goals into collective bargaining; this would politicize members and create bases for alliances with other social actors.

While the "social democratic/institutional" strategy has predominantly defined the role of the environment committees, there continues to be a tension between their institutional and transformative functions, fed by the contradictory pressures on rank-and-file workers and their union representatives, by the demands and influence of the environmental movement (particularly with regard to State regulatory policy), and by the ongoing restructuring of the industry. A number of environmental demands were included in the union's bargaining with Chrysler in 1990. In addition, the national agreement struck with Ford in September of the same year made significant gains in the areas of reduced work time, child care, and the reinforcement of the union's commitment to social justice issues. Local 444 in Windsor recently negotiated an agreement with Chrysler that will provide expanded educational opportunities for the work force.

The CAW case demonstrates the current limits of "social unionism" and suggests the kind of developments that would be evidence of movement towards a counter-hegemonic conception of union strategy. Such a strategy, as explained above, would link together a multiplicity of subject positions on the bases of a shared resistance to relations of subordination and oppression; it would confront both the definition of "the enemy" and alternatives which advance the goals of equality (social solidarity) and self-determination (liberty).

A comparison of the CAW with the Energy and Chemical Workers, or with public sector unions, indicates that, within the existing institutional and political limits on union strategies, there is a range of responses that they may adopt toward the alternative movements. While the CAW has adopted a pro-alliance policy, the ECWU has remained largely passive and sometimes hostile. In the presence of alternative movements of growing political influence, these responses are determined by a complex array of factors.

Public sector unions are "political" by necessity — their employer is the State. Also, the "human service" professions (nurses, teachers, social workers, etc.) and highly-educated white-collar workers (public administration) seem to be key elements of the alternative movement coalitions. Offe argues that this is because their knowledge of decision-making processes, of inefficiencies, of irrational aspects of the system and of its unjust and undemocratic aspects, as well as their expertise about alternatives, gives them both the motivation and the means with which to develop a political critique of the State.

Workers in economic sectors which have been relatively protected from current capitalist restructuring, either through State policies or the luck of the market, may be in a stronger bargaining position vis-à-vis employers, and therefore less defensive toward the environmental or peace movements. This is one factor that may explain the CAW's willingness to ally with the environmental movement. The Auto Pact has provided the Canadian State with some leverage over MNC investment in the sector, while the petrochemical workers have taken no such step. The ECWU functions in an economic sector where huge MNCs have free reign, and the federal and provincial States (since the defeat of the National Energy Policy) have adopted a free-market approach. The Free Trade Agreement offered even more lenient terms of exploitation to the petrochemical companies.[22] However, the social democratic optimism of the CAW leadership could be affected by the deepening recession in the North American auto industry linked to world market saturation and the effects of the free trade agreement on Canadian production.

The ECWU is also a less militant or alliance-oriented union than the CAW.[23] The oil fields, refineries and industrial chemicals sectors have always been highly capital-intensive relative to other industries, and their workforces have been comparatively well-paid. Employers have been able to buy peace with wage increases surpassing those of other sectors. The higher proportion of skilled tradespersons in the ECWU, in addition to employer campaigns, have contributed to the formation of a "professional/elite" culture among ECWU officials which is resistant to militant, grass-roots oriented campaigns and tactics, and to the formation of alliances with non-union organizations (Adkin, 1989). In addition, certain industrial sectors have been more vulnerable to campaigns by the environmental movement than others. The chemical and nuclear industries [areas of ECWU unionization] have been subject to more health and regulatory scrutiny in Canada in recent years than has the auto industry. The threats to ECWU jobs from environmental reforms have been more direct and immediate than the pressures directed toward autoworkers from the environmental movement.

CONCLUSIONS

Issues beyond the environmental regulation of the industrial model of growth, or the management mandate of the social-democratic State, are being posed by the critiques and in the proposals of the radical elements in the environmental movement, and also by some activists in the labour movement. However, the limitations and contradictions of a social democratic response to the economic and environmental crisis have not been confronted by alternative movements in Canada as they have, for example, in West Germany, or — since 1981 — in France. NDP govern-ments at the federal and provincial levels might create new spaces for grass-roots mobilisation, or provoke, as a result of heightened (and frustrated) expectations, a radicalisation of the alternative movements. The development of a new counter-hegemonic party (not currently being proposed by significant numbers of Greens or socialists in Canada) could yet emerge. In the context of a broad social mobilisation around a "new societal paradigm," we can expect movement by some unions towards this bloc, entailing changes in the structures, practices and priorities of these organisations. Another possibility is that union organisations may be — as Gramsci predicted (1975) — abandoned and by-passed by other forms of collective action.

A radical democratic and pluralist project appears to be the only alternative to the impasse likely to be confronted by social democratic solutions, or to a deepening of the economic, social and ecological crisis which could prepare the way for authoritarian responses. The NDP would do well to note the experience of Socialist government in France. The capitulation of the Parti Socialiste (PS) to the liberal-productivist model has disillusioned the alternative movements and contributed to a cynical alienation from politics on the part of the majority of the population. This alienation is often expressed in terms of an inability to distinguish left from right. The old cleavage is indeed disintegrating, as evidenced by the declining memberships and militant bases of the traditional political par-ties and the unions. Alain Lipietz has argued (1989) that the Conservatives, the Liberals and the Socialists now comprise a broad centre in the French political system, whereas the Communists, still attached to the Fordist paradigm, are in crisis and decline. The emerging poles of a new societal paradigm appear to be the Greens and the far right. Within any "historical compromise" there are "frontiers" of social conflict — interests excluded from the hegemonic bloc. There are always poles of conflict, in this sense. The failure of the Canadian NDP to deepen and extend its democratising agenda could lead, as in France, to the temporary fragmentation and marginalisation of the alternative movements. However, in the contexts either of a deepening recession and an environmental crisis, or of a project of radical democratisation, we will confront a reactive pole comprised of those threatened by change. Its discourse may well take the form of an "anti-politics" populism (already present in the Reform Party's contradictory welding together of a political democratisation discourse and a neoliberal economic agenda), xenophobia and/or anti-feminism.

The values of the alternative movements (self-determination, social solidarity) and their linkages to the goals of decentralisation and democratisation of decision-making, suggest the outlines of a new paradigm of social conflict and change. Inevitably, the emergence of this new paradigm is marked by clashes between old and new ways of interpreting a multitude of identities and relations. Yet what is at issue is not the schematic ending of one era and the beginning of another; the "old issues" are not irrelevant, and the "old actors" are not incapable of change. The challenge facing us is rather to view with a critical and fresh eye both all that was known, and the limits of our imagination.

NOTES

1. I would like to thank Colin Leys and Rosemary Warskett for their helpful comments on earlier drafts.
2. I use the term "alternative movements" in lieu of the term "new social movements," which is prevalent in the literature dealing with the grassroots movements which emerged in the advanced industrial societies in the late 1960s. This is first, because of the problem of "newness" versus continuity: the women's, peace, and environmental movements, for example, have roots in the previous century. "Alternative" refers to the association of the post-1960s movements with a critique of the post-World War II model of development. Second, there is the problem of why other "grassroots" movements, like religious fundamentalism, racism, or the gun lobby, are not also "social movements." The Touraine school initially used the term "social movement" to mean a movement which is the bearer of a historical project for grand social transformation. "New" emphasised the historical differentiation of, for example, the anti-nuclear movement, from the "traditional" or older social movement, the workers' movement. "Alternative" refers to this transformative role, distinguishing the women's, peace, ecology, and other movements from movements which are reactive, that is, based on social groups whose interests are threatened by change or whose identities are in dissolution. There are also problems with the conceptualisation of "new social movements" as specific to the liberal democratic model of industrial society (see Hegedus, 1989), but that is beyond the scope of this discussion.
3. Touraine, Alain. *The Voice and the Eye: An Analysis of Social Movements.* Cambridge Univ. Press, and Éditions de La Maison des Sciences de l'Homme, 1981. [Trans. from the original *La Voix et le Regard*, pub. by Éditions du Seuil, Paris, 1978.] p. 9.
4. Hirsch, Joachim. "The Crisis of Fordism, Transformations of the 'Keynesian' Security State, and New Social Movements," *Research in Social Movements, Conflicts and Change.* Vol. 10, 1988. p. 49.
5. Touraine, A., Hegedus, Z., Dubet, F., and Wieviorka, M. *Anti-Nuclear Protest: The Opposition to Nuclear Energy in France.* Cambridge University Press, 1983. [This book was first published as *La Prophétie Anti-Nucléaire.* Paris: Éditions du Seuil, 1980.] p. 178.
6. Offe, Claus. "New Social Movements: Challenging the Boundaries of Institutional Politics." *Social Research.* Vol. 52, no. 4 (Winter 1985). p. 810.
7. Ibid., p. 845.
8. These themes—concerning science, technology, humanism, and democracy— were recently, and quite brilliantly expressed by: Franklin, Ursula. *The Real World of Technology.* Toronto: CBC Massey Lectures, CBC Enterprises, 1990.

9.   Hegedus, Zsuzsa. "Social Movements and Social Change in *Self-Creative Society: New Civil Initiatives* in the International Arena," International Sociology. Vol. 4, no. 1 (March 1989). p. 32.

10.   Offe, C., 1985. p. 835.

11.   In Canada one thinks of conflicts between the immediately affected workforces and environmentalists or health activists concerning asbestos and uranium mining, elimination of lead from gasoline, toxic pollution in the pulp and paper, steel, chemical, and other industries, forestry, nuclear power and hydro-electric megaprojects, to give only a partial list. Similar conflicts have been documented in other advanced industrial countries, and have increasingly emerged in the newly industrialising countries and in the countries of formerly-existing socialism.

12.   For a review of the arguments of Lenin, Trotsky, Luxemburg, and others regarding the trade unions and socialist struggle, see John Kelly, *Trade Unions and Socialist Politics*. London: Verso, 1988. Gramsci's views on the unions are largely to be found in his political writings.

13.   Such an analysis is offered in: Adkin, Laurie. "Counter-hegemony and Environmental Politics in Canada," in W. Carroll, ed. *Contemporary Social Movements in Theory and Practice*. Toronto: Garamond Press, 1992.

14.   It is important to distinguish here between the kind of "fundamentalism" associated with, for example, the "fundos" in the German and other European green movements, which is both ecological and humanist, and the "Earth First" variant. Certain groups of environmentalists in the United States, as well as factions within the Green movements generally described as the "right wing," espouse neo-Malthusian, neo-Hobbesian, or national-populist views.

15.   Citizens' groups studied in my doctoral research (Adkin, 1989) included those formed in the "Chemical Valley" (following the St. Clair River from Sarnia to Windsor), concerned primarily with toxic chemical pollution of the water system, the citizens' coalition against lead, in Toronto, and various groups participating in the Great Lakes Water Quality Agreement Review of 1987 and the remedial action plans for pollution hot spots in the Great Lakes Basin. Another study examined citizens' mobilisation around the waste disposal issue, in the case of the Detroit incinerator (Adkin and Alpaugh, 1988).

16.   In the Canadian case, the responses of citizens' groups, individual corporations and business associations, environmental organisations, and unions, to State efforts to manage environment-economic conflicts, were examined with regard to: the Ontario Spills Bill (a 1985 amendment to the Ontario Environmental Protection Act); the drafting of the Canadian Environmental Protection Act (1986-1987); the Ontario Municipal-Industrial Strategy for [Pollution] Abatement, introduced in June 1986 by the Ontario Minister of the Environment; the 1986-1987 review of the [Canada-United States] Great Lakes Water Quality Agreement and the Remedial Action Plans for the Great Lakes. A detailed study was also made of the responses of these actors to toxic chemical pollution in the cases of the 1950s-1960s air and water pollution of the Chemical Valley; the mercury contamination of the St. Clair River discovered in the 1970s; lead pollution; air pollution in Toronto's "Junction Triangle"; and the discovery of the St. Clair River "blob" near Sarnia in 1985. (See: Adkin, Laurie. "The Prospects for Eco-Socialist Convergence (An Investigation of the Relations Between the Environment Movement and Two Canadian Industrial Unions)." (Doctoral Dissertation, Department of Political Studies, Queen's University, 1989).

17.   This debate, which has penetrated Canadian left intellectual circles in recent years, continues to be preoccupied with Marxism's relationship to the concerns of ecology.

18.   In my interviews and observations of rank-and-file militants in the Canadian Auto Workers Union who were active in environmental issues, I noted that most were either simultaneously or previously involved with environmental groups, and/or had backgrounds in left politics.

19. This term signifies, within the union movement, a recognition of the necessity for unions to address social issues beyond the workplace, to demonstrate solidarity with the struggles of other groups.
20. "Pre-emptive unionism" is a term used by Gavin Kitching in *Rethinking Socialism.* London and New York: Methuen, 1983.
21. Chantal Mouffe used the term "frontiers" to express this idea in a talk given at Queen's University, Kingston, Ontario, March 27, 1991.
22. Other factors which strengthen the CAW's economic/bargaining position include its relatively large membership and its geo-political concentration. The ECWU's membership in the petrochemical sector is concentrated in the Sarnia area, but is much smaller than that of the CAW. [While there are approximately 30,000 CAW members in Essex County, and 95,000 CAW members in the auto industry, located primarily in southwestern Ontario, the ECWU has only about 15,500 members in all of Ontario, with fewer than 3,000 in the Sarnia area.]
23. Regarding the militant rank-and-file culture of the CAW, see the works of Sam Gindin and Charlotte Yates cited in the lists of references.

REFERENCES

Adkin, Laurie. "Counter-hegemony and Environmental Politics in Canada," in W. Carroll, ed. *Contemporary Social Movements in Theory and Practice.* Toronto: Garamond Press, 1992.

Adkin, Laurie. "The Prospects for Eco-Socialist Convergence (An Investigation of the Relations Between the Environment Movement and Two Canadian Industrial Unions)." (Doctoral Dissertation, Department of Political Studies, Queen's University, 1989).

Adkin, Laurie and Catherine Alpaugh. "Labour, Ecology, and the Politics of Convergence," *Social Movements and Social Change,* Frank Cunningham et al., eds. Toronto: Between the Lines, 1988.

Boggs, Carl. *Social Movements and Political Power.* Philadelphia: Temple University Press, 1986.

Cohen, Jean. "Rethinking Social Movements," *Berkeley Journal of Sociology.* vol. XXVIII, 1983. pp. 97-113.

Franklin, Ursula. *The Real World of Technology.* Toronto: CBC Massey Lectures, CBC Enterprises, 1990.

Gindin, Sam. "Breaking Away: The Formation of the Canadian Auto Workers," *Studies in Political Economy.* 29 (Summer 1989).

Gorz, André. *Farewell to the Working Class: An Essay on Post-Industrial Socialism.* Trans. Michael Sonenscher. London: Pluto Press, 1982.

Gorz, André. *Ecology as Politics.* Trans. P. Vigderman and J. Cloud. Montréal: Black Rose Books, 1980.

Gramsci, Antonio. *Ecrits Politiques.* Vol. II (1921-1922). Robert Paris, ed. Trans. M. Martin-Gistucci, G. Moget, and R. Paris. Paris: Éditions Gallimard, 1975.

Hegedus, Zsuzsa. "Social Movements and Social Change in Self-Creative Society: New Civil Initiatives in the International Arena," *International Sociology.* Vol. 4, no. 1 (March 1989). pp. 19-36.

Hirsch, Joachim. "The Crisis of Fordism, Transformations of the 'Keynesian' Security State, and New Social Movements," *Research in Social Movements, Conflicts and Change.* Vol. 10, 1988.

Kelly, John. *Trade Unions and Socialist Politics.* London: Verso, 1988.

Kitching, Gavin. *Rethinking Socialism.* London and New York: Methuen, 1983.

Lessage, Marc. *Les vagabonds du rêve (vers un société de marginaux?).* Montréal: Boréal Express, 1986.

Melucci, Alberto. "The New Social Movements: A Theoretical Approach," *Social Science Information.* 19, 1980.

Mouffe, Chantal and Ernesto Laclau. *Hegemony and Socialist Strategy: Towards a Radical Democratic Politics.* London: Verso, 1985.

Mushaben, Joyce Marie. "The Forum: New Dimensions of Youth Protest in Western Europe," *Journal of Political and Military Sociology.* Vol. 11, no.1 (Spring 1983). pp. 123-144.

Offe, Claus. "New Social Movements: Challenging the Boundaries of Institutional Politics." *Social Research.* Vol. 52, no. 4 (Winter 1985).

Touraine, Alain. *The Voice and the Eye: An Analysis of Social Movements.* Cambridge Univ. Press, and Éditions de La Maison des Sciences de l'Homme, 1981. [Trans. from the original *La Voix et le Regard,* pub. by Éditions du Seuil, Paris, 1978.]

Touraine, A., Hegedus, Z., Dubet, F., and Wieviorka, M. *Anti-Nuclear Protest: The Opposition to Nuclear Energy in France.* Cambridge University Press, 1983. [This book was first published as *La Prophétie Anti-Nucléaire.* Paris: Éditions du Seuil, 1980.]

Williams, Raymond. *Towards 2000.* London: The Hogarth Press, 1983.

Wood, Ellen Meiksins. *Retreat from Class.* London: Verso Books, 1986.

Yates, Charlotte. "The Internal Dynamics of Union Power: Explaining Canadian Autoworkers' Militancy in the 1980s," in *Studies in Political Economy.* 31 (Spring 1990).

Chapter 6

Serge Quenneville

LOCAL UNIONS AND THE ENVIRONMENT: THREE QUÉBEC CASE-STUDIES*

The difficulty in achieving a successful balance between job protection and environmental safety has caused unions in Québec to experience some trying times. A description of environmental activities taking place in three local Québec unions, within the pulp and paper, health and social services, and commercial sectors, illustrates how they are coping with this issue. Unions are often put in the compromising situation of having to choose between job security and environmental safety because of the absence of a long term strategy, on the part of management or the government, to find solutions which are compatible with both these objectives.

Environmental protection has, fortunately, become a major social concern, giving rise to public scrutiny of pollution control, programs of waste and resource management and the designation of green spaces, environmental politics, and many other important activities. In fact, we have moved into a new paradigm, "an ecologization of the social world."[1] No longer is the environment considered as an object to be exploited, but rather as an integral part of the production process, and increasingly as the basis for a new social partnership. For the labour unions, environmental questions represent a relatively new challenge, or rather, a new way of seeing their role in the workplace and in society at large. The unions now find themselves at the centre of a holistic approach in which the economy, the environment and society must be integrated into an overall plan for sustainable development.

The three unions' experiences soon to be described illustrate two points in particular. The first concerns the indivisibility of the environment; it is wider than national boundaries, let alone the limits of any given production site. The links between the health and the safety of working men and women are part of this indivisible environment. The problems

---

* This article was translated by Rev. George Topp, S.J.

connected with health and safety in the workplace, and with the degradation of the environment share a common origin: the production process.
The production process calls for the use of certain primary materials and
products, and generates waste which is dangerous to both the environment and the population. In fact, many of these polluting substances and
dangerous situations traditionally identified simply as occupational
hazards have effects which go far beyond the workplace; professional
illness and accidents at work are also, in reality, ecological accidents and
environmental illnesses.

The increase in major ecological accidents and their effects on entire
communities prove that work-related activities also have considerable
effects on the safety, health and well-being of populations and on the
environment. Industrial activities are directly involved in these problems,
as we know only too well from the accidents at Bophal, Seveso, Love Canal,
Bâle, Tchernobyl or, closer to home and on a smaller scale, at Saint-Basil-Le-
Grand and at Saint Amable. We should also include the growing danger
associated with the increased use of chemical products in the workplace
and in the home. Working men and women are exposed to these hazards
both as working people and as citizens.

Secondly, trade unions have focused attention on the complexity of
environmental questions, with respect both to the nature of the specific
problems, and to the range of social interests and people involved. Today,
environmental issues require workers, both collectively and individually,
to maintain environmental control over both their work environment and
their personal lives. A better understanding of the production process,
more access to information in the firm, the ability to evaluate the social
benefits of work, and the identification of the impact of work on the
environment, are all ways in which workers can become more involved,
and go well beyond health and safety issues.

The relationship between jobs and the environment also has international dimensions. The considerable differences in the norms of environmental protection between countries are just as unacceptable and
inappropriate as the differences in the length of the working week, union
rights, working conditions and the minimum working age or level of social
welfare provision. Workers will not tolerate competition from production
based on working conditions that are inferior to their own; and the same
applies to environmental norms.

Superficially, the relationship between the environment and employment may seem to be relatively simple and direct. If a firm or a factory shuts
down for some alleged environmental reasons, workers will lose their jobs.
Conversely, however, the environment can be a sector in which jobs
associated with ecological production are actually created. The production
of anti-pollution devices such as air purification systems and waste disposal and treatment programs are just a few examples of this. In fact, the
relationship between jobs and the environment is rather complex. The
introduction of environmental measures has short, medium and long term

results. At the local level, the effects may be very serious: factory closures may affect an entire community and result in severe social degradation and poverty. At the global level, several studies have already shown that, in the long run, the employment effects of environmental measures are more positive than negative.[2]

The question of the role of union rights needs emphasising. In the 1970's, Québec labour unions won some of the additional rights that they had been hoping for in the areas of training, compensation and the right to participate in inquiries and have access to information. These rights do not, however, extend to the environment. Since this issue involves other social partners, union locals must above all develop relationships with citizens' committees, ecological groups, company management, local governments and provincial ministries.

The unions must develop unexplored alliances with both old and new partners in order to confront all the issues at stake. The union movement is called upon for the first time to engage in sustained dialogue with the ecology movement, whereas, presently, the relationship between the two is complex, and limited mainly to economic and employment issues. The task ahead is to define the basis upon which we can build this wider social project, in light of the environmental negligence described below.

ALEX COUTURE INC.

Alex Couture Inc. is a meat processing plant located close to a residential area in Charny, a small town in the suburbs of Québec. It has been in operation since 1939, first in Québec City and then, from 1965, in Charny. Although at that time Charny was a small municipality of about 5,000 people, the area underwent a rapid urbanization in the early 1970's. As the residential area expanded, it gradually approached the industrial zone occupied by the plant, and since there was no housing plan, municipal development was left to the whims of the free market. Moreover, in order to begin construction of a highway to La Beauce, much land was expropriated and cleared, further exposing the plant.

The meat processing industry depends on the collection and recycling of about 500,000 tons a year of products from more that 15,000 establishments. These products are non-edible by-products of slaughterhouses, butcher shops and charcuteries (such as chicken feathers, viscera, blood, pork bristle), and also fat and oil remains from restaurants. Added to this is a considerable volume of animals which die on farms and elsewhere. The products are transformed into protein flour and non-edible fat products, which are then recycled or used to produce grain and food for domestic animals, soap, cosmetics, industrial lubricants and other products. The flour is generally sold on the market in Québec, whereas the fat products are partially exported on the international market, which determines the industry's overall marketing and pricing conditions. The industry employs 400 people and generates 70 million dollars in output in Québec annually.

Approximately 60 members of the union work in this industry, 35 of whom are employed in this plant.

Impact on the Environment

Environmental problems caused by the plant include odours released into the atmosphere, and odours caused by the water used in the plant, which is discharged into the sanitary system of the town of Charny.

The process of production itself produces unpleasant-smelling gases which have to be treated before entering the atmosphere. Three primary materials — feathers, pig bristle and blood — produce very concentrated gases. When they are discharged into the sanitary system, besides giving off a bad smell, they aggravate the situation by heating up the municipal water supply which passes through a fairly residential zone. The odours are also carried as far as the Chaudière River, and are being continuously released into the air along the way.

Citizen Action

Since 1965, the citizens of neighbouring regions have, on a regular basis, expressed concern individually or collectively to different municipal, regional and governmental agencies regarding these odours. In 1986, the residents formed the Citizen's Clean Air Committee at Charny to document their complaints and apply pressure on private, public, governmental and judicial agencies to put an end to this situation.

After two years, and after thoroughly frustrating the residents, the firm grudgingly implemented some technological improvements, including the installation of an air-washer, an oxidation tower, gas detectors, electric boilers and a biofilter; they also introduced a dehydration process, a method to treat some gasses and a water treatment system which complied with municipal regulations approved by the MENVIQ (Ministère de l'environnement du Québec). The firm's modification of its air-purification system did not, however, meet the standards set by MENVIQ.

Frustrated by the company's ineffectiveness, the Citizens' Committee brought together the municipalities of Charny and Saint Rédempteur and, in the summer of 1989, established the Coalition for the Relocation of Alex Couture Inc. In response to this pressure, a task force was struck under the direction of Marc Ivan Côté, then Minister of Transportation, with Remi Bujold as president. Representatives of the city, the coalition, the firm, and different provincial and federal ministries made up this task force which brought their report to the table in the summer of 1990. The report rejected relocation of the plant and proposed instead some changes which were far less satisfactory to the coalition: the short term abandonment of the treatment of certain products (feathers and bristles) which generate odours that are more difficult to treat; plans and tenders for a program of sanitation; modification of urban planning to prevent any residential construction less than 450 metres from the plant; the repair of the pipe carrying the waste-waters; a proposal to find an appropriate location for a plant that would treat the waste liquids, and the construction of a system of air-treatment.

Since this time, the case has been stuck in legal wrangling between MENVIQ and the firm. The style adopted by management, its contempt for local citizens and refusal to collaborate with the union, forced the province to intervene on several occasions. It finally issued legal proceedings against the firm. A group of concerned citizens and the city of Charny requested a permanent injunction from the courts and sued the firm for damages. The company, however, systematically exploited all possible appeal procedures and delay tactics.

Union Action

The union has taken several steps to deal with this issue and began by trying to collaborate with the Citizen's Committee. However, since the union opposed the relocation of the factory, considering this strategy a threat to jobs, there was no basis upon which to build an alliance. Instead, the result was a hardening of positions, and the Citizen's Committee, for some time, accused the union of acting on behalf of the employer!

The union did approach management and sought its cooperation. Together they established their own environmental sub-committee with equal representation to study the question. It became clear very early on, however, that the union would have only a small role to play. Still, it did succeed in learning management's position on this issue during this limited collaboration: both the problem of odour emission and the threat of job loss would be solved, according to the company, if workers kept all doors closed, and if production were increased! The company's standards, the management argued, would then comply with environmental regulations. Moreover, management blamed the Minister of the Environment for the failure to make progress and for the present state of working conditions, because he had refused to approve their original plan for air purification. When the union executive took the matter up with MENVIQ, the management of Alex Couture abolished the sub-committee.

Harmful Impact on the Health of Workers

In the case of Alex Couture Inc., environmental negligence had direct repercussions on health and safety at work and on the organization of work. The company sought to promote work practices that would keep the odours inside the workplace. Previously, workers would open the garage doors to improve the ventilation and the quality of the air, but now the employer insisted that they be closed in response to growing complaints by local residents. The union responded by preparing two dossiers on the health and safety of workers. The principal symptoms identified were: eye irritation, sudden perspiration resulting from any effort, headaches, dryness of the lips, sore throats, difficulty in breathing (dyspnoea) and dry coughing. The situation has since deteriorated; there have been reported cases of poisoning and several workers have been hospitalized. These working conditions have also had serious repercussions on the internal organization of the union, as the increased turnover of workers has reduced seniority to one or two years. This has severely affected the overall stability of the union and its ability to deal adequately with all the matters that concern it, including environmental issues. Union vitality is a necessary condition for effective union involvement in environmental matters.

Meanwhile, however, the union has registered a complaint with the Commission de la Santé et Securité au Travail (CSST) and collaborated in an inquiry with the Département de Santé Communautaire (DSC). The CSST, the DSC, the CLSC (Centre Local de Santé Communautaire) and the IRSST (Institut de Recherche en Santé et Securité au Travail) are studying the situation.

Conclusion

It is clear that the union must become involved in environmental issues and develop a strategy of intervention at all levels — citizens' groups, the business community, ecological groups and the government. The union can also play an important role in monitoring and implementing measures to protect the environment in the workplace.

Subsequent to the Bujold report, MENVIQ adopted a new sanitation program submitted by the firm in June 1991. The cost of decontamination will be assumed entirely by the firm, on condition that it has access to existing governmental programs. The implementation of this plan, which includes a projected 3.5 million dollars for a new system to treat odours, will be closely monitored by the union, which will participate in the planned measures to improve working conditions.

THE UNION OF WORKERS OF THE CENTRE-HOSPITALIER ST. VINCENT-DE-PAUL AT SHERBROOKE

Biomedical Waste

Workers cannot remain indifferent to the problem of contamination caused by the absence of effective control of biomedical waste products. Medical establishments and other producers of biomedical waste are not assuming responsibility for these products, nor are they equipping themselves with a management that respects the right of the population to a healthy environment. Although the administrators are aware of the mounting tons of biomedical waste, they claim that financial problems prevent them from taking any action.

The Ministries of the Environment and Health and Social Services have classified biomedical waste into four groups: (1) those of a biological nature, such as human anatomical parts and contaminated biological liquids, bacteria, culture media, contaminated containers, and remnants from contaminated surfaces; (2) those of a physical nature, such as contaminated material, lingerie, bed linen and contaminated hardware; (3) those of a chemical nature, such as solvents; and (4) various kinds of waste such as antineoplastic preparations used for treating cancer, out of date or unused vaccines, products of genetic engineering, or out of date or contaminated medications.

Currently, biomedical waste is dealt with as follows: anatomical parts are sent to a pathology laboratory, where they are classified by size without regard to their pathogenic aspect. The way in which the various parts, containers and the used liquids are handled is, in most cases, inadequate. In certain establishments anatomical parts are frozen before they are disposed of by incineration, an essential procedure which, however, does not prevent their deterioration. Moreover, halogenous substances used for the chemical treatment of anatomical parts in preparation for analysis do not burn and are, therefore, returned to the atmosphere. Physical waste is all placed, after treatment, in containers that are often inadequate before being disposed of on waste disposal sites; this severely contaminates the soil and seeps out as contaminated liquids. Virtually no precautions are taken for chemical waste, which is simply diluted with a lot of water and discharged into the sewage system; other kinds of waste are recovered by waste disposal companies. The hospital management is basically unaware of the disposal methods used by these companies.

Union Action

The CSN local has been concerned with this issue since 1987, following numerous complaints of a physical nature which were later thought to be directly linked to the untreated air due to the absence of control over biomedical waste. The first step taken by the union was to develop a data bank to record the illnesses experienced by workers. In most cases, the symptoms observed were the same: the lowering of arterial tension; excessive dryness of the throat and the sinuses; numbness in the area of the sinuses; headaches; and the appearance of cutaneous lesions at the corners of the mouth. As soon as these people left work, these symptoms disappeared.

The union then conducted a secret independent inquiry, since the employer had refused to listen, assuming the union was incapable of developing any expertise in this matter. In the laboratories, the union discovered to its surprise that many incompatible products were, in fact, found side by side under the sinks, actually causing a premature deterioration of the plumbing system in certain areas. Rather than change the plumbing, a sterilizer was installed, with the result that when contaminated vapour escaped from the steriliser, it spread through all the interconnected units and caused the symptoms described above.

Also, in the laboratory, since there was no filter system, blood and solvents were thrown directly into the sink which then flowed into the sewer system. There was no way to find out what precautions, if any, had been taken to deal with these problems by the municipality.

Similar conditions were observed in the pathology laboratory. Anatomical parts which had remained in a preparation containing formalin for several months had congealed; the liquid was subsequently poured into the sink, and the container was then thrown into the garbage. Due to inadequate ventilation, workers in this section also developed many of the symptoms described above.

The union was surprised to discover equally disturbing conditions in the maintenance areas. Solvents used in carpentry and painting were thrown directly into ordinary garbage cans to be subsequently disposed of in a common dump site. The ventilation was deficient here as well, and maintenance workers were direct victims of the total absence of control over biomedical waste. They were required on a daily basis to move all sorts of contaminated waste which was hazardous to their health and to the environment.

Even within the dietary sector of the hospital, volatile toxic solvents were used to clean the ovens and cooking utensils. It was here that the largest number of workers were suffering from poor health because of inadequate environmental standards.

The union reported this alarming situation to the media, and notified the Commission de la Santé et Securité au Travail (CSST), which had on two previous occasions conducted a thorough inspection of the establishment, accompanied each time by a representative of management. This action resulted in a meeting between the union and the director of the hospital the next day to evaluate the situation.

Action Transcending the Workplace

Many other factors have affected progress on the Saint-Vincent case. The central Council of L'Estrie filed a report on biomedical waste with the Ministry of the Environment in 1989; this was followed by evidence submitted by the Fédération des affaires sociales (FAS) to the Charbonneau Commission in 1990.[3] The union also took numerous other initiatives on the environment. As a result of all these efforts, several changes have been introduced at the Saint Vincent de Paul Hospital Centre: the hospital incinerator has been closed, as it could not maintain an adequate temperature; a container appropriate for the disposal of physical waste products has been provided, permitting the sterilization of this waste before disposal; biomedical waste products continue to be frozen before being sent to the incinerator, but the containers and the liquids are now retrieved and a product has been found to neutralize the formalin; used solvents are all recovered in barrels; and some waste products are sent to the Centre hôpitalier de l'Université de Sherbrooke (CHUS), whose incinerator is still in working order.

Conclusion

A committee representing both management and the union must be established in order to guarantee the continued control of biomedical waste products, as there remains much to be done. In addition, a fact-finding study has been conducted by both union and management representatives, in order to raise the consciousness of workers and to ensure their participation in the planned action. Although the data on the shipment of biomedical waste outside the establishment remains incomplete, a representative of management recently informed the union that the hospital will acquire a larger compacter, and that safe storage capacity will soon be constructed for this waste.

The implications of this case are indeed frightening as all biomedical waste in the system has a direct impact on the air we breathe, and efforts to control it remain unsatisfactory. There are tons of biomedical waste products which should not be burned, for too many pollutants escape at the time of incineration and may cause serious public health problems. Much of the waste should not be deposited in disposal sites, as its decomposition allows volatile organic compounds to escape, which are gases that affect the health of the environment and the population.

It is wrong to assume that good management in the public health sector implies exorbitant costs. Appropriate incentives can force management to assume greater responsibility for the environment, for the population at large and for the men and women employed in the health and social services sector. Improved management within the establishment, better transportation and handling of waste can all be achieved with economic incentives to reduce costs, legislative measures to ensure the strict regulation of biomedical waste disposal, and active participation by the unions in the implementation of such a program. A system of control is currently in place and administrators have already acknowledged that the associated costs are far less than anticipated. Employers' associations and the different levels of government must also become involved; it is their duty to establish a wider system of control for all biomedical waste, whatever the source.

THE CASCADES FACTORY — THE BLACK FLUID SAGA

The cardboard factory located in Jonquière, formerly owned by Abitibi-Price, was purchased in 1984 by the Lemaire brothers' Cascades Company. The pulp and paper industry dominates the economy of the Saguenay — Lac St. Jean region and has been a major industry and employer in Québec. The paper industry also plays an important social role which has shaped the development of several regions of Québec. However, the environmental record of the industry is very poor, and the national union of pulp and carton workers in Jonquière has been directly concerned with the environmental record of the company since 1988, and with its serious repercussions, not only on the environment, but on the social and economic life of the region as a whole.

Impact on the Environment

All aspects of the environment are affected by paper production. The emission of sulphur-based compounds (acid rain) pollutes the air; and the disposal on the factory sites of waste such as gypsum sediment, shavings, fibres, drugs, knots, ashes from the boiler, paper and heavy metals pollutes the soil. However, it is the waste discharged into the water by the paper industry which is most harmful to the environment. This consists largely of organic compounds such as wood and chemical residue, and inorganic compounds such as metal. The 61 factories in this region alone generate more pollution than the whole population of the province combined. The quantity and level of toxicity depend on the procedures used and on the productive capacity of the factory.

The Cascades factory of Jonquière produces cardboard according to a production technique known as the Kraft procedure or sulphate process, the most common production method in use since 1950. This process transforms wood shavings into pulp (Kraft pulp) which is subsequently bleached and dried into cardboard with the use of chemical compounds. In the process, a chemical liquid is used to wash the wood shavings. This white liquid, which contains an alkaline base, turns black in the course of extracting lignin, acids, salts and chemical substances from the wood.

The Black Fluid Saga

In the summer of 1988, a series of "accidental" spills into the Rivière aux Sables (four in one month) of black liquid originating in the Cascades plant, alarmed the population, the media and ecological groups. At the end of July, 9000 gallons of black liquid escaped into the ecosystem of the Saguenay; at the beginning of August, 100 additional gallons were spilled. This mobilized ecological groups and the Environment Committee of Chicoutimi, which revealed the damage caused by these spills to the public. They also presented a series of simple solutions to prevent such ecological accidents, such as the erection of a dyke around the reservoirs containing dangerous chemical products. A third spill was reported to the regional management of the Ministry of the Environment. Since then, Greenpeace has demanded an additional inquiry by the Ministry, this time covering the entire paper industry. For Greenpeace, the daily disposal of approximately 1.5 tons of toxic material into the river was far worse than these accidental spills. The committee also exposed spills in Trois Rivières from the Consolidated Bathurst plant, and asked for an immediate change in environmental regulations and for a public consultation. The media called for fines; the regional division of the Ministry took no action.

A group of workers at the Abitibi-Price plant, on the opposite bank of the Rivière aux Sables, joined the protest, insisting that the now more frequent and numerous spills at Cascades were not accidental but rather the result of negligence on the part of management. The media followed the case very closely.

In less than one month, a fourth spill occurred. The Environment Committee of Chicoutimi decided to conduct its own investigation in collaboration with researchers from the University of Québec at Chicoutimi, especially on the impact of these spills on the aquatic ecosystem (trout cages) and on fishing in general, which is very important to the region. The committee even set up a campsite from which to keep track of the emissions from the factory, thereby drawing attention to the negligence of the Ministry. There was a fifth, then a sixth spill in the days which followed.

Conditions Within the Factory

In 1988, following four years of continuous growth, Cascades Jonquière announced a 45 million dollar project to modernize its cardboard making machinery, news which was, of course, well received in the region. Because of the extensive environmental dossier compiled on Cascades in the summer of 1988, the company now unveiled a plan to counteract the spills. It agreed to introduce a system of protective measures consisting of the installation of two reservoirs of 225,000 gallons for chemical products, and for recovering leakages of black fluid. It also consented to build pumping stations for sewage, to install a system to recover black fluid in the manufacturing process, and to take additional preventive measures. These projects would cost about one million dollars in total.

The union felt that this slim million dollars for environmental protection was insignificant compared with the 45 million dollar investment for production. Cascades claimed to be acting responsibly; according to the manager of the factory, "even subsequent to the spills that had occurred, the firm has never violated the norms set down for it by the Ministry of the Environment, and Cascades is under no obligation to create a protection system such as it intends to instal in the course of the coming months." Moreover, the manager did not fail to add that the company aimed to operate at a profit and to provide lasting jobs for its 400 employees.

The Role of the Union

The intervention of the union in environmental issues was intended first and foremost to protect jobs, for there was a certain danger of job loss in the sector of the factory from which the spills emanated (the Kraft pulp sector). This sector employed almost one half of the 300 workers of the plant. It must be noted that, in the first instance, it was workers from the plant who anonymously alerted the Regional Director of the Ministry of the Environment about the black liquid that was escaping into the out-flow. The union was surprised by the speed with which events unfolded, especially by how quickly this information was captured by the media. Still, it preferred to let the debate take place outside the plant without too much intervention on its part, so that it could devote its energies to the concerns raised by this issue within the union and the firm. The most important of these considerations was job protection, but there was also the need to negotiate the right to refuse to pollute. If the union had been able to obtain this right in the collective agreement, it would have repre-sented a precedent in Québec. However, it did not happen because the company was aware that a precedent of this sort would open the door to a whole new area of negotiations concerning the environment and health and safety.

Instead, an agreement was reached with the company outside the collective agreement, stipulating the right of workers to denounce any work practices which have a negative impact on the environment. The union also made contact with various pressure groups, especially Green-peace. In response to Greenpeace's radical proposal to block the company's sewer, the union urged the groups to recognize the serious impact such a strategy would have on jobs, and that a search for long term solutions was more appropriate.

In this case, the union became a mediator in which it had to take into account the anxieties of working men and women, the ability of the firm to manage the problem, the legitimate concerns of the local population to live in a healthy environment, the demands of ecological groups (which were more political in nature than the demands of the local residents), and the media's need for news.

Conclusion

In a period of environmental crisis, the unions are somewhat on the defensive and are legitimately involved in protecting their members and their jobs. It is therefore not an ideal time to elaborate a positive union approach to environmental issues. As it is, the union continues to struggle to gain the right to refuse work that contributes to pollution, the right to be informed about the environmental impact of a system of production, the right to job security and the right to negotiate.

The black fluid story represents the extent of changes that are neces-sary, and that are also imposed by the market on the pulp and paper sector. If we want to assure job protection in the current context of transforming production to meet environmental needs, the unions must participate at the level of development and in the projects undertaken by the industry. Above all, the unions must achieve, through legislative measures and adequate funding, security for those whose jobs are lost because of environmental reasons.

In 1991 Bernard Lemaire, the president of Cascades, announced the closing of the Kraft pulp section and the loss of 150 jobs in the region. The principal reasons cited for the closure were international competitiveness and the pressure exercised by changing consumption patterns, especially in Europe. Further massive closures at Trois Rivières in early 1992 have reinforced the gravity of the situation. In this context, environmental questions carry little weight; they form only one element in a context of global economic restructuring, increasing competition, regulations and changing consumption habits, which together are imposing radical changes on methods of production and on the choice of final products. The involvement of the unions is therefore essential not only for workers and their industries, but for the whole of society, which has a right to demand that systems of production take environmental issues into account.

There are currently no permanent solutions to the conflicts between economic and environmental considerations. At the local level, different social actors must react to each situation as they arise. The unions perpetually find themselves wedged between management which restricts their involvement in environmental issues and a Ministry with little credibility. For the unions to develop a meaningful alliance with ecological groups and citizens committees means they must have the right to full access to information on the job, and the right to participate actively in monitoring environmental standards at work. They are at the heart of this issue and are only too well aware that jobs should not be protected at unacceptable environmental costs.

The unions are involved in a political struggle: union participation in public consultation, in the planned use of public space, in the evaluation of development projects, in "hot" dossiers such as energy and waste management has grown considerably. Job security must be included in these discussions, especially in those sectors threatened by violation of environmental standards. This situation will worsen in the next decade especially considering the high costs of restructuring production to meet environmental norms in many industries such as mining, paper and related products, rubber and plastics, iron and steel and food processing. Several of these industries may well apply intense economic pressure as closure would devastate the regional economies affected.

The success of environmental politics and the impact on jobs — both gains and losses — depend in part on training programs, recycling and adaptation at work. The trade union movement has, therefore, become involved from the end of the 1980's in a new paradigm in which the "ecologization" of the social and of the economic is irreversible. This requires both a holistic approach to the problem and a new solidarity at the local level (intersectoral cooperation, new alliances) and at the international level (agreements, conventions, etc.). There is much work ahead in order to clearly define the "ecological niche" which the trade union movement in Québec will occupy in the transition to a sustainable development.

NOTES

1. Maffesoli, Michael, "L'écologisation du monde social" in *Revue international d'action communautaire*. 24/64, automne 1990.
2. Report du directeur du Bureau international du travail, "l'Environment et le monde du travail." 1990.
3. The FAS is an organization of all unions in the health and social service sector.

REFERENCES

Maffesoli, Michael, "L'écologisation du monde social" in *Revue international d'action communautaire*. 24/64, automne 1990.

Report du directeur du Bureau international du travail, "l'Environment et le monde du travail." 1990.

Chapter 7

Rosemary Warskett

DEFINING WHO WE ARE: SOLIDARITY THROUGH DIVERSITY IN THE ONTARIO LABOUR MOVEMENT[1]

Solidarity for ever, Solidarity for ever, Solidarity for ever, for the union makes us strong.

Standing to sing "Solidarity for Ever" at the end of every significant union event symbolises for North American unionists the importance of collective action and the strength that derives from workers' unity. It is the moment when labour antagonists look around the hall and recognise the need for differences to be put aside in the interests of the greater whole.

Depending on the occasion, "Solidarity for Ever" may be sung with enthusiasm and sincerity, or it may be recited in a routine and perfunctory manner. In both cases, however, the union activists use the song to clearly express their belief in the underlying message: the general understanding that collective solidarity is the basis on which the labour movement can maintain a distinctive identity, culture and power in a society dominated by private capital, individual competitiveness and mass alienation.

One of the ambiguities associated with this message, however, concerns who is included and who is excluded when this solidarity is evoked.[2] Furthermore, who is to define union goals and place limits on the use of collective action? Who has the power to define the boundaries of solidarity and the uses to which its force will apply? These questions are important because labour activists and leaders sometimes refuse to recognise that some members are more equal than others, in the sense that certain goals will benefit some more than others. Linked to this refusal is an inability to recognise the hierarchical divisions and fragmentations that exist within the labour movement and the working class.

Concern about solidarity and democratic participation leads to even more profound questions regarding the process of decision-making within the union movement. Is the call for solidarity a means by which the decisions of leadership are imposed upon the rank and file, a "club" that is used against marginalised groups of workers and other sections of the working class? Is it evoked to deflect criticism and thwart democratic participation? Or can the culture of solidarity be a means through which democratic decision-making is encouraged at all levels of the union movement? And if it is encouraged, how is the tension that frequently arises between specific group and collective interests to be resolved? During the process of collective and political bargaining only some interests can be met, creating in effect a hierarchy. Who decides the order of the hierarchy and on what basis is this decision to be made? Whose interests will stand over those of others in the name of general solidarity? The answer to these questions is linked both to the conception of solidarity and to the general vision of the current political and economic climate held by a particular labour movement.

Offe suggests that within developed, capitalist industrial societies a problem of unity has arisen recently within the ranks of labour, and has raised some doubts concerning the ability of labour movements within these societies to act in solidarity as they did in the past. "...Arising out of the conditions of economic crisis and tendencies of cultural change," he argues,

> the problem consists...in an accentuation of the economic and 'moral' divisions within the working class. The result...is a growing heterogeneity in the objective situation of different groups of employees, as well as in their subjective perceptions and interpretations. These lines of division emerge more clearly as a consequence of the worsening labour market situation.[3]

It is easy to agree that new problems, such as rising unemployment and an increase in precarious or "flexible" forms of employment, are being presented by labour markets of advanced capitalist societies, perhaps especially in the United States and Canada (Albo:1989; Edwards:1979; Myles:1989). Yet, the problem of labour unity is not new; divisions existed within these western labour movements to a greater or lesser degree both during the postwar period and before. In particular, women, newly arrived immigrants (in European countries guest workers), aboriginal people and the unemployed have long been marginal groups that did not, and still do not, have the power to assert their particular interests within the Canadian labour movement as a whole. What may be closer to the truth is that recent labour market changes, together with the rise of certain popular movements, have provided openings for marginalised identities within the working class to make their particular experience and needs felt. Acting on the basis of their experience, women and minority groups have made existing divisions visible. They bring to the forefront their subordination, within the labour movement and the working class, challenging the ways in which union identity and solidarity have been constructed in the past.

Built into the construction of union solidarity is the understanding that practices and meanings must at least partly be protective and defensive, given the strength and power of international capitalism. Changes in the economy, therefore, give rise to defensive strategies directed towards protecting union members' livelihoods. Furthermore, because they are centred on the work place, unions themselves cannot bring about radical changes in political and economic conditions and in culture. Changes such as these require links to be made with the newly emerging social and political movements which are engaged in exposing the limitations and contradictions of liberal democracy, and are willing to strategise and act locally together to build democracy, and to encourage the creative capacities of people in their communities and work places.[4]

I intend to examine the definition of "who we are,"[5] the goals of union solidarity, and how they are being challenged and changed within the Ontario labour movement. There are signs, however slight, that there is a potential for a much broader conception of solidarity than that which was constructed after World War II, one that may allow the labour movement to move beyond a defensive type of solidarity, and to unite organically with other social forces pressing for radical change. And this is despite, or possibly because of, the difficult times the labour movement in Ontario has lived through since the mid-1970s.

There is a growing recognition amongst some labour activists that if unity is to be reconciled with equality, the differences within the labour movement and the working class need to be recognized and taken into account, rather than subordinated in the name of greater solidarity. Taking differences into account means reformulating traditional goals and strategies. It means adopting a wider and more encompassing vision of labour and the working class, one which goes far beyond mere reaction to capital's restructuring of the economy.

STRUCTURAL CHANGES WITHIN THE ECONOMY AND THE LABOUR MOVEMENT

It is frequently pointed out that the "...position of trade unions, and working class politics in general, have always been historically contingent, and defined vis-a-vis the changing contours of capitalism."[6] However, there is no simple relation between changes in the economy and changes in union organisation, practices or identity. Usually, there are choices to be made about the direction to be taken, the goals to be achieved and the strategies to be employed, even though these may be severely circumscribed by the structures of capital and the State. Changes that take place in the political and economic framework, and the resulting choices available, are interpreted and understood through the "conception of the world" that any labour movement and working class develops. Whether such a conception is independent or at least partially loosened from the hegemony of the dominant classes, in the sense that they spring out of the experience and action of the subordinate classes, will have a direct impact on the kinds of choices and decisions that are made.[7] In this sense the prevailing conception of union solidarity informs union strategies, goals and actions, and in turn the resulting experience acts to change or confirm unionists' conception of solidarity, and their vision of the world in general.

By the mid-1970s the changing contours of capitalism were becoming more and more apparent. Economic restructuring and changes in the labour movement in the postwar years now contributed to class conflict as the crisis of capital deepened. Rapid union growth from the 1940s onwards, especially in Ontario and Québec, was a very important factor in this respect. Growth resulted initially from unionization of mass production and resource industries, followed by the extraordinary rise of public sector unions from 1965 onwards. Both these thrusts meant that by 1983, the union density in Canada reached a postwar high of 40 per cent.[8]

During the late 1930s and 1940s unionisation of the mass production and resource industries occurred under the banner of the Committee for Industrial Organization (CIO), and during the next twenty years this type of unionism increasingly gained dominance and hegemony over the Ontario labour movement.[9] The CIO's commitment to industrial militancy, democracy and equality became a "badge of honour" that was worn with pride by predominately white, male members, on both sides of the border.[10] It was, however, a "badge of honour" that, for the most part, became narrowly focused on the workplace. During the 1930s and 1940's working class mobilization and politicization reached an unprecedented level, but the CIO's culture of militant solidarity was eventually limited in the postwar period to the realm of industrial conflict. Despite the fact that these unions were led by activists who supported the NDP at the ballot box and presented social democratic reforms for approval at Ontario Federation of Labour (OFL) conventions, their conception of solidarity did not lead them farther into the realms of society and politics.

The expansion of Canada's welfare State (both for individuals and businesses) in the period immediately after the war resulted in the rapid growth of State employment, at the federal, provincial and municipal levels. This expansion contributed in turn to the push towards unionisation by State employees, to the point where Canada enjoyed a more rapid unionisation than other capitalist countries in the postwar years (Albo:1989). From 1965 onwards, workers at all levels of the Canadian State (broadly conceived) opted not only to join unions but to advocate militancy as well. In 1951 there were 14 public sector unions with a total of 54,000 members, and by 1981 these numbers had increased to 71 unions with over 1,347,000 members. Also by 1980, 38% of all office workers were covered by collective agreements, the vast majority of them in the public sector.[11]

Moreover, the growth of these unions reflected structural changes, particularly in the labour processes of the State, but also in the growth of information and service employment in the private sector. Between 1941 and 1981 "white collar" occupations, as a percentage of the entire Canadian labour force, more than doubled from 25.2% to 52.2%, while "blue-collar" occupations declined from 48.7% to 42.2%.[12] It was through this growth of "white-collar" employment that large numbers of women entered the paid labour force (Lowe:1987),[13] and hence also the union movement; in fact, women now constitute 36% of total membership, up from 16% in 1965,[14] and they have even unionised at a faster rate than men.[15] At a time when unionism has been in steady decline in the United States, the increased unionisation of women is one important reason why union density in Canada has remained relatively high. It is also linked to the larger size of the public sector in Canada than in the USA.

State sector unions have two important characteristics that distinguish them from the unions that developed in the mass production and resource industries during the postwar period. They include large numbers of women in their memberships and they are completely Canadian, having no affiliations with American unions. Increased unionisation of the public sector, therefore, resulted in a decline in the proportion of members in the Ontario Federation of Labour (OFL) belonging to American international unions.

This decline was accentuated by further developments in the 1980s. With the deepening of the economic crisis, neoconservative governments, federal and provincial, adopted more restrictive labour policies in an attempt to aid the faltering economy.[16] At the level of the firm, management tried to reduce labour costs by contracting-out and increasing part-time employment.[17] The relative weakness of Canadian manufacturing was reinforced by the global restructuring of capital, leading to an increase in service employment relative to manufacturing and to resource industries. Almost ninety percent of net job growth in the 1980s has been in the private service sector, particularly in low-wage jobs (Myles, Picott and Wannell:1988). Declining employment in primary and secondary sectors has impacted dramatically on unionisation. Between 1976 and 1986 union membership in mining and manufacturing declined from 83.2% to 66.4%. (Corporations and Labour Unions Returns Act, *Annual Report*, Part 11, various years.)[18] The severe loss of blue collar manufacturing and industrial jobs, and the rapid expansion of marginal kinds of employment is resulting in a polarization between core and "periphery" workers. Workers in the full-time, permanent, pensionable "core" are, for the most part, male and white, while those on the "periphery" include not only large numbers of women and youth, but also various ethnic and racial minorities. In Ontario, right up to the post-war period the labour movement was dominated by workers of British origin. Large scale immigration since the 1950s brought many more non-British and non-white workers into the labour force. As a consequence, these people's experience of and resistance to racism has impacted on a wide range of institutions, raising questions regarding their role in defining Canadian culture.[19] No less than other institutions, and perhaps even more so because of their commitment to social justice, unions are required to confront racism within their ranks. This confrontation has, in its turn, impacted on the conception of solidarity within the labour movement.[20]

As already indicated, while Offe is correct to argue that changes in the economy of advanced capitalist societies are undermining the past basis of unity within labour movements, it is equally valid to emphasize that these changes also open the possibility for positive change. At the levels of the labour process, labour force participation and union organisation, changing the definition of "who we are," who solidarity is between, and for what ends, has become a distinct possibility. The labour movement now has many more women, more members of non-British origin, more State workers, more "white-collar" workers and more members in Canadian unions. All these "mores" have contributed to the formation of different movements within the ranks of organised labour, and to new challenges to the concept of "who we are" and the goals of union solidarity.

THE IMPACT OF FEMINISM ON UNION IDENTITY AND SOLIDARITY

One of the most significant challenges — perhaps the most significant — to the Ontario union movement's culture of solidarity has been the development of union feminism. This particular brand of working-class feminism flourished and developed from the mid-seventies onwards, following the increased participation of women in the labour force and in unions. Although the expanded ranks of female unionists played a necessary role in the development of feminist culture, the mere existence of more women is not a sufficient condition for the occurrence of fundamental changes in union culture (White:1990). Changes depend on the way in which the increased numbers of women confront and challenge both the existing culture, and the changes that have occurred in the conception of union solidarity over the last fifteen years, which are attributable in large part to the specific way in which union feminists struggled to change their subordinate position in the workplace, the union and the home.

Union feminism seemed to catch fire in Ontario in the mid to late seventies. This occurred through a series of struggles and strikes undertaken mainly by women attempting to gain a first contract. One of the most significant occurrences took place in 1978 at the Fleck Manufacturing auto-parts factory near Exeter, Ontario. It became a *cause célèbre* as each night the entire province turned on their television sets to watch the spectacle of determined women, on the picket line, confronting police who were wearing riot gear, and were determined to use force and violence to keep the factory open.[21] Standing their ground against the onslaught of provincial police, the women on the Fleck line became the symbol of a new breed of working-class feminists.[22] Leaders in the UAW, the parent union, were impressed by their courage and tenacity, and this particular strike was an important landmark in changing the UAW's policies towards women.

In their fight for a first contract, the Fleck workers were joined by others, predominantly women, working at Blue Cross, at Radio Shack and at Mini-Skools.[23] These strikes had a number of important effects on union culture and solidarity. Primarily, they challenged and undermined the view, held by many traditional unionists, that women do not have a strong attachment to the workplace and are unwilling or too frightened to organize. Even at this date, when this stereotype has been challenged by the growing numbers of unionised women, it is frequently argued that women are unwilling to undertake the tough militant action needed to win a good contract. Action by workers at Fleck, and by other female dominated bargaining groups, punched holes in the view

> that women are a docile part of the work force, working for pin money, and afraid to stand up for their rights,...It was similarly shaken during strikes at Radio Shack, Puretex, Sandra Coffee and Irwin Toys.[24]

All these strikes occurred in the late 1970s and early 1980s and were followed by other significant struggles — notably the 1980 Federal Clerks strike (a bargaining unit of the Public Service Alliance of Canada (PSAC) consisting of 76% women) and the 1981 Canadian Union of Postal Workers' (CUPW) fight for paid maternity leave. Among traditional unionists there was a perception that women had won their union stripes through these struggles. It became practically impossible to use female weakness as an excuse for not taking actions in favour of organizing women, or for mobilizing in support of their demands.

On the external union front, these predominantly "women's strikes" were an important element in the development of the connection between feminists and women unionists. It was a connection achieved through very practical ways, such as when feminists' in the International Women's Day Committee (IWDC) organized a women's solidarity picket in Toronto to support the Fleck workers together with the union feminist group of Organized Working Women (OWW).[25] During the 1981 Canadian Union of Postal Workers' (CUPW) strike where paid maternity leave was a key demand, the IWDC called for united action by the women's and the union movement. They had an important influence within The National Action Committee on the Status of Women in Canada (NAC) — the umbrella group for progressive feminist organizations — in persuading other women to support the strike.[26] All these "women's" strikes were important in raising the consciousness of non-union feminists with regard to the importance of unions for women and their potential for effecting change in the workplace and in society as a whole. As a result, feminists "were given a deeper understanding of class conflict..." (Maroney:1981) and they helped to fracture the view that unions are necessarily, or primarily, organizations of blue-collar men whose interests are basically opposed to those of women workers. The support of the NAC for union struggles eventually created a positive impact on the union movement and helped to develop working class feminist demands concerning issues such as abortion and child care.

Another important development in linking feminism and unionism at this time was the formation of a wives' committee in support of the Steelworkers' strike at Inco in Sudbury. Wives Supporting the Strike (WSS) was formed to mobilize women around a programme of action designed to keep the community together both physically and spiritually; the committee organized collective suppers, children's programmes and educational sessions about the strike. The importance of the WSS lay in its "role of class-conscious feminism in promoting solidarity between the union and the community...."[27] It organized activities which caused the private realm of the home to become merged with the realm of work into a community of defence and action. Limits were placed on this initiative, however, when conflicts arose concerning the women who sought to participate in the decision-making process regarding the conduct of the strike and the union leadership.[28] There were many rank and file, including the union leadership itself, who considered such action to be completely outside the purview of wives, families and the general community. Although wives' support became necessary, not just desirable, and by the end of the strike the executive "had come around to a position of respect and support for them,"[29] they were still not welcomed as equal participants in union activity. The boundaries of the union's solidarity were drawn hierarchically and the action of the WSS did not succeed in breaking down the hierarchy of decision-making between men and women, the workplace and the community.

Yet the struggle by the wives (which was admirably illustrated in the film *A Wives' Tale*)[30] raised questions regarding the link between home and workplace, and the relationship between working class communities and unions. It not only provided an inspiration for similar groups of women,[31] but also had the effect of broadening the debate within the labour movement over who has the power to contribute to and make decisions affecting the entire community. Should these not include representatives of both those working at the point of production and those working to reproduce this labour power? In this sense the WSS raised fundamental questions regarding the solidarity of the working class community as a whole.

At the same time that the Ontario union movement's conception of solidarity was undergoing challenges from "outside" the movement, it was also experiencing criticism from feminists within. It was criticism which gathered steam and depth throughout the eighties. Union feminism, in general, demanded a broader approach to bargaining demands, union policy and participation by the membership, and criticised the limitations of the process and policies traditionally found within the movement.(Briskin:1990; Edelson:1987) Initially it was Organized Working Women (OWW), an informal group devoted to bringing together union feminists across union lines, who took up this role. As a non-constitutional body within the OFL, OWW represented union feminists' determination to build their strength within the movement, and although the organisation involved small numbers of women, its influence was felt in the form of resolutions to OFL and union conventions. Thus its very presence raised questions about who has power to assert demands and make decisions.

But the most important aspect of OWW was the "home base" it provided for union feminists to discuss, across union lines, problems experienced both within their own unions and within the OFL. As such, OWW developed energy, ideas and strategies, with which its members could effectively work to change both the policies and the processes of their own particular parts of the union movement.[32] By the end of the seventies union feminists were actively working to change the policies of the OFL and their own unions. The strength of their challenges were rewarded in 1983 when OFL became the first provincial labour federation to implement an affirmative action programme directed at increasing the numbers of women in leadership positions.[33]

While the visibility of women leaders is important both symbolically and materially, union feminists saw other struggles as equally if not more significant. Policies were targeted to address the subordination of women in the work place, internally in the unions, and in the home. This involved addressing women's "triple day" as union activists, and devising policies which relieved women of their duties in the home, such as the provision of paid childcare during union events. By emphasising the relationship between home, the work place and the subordination of women in both spheres, they also had the effect of placing in question the goals of unionism. Should unions be concerned only with work place problems or also with social issues generally?

Union feminism thus had the effect of challenging and widening the vision of the OFL's industrial unionism to include abortion, childcare, affirmative action, pay equity and sexual harassment (Briskin:1990). It is now well established among most OFL unions that contract demands can address the concerns of women and other groups; and more generally, that unions can move beyond bread and butter issues of the work place into social concerns which reflect the relationship between the work place and the community as a whole. Challenging the idea of work as a sphere separate from that of the community has a very positive effect on the concept of solidarity and on the cultural radicalisation of workers in general. Debating the implications of sexism had quite wide implications for the unions' vision of the relationship between work and society.[34]

The wider feminist struggle against sexism, sexual harassment, violence against women and the right of women to control their own bodies also had far-reaching implications for the labour movement (Maroney:1981). During the eighties, sexual harassment was uncovered as a major problem within the union movement. In struggling against it union feminists exposed and challenged the sexual power divisions within the working class.[35] Union feminists, through various forums, confronted fellow unionists, both in the work place and within the unions, with the fact that male sexual power is used to subordinate and silence "union sisters" at meetings, conventions and educational forums. Sexist language, sexist activities and the absence of women in positions of authority and power were scrutinised and criticized.

Union women also learned new ways of supporting each other, and examined their own sexist behaviour in terms of language and behaviour. Their situation led to an examination not only of sexism but also of other forms of worker oppression including racism and homophobia.[36] As a result, the OFL and many of its affiliate unions instituted procedures for dealing with sexual and other kinds of harassment between members. Such policies challenged the way in which traditional forms of union solidarity had condoned and protected discrimination and harassment of some union members by others. A revitalised concept of solidarity was thus proposed, which requires that all forms of oppression and subordination within the union movement, including sexism, racism and homophobia, be rooted out and replaced by democratic participation and processes.[37]

While recognizing the ways in which union feminism has challenged and changed union solidarity, we need to go further and ask whether it can also affect our understanding of class, and contribute to a different and more progressive vision of the relationship between labour and society. Certainly union feminism raised, and continues to raise, questions concerning democratic process and participation and therefore, in a general sense, also questions the relationship between the leaders and the led. There are some ways, however, in which the discourse of feminism has also limited the reconstruction of "who we are." In particular, the debate regarding the unequal pay of women was framed in terms of the liberal State's discourse about equality. If anything the current concept of pay and employment equity has tended to endorse the liberal ideology of "fair" pay and equality of opportunity (Warskett: 1990; Brenner:1987). It fails to address the process in which both women and men are involved in selling their labour power where the all dominating goal is the accumulation of capital. It remains to be seen whether the labour movements' experience of implementing the Ontario Pay Equity legislation will contribute to the development of an analysis of the relationship between gender and class, and a broader vision of how to overcome the divisions, competition and alienation that occurs between workers of different genders and different cultural backgrounds.

SOLIDARITY AND INTERNATIONAL UNIONISM

Of course, a broader vision regarding the relations of production and their impact on working class culture necessitates going beyond an analysis of the internal divisions within the labour movement. It requires the development of a vision of international unionism in the context of the international division of labour, and the examination of the reasons for the competition between workers of different nationalities.

Because of the declining numerical strength of American unions (the union density now stands at 16%) and the acceptance of concessions by unions such as the formerly militant United Auto Workers (UAW), American international unionism no longer offers a model for Canadian unions. Indeed, today

> ...American unions are crushed and caught in a vicious circle of competitive concessions. American rank-and-file movements are already looking north of the border for inspiration, to unions that are more political, less conservative, and less willing to accept concessions.[38]

Acceptance by American unions of concessions and layoffs, and their generally declining militancy, are important reasons the Canadian sections of such unions have been seeking autonomy, whether through greater Canadian decision-making within the parent "international" union, or through complete separation as in the case of the CAW (Gindin:1989). Breaking away or becoming more independent from American international unions has provided Canadian unions with space for the growth of a different concept of international solidarity than that of the AFL/CIO. This development has been reinforced by the fact that, in general, Canadian unionism has held its own, with union density declining only slightly during the same period that American unions have been in rapid decline.

Amongst activists in Ontario labour councils and OFL locals, there was an attempt in the 1980s to define a different and more progressive concept of international solidarity. In practice this took the form of inviting labour delegations from liberation movements in Nicaragua, El Salvador, South Africa, and from the British National Union of Mineworkers (at the time of its 1984-1985 strike) to speak and explain their position. Also, many union locals and councils sent donations to and made connections with international solidarity organizations such as SACTU and "Tools for Peace," sent delegations to countries with "left leaning" labour movements and generally started a move away from the cold war thinking and rhetoric of the CLC International Affairs Department.[39] In the process, some of these organizations have developed a broader and more militant approach to international solidarity.

In recent years, it became apparent to some OFL delegates that the official CLC policy in support of the liberation struggles of international movements, set by directives from delegates at each biennial convention, was frequently at odds with the policy actually pursued by the CLC's Executive and International Affairs Department. CLC representatives advised activists not to receive socialist and left-leaning delegates from international organizations who were not officially invited by the CLC, even when official policy supported these movements. Inevitably this resulted in conflict between CLC staff members of the International Affairs Department and activists in the OFL. As a result, the OFL Executive Board Subcommittee on International Affairs issued a report where, after noting the political changes that have taken place around the world, it remarked that frequently

> ...we are surprised by the reaction of our Canadian Labour Congress to these world events. Sometimes it seems that there is a 'made in Brussels' line, *not* a 'made in Canada' perspective. It sometimes seems that the role of our CLC International Affairs Department is to disseminate the ICFTU view *into* Canada, rather than to reflect the Canadian workers' views out to the world.... The CLC should play a major role in promoting progressive workers' causes in other countries. It should be challenging often regressive Canadian government positions. We should be offering balance to the US trade unions who often reflect or are restricted by their government's foreign policy, which hurts many workers. We have a special role to play in Latin, Central and South America.[40]

The critical nature of the report resulted in a resolution being passed at the 1989 OFL convention held in Toronto. Known as the "Made in Canada" policy, the resolution was essentially a criticism of how international solidarity is defined, organized and articulated by the CLC International Affairs Department. It explicitly attacked the CLC's support for the International Confederation of Free Trade Unions (ICFTU) which had a strongly anti-communist position with respect to people's liberation movements.[41] Although the report and the "Made in Canada" resolution had a strong nationalist orientation, in the context of international solidarity this orientation exhibited both an awareness and an opposition to American imperialism and support for liberation movements struggling to free themselves from its effects. [42] It remains to be seen, however, whether the solidarity support of OFL affiliates will be translated into a wider set of actions and alliances.

CONCLUSION

The Canadian labour movement emerged in the postwar period with nearly double its prewar membership. Significant numbers of its members worked in mass production industries, mainly in Southern Ontario and the resource industries of Northern Ontario. They were proud to belong to the CIO tradition of industrial unionization built through pain and struggle in the battles that took place around the right to collective association. By the early 1950s, the leadership of these unions had become cold war warriors who propounded an aggressive business unionism. Its culture of solidarity excluded, for the most part, women, newly arrived immigrants, those in marginal forms of work, the unemployed, native people and many others who did not work in the core manufacturing and resource industries. Its vision became narrowly confined to the workplace and to making economistic demands, which were satisfied to a certain extent during the expanding period of Fordism. Beginning in the 1970s, however, and with gathering momentum during the 1980s, partly as a result of political-economic changes, there were significant changes in and challenges to the culture of the Ontario labour movement.

Offe (1985) presents a somewhat pessimistic view of the divisions created by changes in the economy, whereas the argument in this chapter, in contrast, is optimistic. There were always divisions within the Canadian and Ontario labour movements — between more established "core" workers of British origin and newly arrived peoples, between immigrants and indigenous peoples, and between men and women, etc. Labour market changes have now made these divisions more salient making it more obvious that the solidarity that existed among male core workers must be broadened and changed if union solidarity is to be sustained, and if there is to be any progressive potential for the working class as a whole.

Offe is right when he says that the form of solidarity must change in keeping with the changing structure of the labour movement. But he believes that this is positive

> ...only under the somewhat paradoxical condition that trade union organization does not limit its political activity to the fact that its members are *employees*, but rather concentrates addition-ally on those living conditions that are not determined directly by wage labour relations and have, therefore, traditionally been included under the jurisdiction of the state rather than union policy.[43]

But it does not necessarily involve a paradox. In Ontario, the decline of the manufacturing sector and the weakening of industrial unionism opens up the possibility of a new concept of solidarity, resulting from the in-creased power of formerly marginalised groups. In fact, the growing power of women, minority groups and anti-imperialist activists, together with the decline in influence of American international unionism, has provided an opening for the development of a different kind of unionism — one in which it is possible to make connections between the work place, society and international labour. Formerly marginalised groups have al-ways had experiences and needs different from those of the members of the male-dominated American international unions during the postwar period. Because women, members of minority groups and anti-imperialists have always been largely excluded from power, they have challenged and posed questions about the relationships between the leadership and rank and file, between workers in the core sectors of the economy and those in marginalized and precarious sites, and between workers in liberal democratic industrial societies and those in the industrialising societies who are so often working under oppressive dictatorial conditions. Inevitably such questions raise the issue of democratic participation in the unions, and of building a movement in which the meaning of solidarity is greatly broadened.

As Gramsci pointed out, the experience of a particular group that is out of step with received "common sense" creates possibilities for a different vision of society and politics. [44] The democratic processes that have become increasingly crucial for Ontario unionism offer the possibility of important new connections between the unions and other popular and progressive political movements, because it is now necessary to construct a union solidarity that is critical and democratic in nature, that continually questions and pushes back the boundaries between the work place, society and politics. It remains an open question whether the recent challenges and changes within the Ontario labour movement will eventually lead to the achievement of such a concept of solidarity, but recent developments point in the right direction.

NOTES

1. I would like to thank Marguerite Mendell and Colin Leys for their fine editorial work and suggestions.
2. Notions of who is with us and who is against us, and perhaps more importantly who and what our solidarity is directed towards and against, are a crucial part of union identity. In other words, ideas concerning the ends to which union solidarity and collective power are to be directed, and who these will benefit, are also crucial to the formation of union culture.
3. Offe, Claus. *Disorganized Capital: Contemporary Transformation of Work and Politics.* John Keane (ed.). Cambridge Massachusetts: The MIT Press, 1985. p. 154.
4. The People's Agenda conference held under the auspices of the Canadian Labour Congress in Ottawa, December 1991, invited participation from members of unions, social movements and progressive political parties. It can be seen as a move in this direction.
5. I have framed my approach to union solidarity purposely in terms of "who we are" and "what is our understanding of solidarity" because it is in large part based on my own experiences and observations within the Ontario Labour movement as a union staffer working for a large public sector union. It also reflects my experience and development as a union feminist.
6. Albo, Gregory. "The 'New Realism' and Canadian Workers," in *Canadian Politics: An Introduction to the Discipline.* A. Gagnon and J. Bickerton, eds. Peterborough: Broadview Press Ltd., 1990. p. 471.
7. Gramsci, Antonio. *Selections from Prison Notebooks.* London: Lawrence and Wishart, 1971. pp.323-343.
8. Meltz, N. "Labour Movements in Canada and the United States," in *Challenges and Changes Facing American Labour.* T. Kochan (ed.) Cambridge: MIT Press, 1985. pp. 316-7.
9. For the most part the CIO organized in the industrial plants of South Western Ontario, the heartland of industrial Canada and less successfully but nevertheless significantly in the mining communities of Northern Ontario. Unions carrying the CIO banner such as the United Auto Workers (UAW), The United Steelworkers of

America (USW) and The United Electrical, Radio and Machine Workers (UE) provided the organizing framework for the conflict that boiled over between workers and managers in the rapidly expanding factories and mines in this period.

10. Donald Swartz coined the term "badge of honour" during a discussion of CIO unionism. It carries with it the recognition that it was a badge won as a result of struggle and determination by workers in the 1930s and 1940s.

11. Rose, J.B. "Growth Patterns of Public Sector Unions," in *Conflict or Compromise: The Future of Public Industrial Relations.* M. Thompson & G. Swimmer (eds.), Montreal Institute for Research on Public Policy, 1984. pp. 83-119.

12. Rinehart, James W. *The Tyranny of Work: Alienation and the Labour Process.* Toronto: Harcourt Brace Jovanovich, 1987. p.77.

13. The labour market participation of women grew rapidly and dramatically between 1950 and 1985, rising from 26.2% to 62.4%. Bakker, Isabella. "Women's Employment in Comparative Perspective," *Feminization of the Labor Force: Paradoxes and Promises,* J. Jenson, E. Hagen & C. Reddy (eds.). New York: Oxford University Press, 1988. p. 19.

14. Canadian Labour Congress. *Empowering Union Women: Toward the Year 2000.* Ottawa, 1990. p.7.

15. For example, between 1966 and 1976 male union membership increased by 40%, whereas the ranks of female unionists expanded by 160% (White:1980).

16. The crisis impacted on the labour movement in the form of fiscal policies and further restrictions on strike activity. Panitch and Swartz(1988) refer to the Canadian State's use of special measures to restrict the use of the strike weapon as permanent exceptionalism.

17. Albo, G. 1990. p.24.

18. These figures do not take into account the further reduction in unionisation as a result of the overall declines in these industries as a whole. For example during the 1981-82 recession the largest losses of membership were by Auto and Steelworkers. Albo, G. 1990. p.17.

19. Abele, Frances and Davia Stasiulis. "Canada as a 'White Settler Colony': What about Natives and Immigrants?" in *The New Canadian Political Economy.* Wallace Clement & Glen Williams (eds.) Kingston & Montreal: McGill-Queen's University Press, 1989. p. 265.

20. This confrontation does not apply to native peoples, who remain for the most part outside the paid labour force and hence also outside the unionised labour force in Ontario.

21. The influence of the company on the Ontario government was an important element in the entire conflict. It is pointed out that "Thanks to Fleck's government connections, the Ontario government kept nearly 500 police on standby during the strike — at a cost of more than half a million dollars for the first two months of the strike alone." Darcy, Judy and Catherine Lauzon. "The Right To Strike" in Briskin & Yanz (eds.), *Union Sisters: Women in the Labour Movement.* Toronto: Women's Press, 1983. p.176.

22. After five months on the picket line they won their demand for union recognition and a wage increase. Ibid., p.176. Maroney, Heather Jon. "Feminism at Work," *New Left Review,* No.141, September/October, 1983. pp. 60-61.

23. Briskin, Linda. "Women's Challenge to Organized Labour," in Briskin & Yanz (eds.). 1983. p. 259.

24. Darcy, Judy and Catherine Lauzon, 1983. p.176.

25. IWDC, an explicit grouping of socialist feminists, played the important role of mediating between feminists and the union movement. By organizing strike support activities, such as rallies and mass pickets, they acted with the intention of politicizing "feminists about the importance of the trade union movement in the struggle for women's equality and mobilized feminists around trade union issues and women's struggles in unions." (Egan & Yanz:1983:369) It has been pointed out that the "...connections made between the Fleck strikers, the women's movement and the UAW had a long-term impact. Two feminist film makers produced a videotape with the Fleck strikers that has been used as a tool to politicize both the

women's movement and trade unionists about the experiences of women becoming trade union militants." Egan, Carolyn and Lynda Yanz. "Building Links: Labour and the Women's Movement," in Briskin & Yanz (eds.) 1983. p.366.

26. Ibid.,pp. 369-371.
27. Maroney, H.J., 1983. pp. 60-61.
28. As one of the women who had formed WSS perceived the situation: "At one point during the 1978 strike, WSS suggested that we be allowed to attend union membership meetings to voice our opinion. At that time, the idea was rejected as ridiculous by the union executive board. Can you imagine how women's input would inspire and broaden the scope of issues that the labour movement is presently concerned with? Union meetings could become revolutionary if women attended and began discussing the effects of Inco operations on our lives." Lane, Arja. "Wives Supporting the Strike," in Briskin & Yanz (eds.), 1983. p. 332.
29. Luxton, Meg. "From Ladies' Auxiliaries to Wives' Committees," Briskin & Yanz (eds.),1983. p. 342.
30. A Wives' Tale (Canada 1980, Sophie Bissonnette, Joyce Rock and Martin Duckworth. 73 min., colour, 16mm. DEC Films.
31. Luxton, M., 1983. p. 34.
32. My knowledge of OWW results from my direct involvement in the organisation. In 1988 I took on the role of President of the Ottawa chapter of OWW and learnt more about the organisation at that point although I had been a member for many years.
33. The constitution was amended "to create five affirmative action positions on its executive board. The convention then elected five more women, increasing the participation of women on the highest decision making body of the Ontario movement by one-third... (OFL: undated)." In 1984 the CLC "followed suit by adopting a constitutional change calling for a minimum of 6 female vice presidents..." (Briskin, Linda. "Women, Unions and Leadership" Canadian Dimension. January, 1990). Other major provincial federations followed with similar resolutions.
34. Of course it is not only union feminism that has broadened the vision of the labour movement in this way. For example health and safety concerns by the rank-and-file have raised the debate concerning the environment and the work place, in spite of many difficulties, as are discussed in the chapters by L. Adkin and S. Quenneville in this volume.
35. In this case the reference to sexual harassment in the work place is quite apart from the question of how the power of the employer, through the agency of managers and supervisors, is used to demand sexual favours and create an atmosphere of male sexual dominance in many work places. The case of Bonnie Robichaud established that employers are liable for the discriminatory actions of their employees. Robichaud vs. Canada (Treasury Board), [1987] 2 S.C.R. 84.
36. A good example of the linkages that are made between different kinds of oppression is found in the CAW's film "Call Me Sister, Call Me Brother." It "powerfully portrays the costs of sexual and racial harassment and outlines the union's tough policy." Canadian Labour Congress, 1990. p. 14.
37. As union feminism gained more power and force in challenging the conception of solidarity and "who we are" and also effected material changes in policies and programs of both the OFL and affiliated unions, a "backlash" against feminism took on more coherence and strength fuelled by neoconservative ideology. But in the face of this reaction and especially in the wake of the Montreal massacre, union feminists have become more alert to the need to "include ways and means of defending and mobilizing support" for the changes they have wrought within the labour movement. Ibid.,
38. Noel, Alain & Keith Gardner. "The Gainers Strike: Capitalist Offensive, Militancy and the Politics of Industrial Relations in Canada," Studies in Political Economy, 31, Spring, 1990. p. 61.
39. John Harker was Director of the CLC international Affairs Department until quite recently. He was well known for his strong cold war views. In 1986 allegations were

made "that he advised South African mining company executives to give money to the International Metalworkers Federation which presumably would be then brought back to South Africa for the purpose of financing trade union organizations in the mines." (Letter from Jean-Claude Parrot, National President CUPW to President of CLC, dated February 24, 1986). These allegations were a catalyst in the formation of the OFL's Made in Canada policy.

40.   "Starting at Home — A Discussion Paper on CLC International Solidarity," September 1989. The ICFTU or International Confederation of National Trade Unions was a confederation of Western labour movements and is in direct opposition to the World Federation of Trade Unions (WFTU) which was perceived to be controlled by Moscow. The case of Nicaragua demonstrates the conflict between the two organizations. ICFTU supported the Confederation of Trade Union Unity (CUS) which was one of only two labour organizations (the other was Christian Democratic) allowed by Somoza to function legally. (Gandall, Marv. "Foreign Affairs, The CLC Abroad" *This Magazine*. vol. 19, no.6, February, 1986. p. 7.) Although the CUS did not support the Somoza regime it was not part of the underground resistance. After the revolution the pro-Sandinista unions became the main organizing vehicle for workers and are affiliated with the WFTU. The CLC supported the CUS and tried to prevent labour delegations coming from the Sandinista unions.

41.   The following is the resolution passed at the OFL convention November, 1989:
Made in Canada International Affairs Policy
WHEREAS it is in the interest of all workers to support our common struggles;
WHEREAS, in many instances, the international affairs policy of the Canadian Labour Congress does not reflect the wishes of Canadian workers, but instead appears to reflect the policies and priorities of the International Confederation of Free Trade unions.
BE IT RESOLVED that the leadership of the Federation of Labour demand that the Canadian Labour Congress adopt a "made in Canada" international affairs policy based on the principles of labour solidarity.
BE IT FURTHER RESOLVED that the Federation leadership demand that the CLC promote such "made in Canada" policies at all international forums and conferences.

42.   Panitch, Leo & Donald Swartz. *The Assault on Trade Union Freedoms*. Toronto: Garamond, 1988. p. 111.

43.   Offe, C., 1985. p. 152.

44.   "...the contrast between thought and action cannot but be the expression of profounder contrasts of a social historical order. It signifies that the social group in question may indeed have its own conception of the world, even if only embryonic; a conception which manifests itself in action, but occasionally and in flashes — when, that is, the group is acting as an organic totality" Gramsci, A., 1971. p. 327.

REFERENCES

Albo, Gregory. 1990. "The 'New Realism' and Canadian Workers," in *Canadian Politics: An Introduction to the Discipline*, A. Gagnon and J. Bickerton, eds. Broadview Press Ltd. Peterborough.

Abele, Frances and Davia Stasiulis. 1989. "Canada as a 'White Settler Colony': What about Natives and Immigrants?" *The New Canadian Political Economy*, Wallace Clement & Glen Williams (eds.) McGill-Queen's University Press, Kingston & Montreal.

Bakker, Isabella. 1988. "Women's Employment in Comparative Perspective," *Feminization of the Labor Force: Paradoxes and Promises*, J. Jenson, E. Hagen & C. Reddy (eds.) Oxford University Press, New York.

Brenner, Johanna. 1987. "Feminist Political Discourses: Radical Versus Liberal Approaches to the Feminization of Poverty and Comparable Worth," *Gender & Society* 1/4, December.

Briskin, Linda. 1983. "Women's Challenge to Organized Labour," in Briskin & Yanz (eds.) 1983. *Union Sisters: Women in the Labour Movement*, Women's Press, Toronto.

1990. "Women, Unions and Leadership," *Canadian Dimension*, January.

Briskin, Linda & Lynda Yanz (eds.). 1983. *Union Sisters: Women in the Labour Movement*, Women's Press, Toronto.

Canadian Labour Congress. 1987. *...A Time to Stand Together... A time for social solidarity, A Declaration on Social and Economic Policy Directions for Canada* by Members of Popular Sector Groups, November, Ottawa.

——1990. *Empowering Union Women: Toward the Year 2000*. Ottawa.

Darcy, Judy and Catherine Lauzon. 1983. "The Right To Strike" in Briskin & Yanz (eds.). 1983, *Union Sisters: Women in the Labour Movement*, Women's Press, Toronto.

Edelson, Miriam. 1987. "Making it Work Takes Time," *Our Times*, March.

Egan, Carolyn and Lynda Yanz. 1983. "Building Links: Labour and the Women's Movement," Briskin & Yanz (eds.), 1983. *Union Sisters: Women in the Labour Movement*, Women's Press, Toronto.

Frager, Ruth. 1983. "No Proper Deal: Women Workers and the Canadian Labour Movement, 1870-1940," Briskin & Yanz (eds.) 1983. *Union Sisters: Women in the Labour Movement*, Women's Press, Toronto.

Gabin, Nancy. 1990. *Feminism in the Labour Movement*, Cornell University Press.

Gandall, Marv. 1986. "Foreign Affairs, The CLC Abroad," *This Magazine*, vol. 19, no.6, February

Gindin, Sam. 1989. "Breaking Away: The Formation of the Canadian Auto Workers," *Studies in Political Economy*, 29, Summer.

Gramsci, Antonio. 1971. *Selections from Prison Notebooks*, London, Lawrence and Wishart.

Kumar, P. 1986. "Union Growth in Canada: Retrospect and Prospect." C. Riddell (ed.) *Canadian Labour Relations*, Toronto.

Labour Canada. 1985. *Strikes and Lockouts in Canada*, Ottawa.

Lane, Arja. 1983. "Wives Supporting the Strike," Briskin & Yanz (eds.) 1983. *Union Sisters: Women in the Labour Movement*, Women's Press, Toronto.

Luxton, Meg. 1983. "From Ladies' Auxiliaries to Wives' Committees," Briskin & Yanz (eds.) 1983. *Union Sisters: Women in the Labour Movement*, Women's Press, Toronto.

Maroney, Heather Jon. 1983. "Feminism at Work," *New Left Review*, No.141, September/October.

Meltz, N. 1985. "Labour Movements in Canada and the United States," *Challenges and Changes Facing American Labour*, T. Kochan (ed.) Cambridge: MIT Press, 315-34

Myles, J., G. Picott and T. Wannell. 1988. *Wages and Jobs in the 1980s*, Statistics Canada Research Paper N.17

Noel, Alain & Keith Gardner. 1990. "The Gainers Strike: Capitalist Offensive, Militancy and the Politics of Industrial Relations in Canada," *Studies in Political Economy*, 31, Spring.

Offe, Claus. 1985. *Disorganized Capital: Contemporary Transformation of Work and Politics*, John Keane (ed.) The MIT Press, Cambridge Massachusetts.

Ontario Federation of Labour. undated. "Affirmative Action: How We Got Started," Pamphlet produced by the Women's Committee, mid-eighties approximately.

——1988. *Still a Long Way From Equality*, Document 3, 32nd Annual Convention, Nov.28 — Dec.1, Toronto.

——1989a. Report of the Executive Board Subcommittee on International Affairs, September.

——1989b. "Starting at Home — A Discussion Paper on CLC International Solidarity," September.

——1989c. "Made in Canada" policy, November.

Palmer, Bryan D. 1983. *Working-Class Experience: The Rise and Reconstitution of Canadian Labour, 1800-1980*, Butterworth & Co. (Canada Ltd.) Toronto.

Panitch, Leo & Donald Swartz. 1988. *The Assault on Trade Union Freedoms*, Toronto, Garamond.

Rinehart, James W. 1987. *The Tyranny of Work: Alienation and the Labour Process*, Harcourt Brace Jovanovich, Toronto.

Rose, J.B. 1984. "Growth Patterns of Public Sector Unions," in *Conflict or Compromise: The Future of Public Industrial Relations*, M. Thompson & G. Swimmer (eds.), Montreal Institute for Research on Public Policy, pp. 83-119.

Stinson, Jane. 1991. "Conditions for Feminist Organizing in Trade Unions: An Analysis of the UAW in the Forties Compared to the CAW Today," Unpublished Paper, Carleton University.

Supreme Court of Canada. 1987. *Robichaud* vs. *Canada* (Treasury Board) 2 S.C.R. 84.

Swimmer, G. 1989. "Critical Issues in Public Sector Industrial Relations," *Collective Bargaining in Canada*, A. Sethi (ed.) Scarborough, Nelson.

Warskett, Rosemary. 1988. "Bank Worker Unionization and the Law," *Studies in Political Economy*, 25, Spring.

——1990. "Wage Solidarity and Equal Value: Or Gender and Class in the Structuring of Work Place Hierarchies," *Studies in Political Economy*, 32, Summer.

White Julie. 1980. *Women in Unions*, Supply and Services Ottawa

——1990. *Mail and Female*, Toronto.

Wilson, Gordon F. 1989. "Confronting the Nineties: Fashioning a Strategic Response by the Canadian Labour Movement to the Problems of Economic Restructuring," Remarks by the President of the Ontario Federation of Labour to the Harvard Centre for International Affairs. Conference on "North American Labor Movements in the 1990s: Similarities and Difference." Harvard University, Cambridge, Mass. Feb. 3.

Yeats, Charlotte. 1990. "The Internal Dynamics of Union Power: Explaining Canadian Autoworkers," *Studies in Political Economy*, 31 Spring.

Chapter 8

Micheline De Séve

WOMEN, POLITICAL ACTION AND IDENTITY*

There is a paradox at the core of the women's movement that distinguishes it from many, if not most, of the older social movements. The centuries-old confinement of women to specific conditions of life and work, places them in a common position that can only be transformed through a united effort. Women are strongly united by their socio-sexual gendered identity and by their life experiences; they can use these bonds to break away from the prison of roles that enforces their alikeness. Thus, if each woman is to succeed in asserting herself as subject, she must begin by acting upon her basic life experience; she must actively transform it to correspond with her desires, yet, in doing so, undermines her unity with other women. Thus, women's collective entrance into the public sphere is highly problematic, as the very categorization they intend to lift as a constraint also serves as their rallying point (Scott, 1988).

The first stage of transforming the female societal position occurs when collective action works to unveil the systematic exclusion of entire sections of human experience from the fields of political thought and action. Women's culture is portrayed as arbitrarily confined to automatic reflexes commanded by nature, as if men and women do not belong to the same species (Conway and al. 1987). The false neutrality of traditional politics is thereby exposed. From the moment women begin to speak out, to contemplate their own independent views as men do, the usual norms based exclusively on male conceptions of rationality and forms of social organization prove inadequate; they are unable to accurately describe, let alone transcend, the variety and richness of both the male *and* the female life experiences (Conway and al., 1987).

Women, however, cannot restrict their politics to one based on socio-sexual gendered identity, as this would tend to solidify the very parameters they want to remove (Manson and al., 1989; Nicholson, 1990). Instead, the feminist movement rejects the omnipresent rigid link between sex/gender

---

* This article is the author's own translation.

and socio-cultural roles. Its radical goal of dissolving all criteria ascribed to socio-sexual characteristics prevents it from substituting a new unitary discourse for the old one, even if that means weakening its collective power of political self-representation.

Thus the women's movement cannot be categorized according to the characteristics of traditional social movements, which concentrate on completely mobilizing the energies of every man or woman on behalf of whatever "cause" it may be. Of course, great mass gatherings are a component of women's struggles to preserve their full civic rights, and especially to guarantee their bodily integrity, i.e. free reproductive choice. However, beyond these defensive coalitions, women yearn to discover the unexplored potential of their capacities as full-fledged, equal citizens. From a feminist perspective, the attempt to delineate a feminist political space is irreconcilable with the principle that every woman should determine her own political choices (Nicholson, 1990). Does this imply that sorority cannot exist beyond purely defensive strategic demands? Is feminism as a collective movement, one which is mobilizing women together, just a temporary form of political organisation, doomed to disappear once women's victimisation has been eliminated?

Women's collective political mobilisations certainly are often sporadic, because the more they want to be aware and self-conscious, the more they want to be able freely to pick issues and causes, even when women's issues never cease to remind them of the collective oppression they mean to overcome. Women shun any *a priori* stand that takes their involvement for granted, and most of all, any position that will enclose their modes of political participation in a one dimensional fashion. That is why the women's movement, the first in history to move along the paradigm mapped by Offe (1985) for new social movements, appears to be nebulous, like a multitude of groups clustered together according to the trends they opt for under all sorts of differing circumstances.

This centrifugal tendency asserts itself even more strongly as the active involvement of women in public life lessens the social pressure to conform. As a result, there are serious disturbances in the effort to integrate the diverse movement, except with regard to a few uncontested rallying issues such as pro-choice policies or affirmative action programs. Every time the women's movement tries to build its unity as a collective force in the public arena, it comes up against the limit which ultimately constitutes and legitimizes it: the principle of the sovereignty of every woman as the subject of her own destiny, with her own means of transforming the world and making it correspond with the personal identity she claims as her own.[1]

Feminism wants the full integration of women into civic life. This can only occur if society recognizes that women have demands inspired by different existential experiences; they require a specific place in the world, especially with regard to the realm of motherhood, a distinct position whose scientific exploration is just beginning, since science has never before focused on women's experiences. The difference between the sexes, experienced daily to the point where they are considered culturally distinct, is no longer *reified,* as *if* it were automatically dictated by sheer male or female instinct. The world of women is finally interpreted as an open cultural space similar to that of men; women no longer consent to endorse a definition of feminine essence fabricated upon an essentialist representation of their specific biological function. In fact, a request to validate such an endorsement would be parallel to asking men to agree with a specific, genetic explanation of the causes of male violence (De Sève, 1985; Kokopeli, 1982; Ruddick, 1990).

It is at this point that the hierarchy in the division of labour, wealth, and power between the sexes begins to be disputed; human will, and not the "nature of things," is revealed as the basis of the prevailing order in both domestic and civic affairs. Taking into consideration the political character of their sexual subordination, more and more women are refusing to comply with a damaging gender ascription, which is used as a pretext to discredit, marginalize and radically shrink the participation and influence of women in society. But once the mould of traditional femininity is broken, on what basis can the foundations of sorority between women be established? Does the unity of women as a political category crumble as soon as women cease to be trapped in the enclosure of the feminine condition? The rejection of sexism aims at refuting any prescriptive claim linking gender characteristics to one or the other sex.

Contemporary feminism is thus plagued with contradictory intentions. On one hand, the demands for collective solidarity between women, gathered as sisters around their common socio-cultural gendered identity, urges them to downplay, at least for the time being, any other pole of identification, be it nationality, class or ethnicity. "To define oneself as woman," states François Collin, "(rather than as French, white, European, intellectual, female worker etc.) is an option; put into concrete form by feminism, it emphasizes this dimension of one's identity in relation to other women, from the basic awareness of a discrimination demanding individual as well as collective protest."[2] Thus, to single out sources of identification other than gender can be attributed to a lack of feminist consciousness and may even be denounced as a defection from the ideals of the movement. On the other hand, the search for individual autonomy, which drives every woman to situate herself as a subject independent of any other-determined identity like sex, gender, class, ethnicity or race, constitutes the cornerstone of feminist theory (Collins, 1987).

The first school of thought advocates the accumulation of collective force on a large scale, a unified movement of protest, even if it absorbs most of the subject's energies, as is usually the case with the traditional activism of old social movements (Miles, 1981; Morgan, 1984). The second directs each woman towards multiple channels of expression, with the risk of dissolving the global potential of the movement into a myriad of fragmented acts (Zavalloni, 1987). Striving to "undermine the social codification which gave it birth,"[3] and to lift the constraint of the feminine condition, confronts feminism with highly unstable options, "swinging from unanimity to impotence."[4]

This paradox is real. Indeed, feminism is condemned to lose what it has gained if women refuse to take part in collective political action, which is a necessary instrument of societal change, in order to pursue their own individual plan of action as soon as sexism is removed from their individual paths: "Since power necessarily exists in any society, those who do not participate in this power on an equal footing stay under the domination of those who participate and make use of it; they are not free — even if they have the *idiotic* delusion of being free because they had decided to live and die as *idiots*, that is, as ordinary citizens (*idioteuein*)."[5] Fortunately, this trend to depoliticize would constitute an *aporia* only if political action were to proceed along an evolutionist pattern, the relativist nihilism of post-feminism following die-hard feminist activism. The evident pluralism of the women's movement, however, points to a more complex situation.

Regardless of how much women's oppression is alleviated, new issues emerge along with the formation of new women's groups. What occurs is the infiltration of women and their radical way of reshaping things into all sectors of political and social organization to which they were hitherto denied entry, or which they had previously disregarded for strategic reasons. Breaking through one barrier after another, which had arbitrarily limited their field of action to "women's issues," i.e. issues strictly related to so-called feminine matters, feminists are discovering new grounds for concern. Indeed, it is quite impossible for women to stay uninvolved even when they cannot agree upon a common standpoint. They must constantly debate amongst themselves about the many crucial problems encountered by society at large. Different groups of women display incredibly diverse convictions in spite of the permanence of their primary socialization. Nevertheless, following feminist theory, they come together to strategize about all questions on the agenda, whenever and wherever women are required to take action. "The liberatory possibilities present in women's experience," writes Nancy Hartsock, "must be, in a sense, read out and developed ... A feminist standpoint may be present on the basis of commonalities with women's experience, but it is neither self-evident nor obvious."[6]

As a result, all political issues now involve both women and men. Also, all issues will likewise involve the opposition that exists to women (as is, for example, the case with the national debate in Canada). What distinguishes feminists is their determination to examine the effects of every proposal on gender relationships, on the empirical life conditions of women, and on the partners and companions with whom they feel united. To put oneself in a woman's situation — to rely on one's subjective position "to construct, and take responsibility for our gendered identity, our politics, and our choices"[7] — subverts analytical categories based on systematic indifference to the reservoir of female or feminine knowledge. Yet, this does not dispose of the cultural differences that exist between women's groups based on differences of history, language or immediate political experiences, not to mention profoundly divergent ideological beliefs.

It is true that disparities between the life histories of women of different origins, ages, classes and cultures impedes the creation of a single, unified feminist movement. The self-determination of each feminist as subject militates against any attempt to merge in an abstractly defined "sorority." The project of international solidarity of women all around the world, as witnessed by the closing assembly of the Decade of Women Conference in Nairobi in 1985, has the potential for growing into a political movement, although it will most likely take the form of a debating arena for various issues. Unless individual women and women's groups resign themselves to apolitical powerlessness and complete fragmentation, common needs still dictate the coming together of groups and individuals in order to attain specific goals.

So what would feminist politics be like, if we imagine ourselves in a future non-sexist society? For Touraine, an authority in the field of social movements, feminism, precisely because it challenges and deconstructs any static definition of womanhood, is unable to present an alternative draft for a new society. "Any sociologist knows," he declares, "that the call for difference cannot serve to build a social movement, which would involve interrelations and power, not distance or specificity."[8] In previous exchanges with Antoinette Fouque he asked, rhetorically, on what base could one institute a movement intended to destroy the very source from which it is launched into existence? If feminism contests the disparities between man and woman as a false criterion on which to organize society, should we not measure success by the fading away of "womanhood" as a significant analytical category for action ? (Bordo, 1990) The gendered woman-subject would become visible only long enough to self-explode into multiple identity fragments, and post-feminism would result in a political blankness after the brief cultural flamboyance of the women's liberation movement during the glorious seventies...

Nevertheless, women's identities as autonomous subjects are not formulated in a vacuum. Self-development, this axiom of postmodern discourse, cannot occur unless it finds its way out of the constraints of the present, which invariably involves forming links with peers. Therefore, political action means structuring relationships with others who are both equals in democratic interaction, whether alike or different, and who are also partners willing to shape decisions on common grounds. Indeed, women, however diverse their aims may be, in a society where their recognition depends on adequate implementation of equity policies, encounter in their everyday life experiences motives which enable them to close ranks with autonomous political allies. Some will no doubt begin to explore new avenues, but the main framework of their political action will for a long time continue to be grounded in their recent past histories.

We can imagine a society where non-mixed organizations would no longer be required; but overwhelming sexual oppression, increasing violence against women, the intense debates about women's right to control their own bodies, and the prevalence of systematic discrimination rule out any premature celebration of victory. Meanwhile, in reality, links are woven between these everyday objective allies: women are interconnected by common ideas based on shared experiences, and by common reflexes acquired in repeated similar circumstances; these bonds evolve into networks that are solidified by the passage of time and the common recognition of values grounded in a new vision of history. Thus, there emerges alongside the famous "old boys" network an alternative women's network, one that leads more and more women to attach greater importance to women's comradeship as an efficient tool of social change and a powerful strategic asset, while at the same time working to validate women's individuality and mutual differences:

> In this sense, the notion of identity simultaneously points to a conscious feeling of individual specificity (from and beyond multiple identifications), to a conscious intent to establish continuity in lived experience (beyond role diversity and temporal discontinuities) and to individual involvement in collective ideals or cultural patterns, deemed positive.[9]

The dispute between federalists and Québec nationalists inside the Canadian women's movement is a good example of feminist groups immersed in different cultural environments choosing whether or not to identify with the common links between themselves, using the particular materials they had at their disposal: learning how to bridge — or not to bridge — some disturbing disagreements.

Canadian feminists are rightly proud of having obtained tremendous gains in convincing the Canadian government to enshrine women's formal rights to equality in Section 28 of the Canadian Charter of Rights and Freedoms, which cannot be superseded by any other clause in the legislation. This outstanding victory is especially cherished by Canadian feminists, the more so since American women lost their decades-long battle to ratify the Equal Rights Amendment to the United States Constitution. The victory of the Canadian women's movement was achieved by a strategy based primarily on applying constant pressure to the central agencies of the federal government. The remarkable gain resulting from this strategy is illustrated by the way the National Action Committee on the Status of Women successfully called for a public debate between the leaders of the three federal political parties during the 1987 national election campaign. It is difficult to think of many other countries where the leaders of the major political parties could be summoned to address feminist issues in a televised public debate, such as the one aired by the CBC during prime time before the vote took place. Whatever their regional differences, women from Newfoundland to British Columbia learned how to support and trust one another through the large scale national coalitions that have been a trade-mark of the Canadian feminist movement. There is but one exception to this picture, that of Québec, which, while being present for the most part in these alliances, has opted for a more cautious stance in order to save its autonomy for actions focused on its own claims to national representation.

Since 1975, Québec has had its own Charter of Rights, which recognized the legitimacy of affirmative action programs for women long before its Canadian counterpart. Also, Québec women's demands related to family and welfare policies have been directed towards revising the Québec civil code, which is different from Canadian law. Applications made by groups of women for grants are also frequently directed towards the provincial government rather than the federal one, because requests are not considered by the federal government unless they are merged into those of Canadian coast-to-coast national organizations; as a result, the specific cultural demands made by Québec's groups, based on French-Canadian national identity, are apt to be ignored.

Moreover, language acts as a barrier to isolate the two cultures that have evolved from distinct origins and socio-economic experiences: Québec and other Canadian women read different authors, evaluate events within different frames of reference, celebrate different artists, and are often unaware of the experiences of the other — each "milieu" evolving along its parallel path. Distance grows between the separate blocks; global Canadian feminist movements occasionally estrange women's groups from Québec without even being aware of it. Canadian feminists are often unable to grasp that beyond a few bilingual spokespersons, the majority of Québécoises are exclusively French-speaking women with their own historical baggage; they are living under a distinct civil law code, being educated under a different system, becoming used to different "maîtres à penser," and, in general, living and thinking in a distinct cultural context (Langlois, 1990). It is not surprising, then, that communication between them and the Canadian women's movement often becomes unclear.

The Meech Lake Accord exemplified how misunderstanding can occur. The Canadian women's movement succeeded in getting Section 28 inserted into the Charter of Rights and hence Canadian feminists relentlessly defended what they rightly viewed as their major achievement, the guarantee of their constitutional right to equality with men. On the other hand, Québec feminists wanted to politically assert their cultural identity as full citizens involved in a collective struggle towards self-representation. Indeed, if every woman subject claims for herself the right to speak, how could a group of self-conscious women, identifying with their own cultural community, let others silence their demands and their voice in the name of a so-called global Canadian perspective? Hence, many of them considered the Meech Lake agreement as granting quite minimal protection for Québec's aspirations to self-determination and could not accept, as Québec nationalists, that this self-determination should be denied to them.

Of course, pan-Canadian women's organizations which are sensitive to regional disparities, and most anxious to let individual members voice their differences, are generally concerned with providing special arrangements for their members from Québec. But, regardless of their diplomatic skills, their need for consensus regularly collides with the distinct feminist culture of "les Québécoises." Contrary to other Canadian women's groups, Québec feminists do not endorse federalism as a tool of collective emancipation. Rather, they are working towards being heard and recognized "en français" in the political sphere, outside as well as inside Québec.

Not surprisingly, some Canadian feminists discredit such nationalism and see it as opposed to feminism: "The notions of commonality based on shared blood, ancestors, territory and a language learnt 'at his mother's knee'," states Vickers, "reflect the outlines of this technique of bonding men together *as if they were kin.*"[10] Vickers thus rightly exposes a male-dominated vision of national identity-building. Rather than see national identity as a potential tool for creating adequate space for all kinds of individual and group self-awareness, nationalism is seen as a "fundamentalist" movement which can only adopt the form of a closely knit, inward looking community — the very image which many of its critics have of feminism, in fact.[11]

Overcoming this stumbling-block is a major challenge for Canadian and Québec feminists alike. It involves the capacity to develop new types of relationships between their respective movements, and to be respectful of each other's distinct goals and subjectivities. It is only if the women's movement discovers how to translate its respect for cultural differences into concrete guidelines for action that the hyper-sensitive issue of ethnicity will not lead to the breakdown of feminist sorority and accusations of mis-representation. It is possible to adopt more flexible patterns of organization for new social movements; the result would be an opening up of infinitely more promising avenues than the perpetuation of an essentialist feminism which ignores cultural or racial differences. It is through the recognition of mutual differences that tolerance is fostered, even if this means that the strength of the movement must be measured partly by its ability to gauge the *distance* between its members; homogeneity is after all, not preferable, especially when it is more apparent than real.

The women's movement is not alone in this respect. It was the movement of May 1968 in France which broke the mould of the old social movements. For the first time, every individual was invited to speak his or her mind in a movement based on "a prohibition against prohibiting." Taking advantage of this golden opportunity, women seized the "parole" and began to explain their experience without having to adapt their discourse to any conventional pre-established format or norms about what language was legitimate. It was a celebration; a brief and illuminating flash of social and political imagination!

The impact of May '68 was felt in Québec: there were sharp debates on the national question and social issues, accompanied by an open struggle to modernize social and political institutions (Descent et. al, 1989). However, the new political culture eventually originated in the middle of an epoch, the seventies, which in Québec was characterized by the domination of fundamentalist Marxist *groupuscules,* and the polarization of antagonistic social forces in a way that prevented pluralism. During the following ten years political parties, unions, grass-roots movements and Marxist-Leninist groups continued to compete for the exclusive allegiance of activists, both male and female. Individuals who longed for autonomy of thought continued to be sacrificed to the exigencies of causes, all of which were noble, just and above all, mutually exclusive.

Although this quest for power would occupy the centre stage for a long time to come, there was also something else taking shape on the borderlines: the enlargement of the political arena in order to incorporate new categories of active members and issues. Due to economic growth, an increasing number of centrifugal trends appeared as diverse interests were articulated and claimed representation. Beyond the conflicts between movements and political organizations, a major shift was brewing: instead of the oblivion of the self there was a redistribution of energies directed at the numerous objectives of a multiplicity of autonomous political subjects (Ollivier, 1990, Thériault, 1987).

Alternating and sporadic actions corresponding to complex identity-building strategies began to replace comprehensive involvement in a pursuit of one specific cause. Individuals were developing their own political analyses on the basis of a new situation which resulted from victories won by the older social movements, such as the trade-unions. Having increased their self-confidence through the better protection of their rights, activists began to distance themselves from overly insistent pressures for mobilization by their respective organizations.

The trajectory of French-speaking Québec feminists illustrated this, as they were confronted at the very beginning of the seventies with the double dynamic of power and identity. Sensitive to systematic discrimination and social inequalities between men and women, their desire to eliminate the inferior gender status ascribed to them by society drove them to focus their collective energy on a common defensive project. Whatever the strength of their nationalist feelings, as women, their split identity made them have reservations about dealing with mixed-sex independentist associations. Even now, they must still remain united; otherwise they cannot accumulate enough power to force existing institutions to suppress the socio-sexual divisions that reproduce their gendered minority political status generation after generation, in spite of their demographic weight.

Nevertheless, there are numerous women everywhere who refuse to define themselves as feminists even when they share the global values of the movement. They fear a reductionist vision of their composite identity:

Any feminist standpoint will necessarily be partial. Thinking about women may illuminate some aspects of a society that have been previously suppressed within the dominant view. But none of us can speak for 'woman' because no such person exists except within a specific set of (already gendered) relations to 'man' and to many concrete and different 'women'.[12]

Ambivalence is thus omnipresent in women's self-definitions. Even within the ranks of organized feminism there are regular divisions produced by the conflict between the aspirations of anarchist feminists and the pressure which the prevalence of sexism exercises on women to minimize their individual inclinations in order to maximize their collective strength. The history of the Canadian and the Québec women's movements is similarly interwoven with complex relationships between equally feminist tendencies, reflecting the diverse and composite identities of the women's groups at various times. Seen in this perspective, the nationalist tendency of Québécois feminists, who insist on being able to speak in their own language and claim political recognition for their cultural specificity, is no more objectionable than the federal option chosen by Canadian feminists. The women's movement, by virtue of the flexibility of its organisation and the multiplicity of its interventions, as well as its ability to react positively to the cultural diversity of its rank and file membership, thus allows for more creative debates amongst its various constituencies.

Eleven years after the failure of the referendum on sovereignty-association, the notion of sovereignty re-emerged in Québec with vigour; even pro-federalist associations presented to the Bélanger-Campeau Commission, in charge of elaborating the position of Québec after the failure of the last round of federal-provincial constitutional negotiations, a list of powers to be returned to the province of Québec that is much longer and more demanding than the five basic conditions stated in the defunct Meech Lake Accord. Yet the atmosphere remained calm and the twentieth anniversary of October 1970 — when war measures were imposed to break the so-called threat of insurrection in Quebec — could just as well have been the hundredth, so much had emotions cooled down. Is this not an indication that a new political culture, pluralist and open, is already gaining ground?

NOTES

1. Personal identity refers to "the organised unity of self-referring feelings, ideas, experiences and projects for the future, ... the subjective appropriation of social identity," while social identity refers to "the position of a subject in culture and society as well as to the pertaining to different biosocial categories (civil status, sex, age, ethical identity, nationality, class, profession, social roles, ideological, philosophical or religious affiliations, etc.)." Camilleri, Carmel et al., *Stratégies identitaires*, Paris, Presses Universitaires de France, 1990, p. 173.

2. CIACCIA, Fulvio, "Entrevue avec Françoise Collin," *Vice-versa*, 30, September-October 1990, p.49.
3. Lamoureux, Diane, "Le mouvement des femmes: entre l'intégration et l'autonomie," *Canadian Issues/Thèmes canadiens*, 12, 1990, p. 135.
4. Lamoureux, Diane and De Sève, Micheline, "Faut-il laisser notre sexe au vestiaire?," *Politique*, 15, hiver 1989, p. 16.
5. Castoriadis, Cornélius, *Le contenu du socialisme*, Paris, UGE, 1979, pp. 19-20.
6. Hartsock, Nancy, *Money, Sex and Power: Toward a Feminist Historical Materialism*, N.Y., Longman, 1983, p. 246.
7. Alcoff, Linda, "Cultural Feminism versus Post-Structuralism: The Identity Crisis in Feminist Theory" in Malson, M. R. et al., (eds.), *Feminist Theory in Practice and Process*, Chicago, Chicago University Press, 1989, p. 322.
8. Touraine, Alain, *Mouvements sociaux d'aujourd'hui. Acteurs et analystes*, Paris, Ed. ouvrières, 1982, p. 237.
9. Camilleri, Carmel et al., 1990, p.11.
10. Vickers, Jill McCalla, "At His Mother's Knee: Sex/Gender and the Construction of National Identities" in Nemiroff, Greta H. (ed.), *Women and Men. Interdisciplinary Readings on Gender*, Montreal, Fitzhenry and Whiteside, 1987, p.482.
11. Thériault, J. Yvon, "Mouvements sociaux et nouvelle culture politique," *Politique*, 12, Autumn 1987, pp. 26-27.
12. Flax, Jane, "Postmodernism and Gender Relations in Feminist Theory" in Malson M. R. and al., (eds.), *Feminist Theory in Practice and Process*, Chicago, The University of Chicago Press, 1989, p. 72.

REFERENCES

Alcoff, Linda, "Cultural Feminism versus Post-Structuralism: The Identity Crisis in Feminist Theory" in Malson, M. R. et al., (eds.), *Feminist Theory in Practice and Process*, Chicago, Chicago University Press, 1989, pp. 295-326.

Belanger, Paul-R., Deslauriers, Jean-Pierre, "Mouvements sociaux et renouvellement de la démocratie," *Nouvelles pratiques sociales*, 3, 1, Spring 1990, pp. 21-28.

Bordo, Susan, "Feminism, Postmodernism, and Gender-Scepticism," in Nicholson, L. J. (ed.), *Feminism and Postmodernism*, N. Y., Routledge, 1990, pp. 133-56.

Ciaccia, Fulvio, "Entrevue avec Françoise Collin," *Vice-versa*, 30, September-October 1990, pp. 49-51.

Camilleri, Carmel and al., *Stratégies identitaires*, Paris, Presses Universitaires de France, 1990, 232p.

Castoriadis, Cornélius, *Le contenu du socialisme*, Paris, UGE, 1979.

Cohen, Jean, "Strategy or Identity: New Theoretical Paradigms and Contemporary Social Movements," *Social Research*, 52, 4, Winter 1985, pp. 663-716.

Collin, Françoise, "Il n'y a pas de cogito-femme" in Zavalloni, Marisa (ed.), *L'émergence d'une culture au féminin*, Montréal, Ed. Saint-Martin, 1987, pp. 107-16.

Conway, Jill K., Bourque, Susan C., Scott, Joan W. (eds.), *Learning About Women. Gender, Politics and Power*, Ann Arbor, The University of Michigan Press, 1987.

De Sève, Micheline, *Pour un féminisme libertaire*, Montréal, Boréal, 1985.

Descent, D., Maheu, L., Robitaille, G., Simard, G., *Classes sociales et mouvements sociaux au Québec et au Canada*, Montréal, Ed. Saint-Martin, 1989.

Di Stefano, Christine, "Dilemmas of Difference: Feminism, Modernity, and Postmodernism" in Nicholson, L. J. (ed.), *Feminism and Postmodernism*, N.Y., Routledge, 1990, pp. 63-82.

Ferry, Jean-Marc, "Qu'est-ce qu'une identité postnationale?," *Esprit*, September 1990, pp. 80-90.

Flax, Jane, "Postmodernism and Gender Relations in Feminist Theory" in Malson M. R. and al., (eds.), *Feminist Theory in Practice and Process*, Chicago, The University of Chicago Press, 1989.

Hartsock, Nancy, *Money, Sex and Power: Toward a Feminist Historical Materialism*, N.Y., Longman, 1983.

Hegedus, Zsuzsa, "Social Movements and Social Change in Self-Creative Society: New Civil Initiatives in The International Arena," *International Sociology*, 4, 1, March 1989, pp. 19-36.

Juteau-lee, Danielle, Roberts, Barbara, "Etnnicity and Femininity (d')après nos expériences," *Canadian Ethnic Studies*, 12, 1, 1981, pp. 1-21.

Kokopeli, Bruce, Lakey, George, "More Power than We Want: Masculine Sexuality and Violence" in McAllister, Pam (ed.), *Reweaving the Web of Life. Feminism and Non-Violence*, Philadelphia, New Society Publishers, 1982, pp. 231-40.

Lamoureux, Diane, "Le mouvement des femmes: entre l'intégration et l'autonomie," *Canadian Issues/Thèmes canadiens*, 12, 1990, pp. 125-36.

Lamoureux, Diane, De Sève, Micheline, "Faut-il laisser notre sexe au vestiaire?," *Politique*, 15, hiver 1989, pp. 5-22.

Langlois, Simon (ed.), *La société québecoise en tendances 1960-1990*, Québec, IQRC, 1990.

Lipovetsky, Gilles, *L'ère du vide, essais sur l'individualisme contemporain*, Paris, Gallimard, 1983.

Maheu, Louis, Descent, David, "Les mouvements sociaux: un terrain mouvant," *Nouvelles pratiques sociales*, 3, 1, Spring 1990, pp. 41-51.

Malson, Micheline R., O'Barr, Jean F., Westphal-Wihl, Sarah, Wyer, Mary, *Feminist Theory in Practice and Process*, Chicago, The University of Chicago Press, 1989.

Melucci, Alberto, "Mouvements sociaux, mouvements post-politiques," *Revue internationale d'action communautaire*, 10/50, Autumn 1983, pp. 13-30.

Miles, Angela, "The Integrative Feminine Principle in North American Feminist Radicalism: Value Basis of a New Feminism," *Women's Studies International Quarterly*, 4, 1981, pp. 481-95.

Morgan, Robin, *The Anatomy of Freedom. Feminism, Physics and Global Politics*, N. Y., Anchor Books/Doubleday, 1984.

Nicholson, Linda J. (ed.), *Feminism and Postmodernism*, N. Y., Routledge, 1990.

Offe, Claus, "New Social Movements: Challenging the Boundaries of Institutional Politics," *Social Research*, 52, 4, Winter 1985, pp. 818-68.

Ollivier, Nicole, "Individualisme et mouvements sociaux," *Nouvelles pratiques sociales*, 3, 1, Spring 1990. pp. 53-60.

Roberts, Barbara, "Beau fixe ou nuages à l'horizon? L'Accord du Lac Meech jugé par les groupes féministes du Québec et du Canada," *Feminist Perspectives Féministes*, 12 b, février 1989, 46p.

Ruddick, Sara, *Maternal Thinking: Toward a Politics of Peace*, N.Y., Ballantine, 1990.

Scott, Joan W., "Deconstructing Equality Versus Differences or the Uses of Post-Structuralist Theory for Feminism," *Feminist Studies*, 14, 1, Spring 1988, pp. 33-50.

Theriault, J. Yvon, "Mouvements sociaux et nouvelle culture politique," *Politique*, 12, Autumn 1987, pp. 5-36.

Touraine, Alain (debates directed by), *Mouvements sociaux d'aujourd'hui. Acteurs et analystes*, Paris, Ed. ouvrières, 1982.

Touraine, A., Wieviorka, M., Dubet, F., *Le retour de l'acteur*, Paris, Fayard, 1984.

Vickers, Jill McCalla, "At His Mother's Knee: Sex/Gender and the Construction of National Identities" in Nemiroff, Greta H. (ed.), *Women and Men. Interdisciplinary Readings on Gender*, Montréal, Fitzhenry and Whiteside, 1987, pp. 478-92.

Young, Iris Marion, "The Ideal of Community and the Politics of Difference" in Nicholson, L. J. (ed.), *Feminism and Postmodernism*, N. Y., Routledge, 1990, pp. 300-23.

Zavalloni, Marisa (ed.), *L'émergence d'une culture au féminin*, Montréal, Ed. Saint-Martin, 1987.

Chapter 9

Gregory Baum

THE CATHOLIC LEFT IN QUÉBEC[1]

In the sixties and seventies, a series of important events created an extensive network of Catholic socialists in many parts of the world, the history of which has not yet been written. At the Second Vatican Council (1962-1965), the Roman Catholic Church left behind its defensive stance towards modern society and solemnly declared itself in solidarity with the entire human family, beginning with the poor. The Council also placed a new emphasis on freedom of conscience, and urged Catholics to react in novel and untried ways to the social and economic problems of their societies.

In response to the Council's new open-minded attitude, large numbers of Catholics in Latin America joined the liberation movements on their continent and formed networks of socialist "base communities" that produced their own theological reflection. Their "liberation theology" was to exercise enormous influence in all parts of the Catholic Church, including Québec. The Latin American Bishops Conference held at Medellin in 1968 adopted several principles that were drawn from liberation theology, and were confirmed by subsequent ecclesiastical assemblies, including certain Roman documents.

One of the first of these principles, is that in order to announce the Gospel authentically it is necessary to analyse the "social sin," the structures of oppression, in which the people find themselves, because the Gospel promises to rescue people from sin and the damage done by sin. Secondly, society must be analysed by looking at it from the perspective of its victims, because the Hebrew Scripture, especially the core story of Moses, was written from the perspective of the victims; and more especially because Jesus, faithful to this tradition, identified himself with the poor, the downtrodden and the excluded. This second principle, often called "the preferential option for the poor," demands that the Christian community look upon its social context from the viewpoint of the oppressed and act in solidarity with their struggle for liberation. According to a third principle, the Church's pastoral task includes the "conscientization" of the people, which means raising people's awareness of the societal obstacles that prevent them from assuming responsibility for their own future. This third principle fulfils the Gospel's role as a liberatory force in human history.

These principles, as we shall see, were adhered to by many Catholics in Québec. It is also interesting to note that Pope Paul VI, in a circular letter written in 1971, lifted the Catholic taboo on socialism.[2] Although the papacy had condemned socialism in all its forms for over a century, Paul VI now distinguished between various forms of socialism, some of which — if non-revolutionary and not committed to a deterministic social theory — could be reconciled with the Christian message.

In the seventies, a significant Catholic left spread in many parts of the world. Some Catholics followed the new teaching of the Church and became engaged in reformist, socialist or social democratic politics, while others disagreed with their Church and became revolutionaries. They appreciated the radical analysis of the ecclesiastical documents, but rejected their mild, reformist response. In the seventies and early eighties, Latin American liberation theology, in particular, defined itself in revolutionary terms against the Church's new teaching.

THE CATHOLIC LEFT IN QUÉBEC IN THE 1960s AND 1970s

The Quiet Revolution, beginning with the election of a Liberal government in June 1960, released a movement of secularization that dissolved the cultural monopoly exercised by the Catholic Church in Québec. A vast number of Catholics welcomed this change, and were encouraged by the modernizing trend affirmed by the Second Vatican Council. The Catholic Church immediately lost the cultural power to define French Canadian identity, and it also soon lost its institutions of public health and social welfare. Within a few years it lost over half of its members,[3] and towards the end of the sixties, practising Catholics had become a minority in Québec. Still, the combination of the Quiet Revolution and the Second Vatican Council produced an enormous vitality among those Catholics who decided to remain in their religious tradition. Moreover, the bishops themselves did not react with resentment to their loss of power; they wanted the Catholic people, now a minority, to make their contribution to the building of the new Québec.

In the sixties and seventies, Québec became a highly politicized society, and Québecers increasingly saw themselves as participants in a liberation movement for national self-determination. The anti-colonial struggles in Africa, the Algerian War, and the civil rights movement in the United States produced a political discourse that growing numbers of Québecers used to define their own political and cultural endeavour. The sense of urgency was intensified by the so-called October crisis of 1970: although vast numbers of Québecers were attracted by the newly-formed separatist and social democratic Parti Québecois, many Québecers, especially labour leaders and intellectuals, opted for more radical forms of socialism. Marxism achieved a strong cultural presence in Québec, unparalleled in any other part of North America.

The emergence of a Catholic left in the world-wide Church, and the shift to the left in Québec society, exercised a profound influence on the Québec Catholic community. Latin American liberation theology now became important reading, and the end of the sixties witnessed the emergence of a Catholic left in Québec. The bishops of Québec and Canada offered progressive social teaching that criticized capitalism, favoured liberation, and recognized socialism as a Christian option.[4] Left-wing Catholics did not necessarily follow the bishops' reformist teaching. They constituted a political spectrum that ranged from options in keeping with this teaching to more radical options that aimed at dismantling the capitalist system and the State that protected it.

In the seventies the Québec Catholic left embraced thousands of deeply committed men and women. It survived on a more modest scale in the period of cultural malaise after the lost referendum of 1980, and it is presently regaining some momentum. This chapter aims to give an account of the organizations that constituted the Catholic left in the seventies, to specify the ideological orientation of their social practice, and then to show how the Catholic left understands its social engagement today. It is based for the most part on published reports or reports in Catholic reviews such as *Vie ouvrière* and *Relations*.

Already in the mid-sixties, the specialized Catholic Action organizations — Jeunesse ouvrière catholique (JOC), Jeunesse étudiante catholique (JEC), Jeunesse rurale catholique (JRC) and Mouvement des travailleurs chrétiens (MTC) — became increasingly politicized. The bishops were worried about a growing Marxist influence, and created a commission, directed by the well-known sociologist Fernand Dumont, with a mandate to recommend new directions for Catholic Action. The Dumont commission was eventually asked to broaden its perspective, to produce a critical study of the entire Church in Québec, and to come up with proposals for the Church's pastoral orientation in the new age. When the remarkable Dumont Report, comprising several volumes, was published in the early seventies, it recommended a liberal, democratic programme for the Church, tolerant of dissent and allowing for participation.[5] Yet even so the social perspective of the Dumont Report did not reflect the socialist aspirations of an increasing number of Catholics. Although the labour representative on the Dumont commission, Jean-Paul Hétu, clearly expressed his dissatisfaction, his voice was somehow not heard.[6]

The socialist mobilization of Catholics spread rapidly during the 1970s. In response to pressures from the base and from Catholic Action (especially MTC and JOC), a group of engaged Catholics, including several Oblate priests, founded le Centre de pastorale en milieu ouvrier (CPMO), with a view to providing intellectual and spiritual resources for Catholics active in working class organizations and low-income neighbourhoods (*les quartiers populaires*). The CPMO was to engage in education and research, set up courses, meetings, and forums for discussion, and publish material useful for the conscientization and mobilization of Catholic working people.

The activities of the CPMO and the spiritual and political ideas debated at its meetings were recorded in the Oblate monthly, *Pretres et laics*. One of the main topics that preoccupied these left-wing Christians was the approach they should take to Marxist theory and practice. A formal debate on the subject took place in September 1973 which left the participants deeply divided. The Catholic Marxists eventually organized their own network, les Politisés chrétiens (PC), while the CPMO became increasingly pluralistic, extending its solidarity not only to workers but to all marginalized groups.

In November 1974 the CPMO organized a major meeting at Cap Rouge, bringing together all Catholic groups and organizations in solidarity with labour to engage in a critical examination of the Church's role in Québec's working class. The participants regarded their conclusions as a counter-statement to the Dumont Report, which had neglected the viewpoint of the working class. The same meeting brought to light the increasing tension between Marxist socialists and more pluralistic socialists.[7]

In 1974, the Oblate monthly *Pretres et laics* became the independent review, *Vie ouvrière*, published in collaboration with CPMO, MTC and JOC. In its new format the review continued to be of service to Christian activists in working class environments. During the later seventies and into the eighties, *Vie ouvrière* remained loyal to the labour movement, but while it was reflecting the shifting orientation of the CPMO, it paid increasing attention to unorganized workers, the working poor, the unemployed, welfare recipients, and all the marginalized in Québec society — the so-called *"milieu populaire."* *Vie ouvrière* also expressed solidarity with women struggling for emancipation. This new orientation, as we shall see, was eventually accepted by the entire Catholic left.

The CPMO and *Vie ouvrière* survived the lost referendum, the ensuing political nausea, and the dramatic decline of the left. Both CPMO and *Vie ouvrière* continue to exercise their educational function in solidarity with labour and the popular sector. They continue to provide a Gospel-inspired critique of contemporary capitalism, the social policies of the Québec government, and today's cultural indifference to the suffering of others.

In a recent series of articles published in *Vie ouvrière*, Pierre Vallière tells the story of this radical publication which under several names and in different formats has existed for a period of forty years. His closing paragraph reads:

> *Vie ouvrière* is one the rare instruments left in Québec in which communitarian and popular organizations are able to publish their own views and read a critical evaluation of present-day society. At this time in history when those in power and the elites try to exclude the majority of the population from defining and building its own future, publications like *Vie ouvrière* are more indispensable than ever.[8]

MARXISM AND NON-MARXIST SOCIALISM AND THE CATHOLIC LEFT

The Marxist Réseau des politisés chrétiens (PC), founded in 1974, was an interesting Catholic organization that I have analysed in another publication.[9]

Already in 1971 Yves Vaillancourt, writing in the Jesuit publication *Relations*, had proposed the creation of a Catholic Marxist organization. Pointing to recent declarations made by the three major labour federations, la Confédération des syndicats nationaux (CSN), la Fédération des travailleurs du Québec (FTQ) and la Centrale des enseignants du Québec (CEQ), Vaillancourt argued that after October 1970 the labour movement had moved from a social democratic to a Marxist-socialist orientation. Christians in solidarity with labour, he urged, were now bound to follow the same course.

In September of the same year Vaillancourt had an opportunity to present his ideas at a public meeting organized by the CPMO dealing with the relevance of Marxism. On this occasion Yves Vaillancourt and Jérome Régnier, two Catholic socialists of different stripes, engaged in a debate on the meaning of Marxism for the Catholic left. Vaillancourt defended scientific Marxism along Althusserian lines, while Régnier advocated a more humanistic, open-ended Marxism, respectful of culture and human subjectivity. When the network of the PC was formally constituted in 1974, embracing several hundred members, it adopted the scientific approach to Marxism, and retained it during its entire existence.

Yet toward the end of the seventies, left-wing Catholics moved increasingly in the pluralist direction, and without abandoning their loyalty to labour, extended their solidarity to other popular sector struggles. They continued to demand that the Catholic Church itself become "*une église populaire*," which meant that it should adjust its structure and ministry to the needs and aspirations of the popular sector. In May 1979 the CPMO organized a well-attended assembly at the Collège Marie-Victorin in Montréal to promote the idea of "*une église populaire*."[10] What emerged from these discussions was a double imperative: first, the entire Church should be in solidarity with the workers and the marginalized, and second, the workers and the marginalized should enter into solidarity among themselves. These Catholics believed that the Church's pastoral mission among these various groups was to help raise their consciousness, promote their self-organization, and encourage the creation of networks of solidarity.

Under the impact of this alternative approach, membership in the PC declined. In 1982, during the aftermath of the lost referendum, the PC's central co-ordinating committee decided to dissolve the network.

It is worth noting in this connection that in 1976 a group of Catholic women belonging to or in sympathy with the PC decided to form their own independent collective, l'Autre parole, which, while in solidarity with the PC, developed a feminist critique of both the Catholic tradition and the socialist movement. This collective survived the demise of the PC.[11]; it is still active today and it continues to publish its bulletin, *l'Autre parole*.

THE QUÉBEC CATHOLIC LEFT AND THE THIRD WORLD

Other organizations of the Catholic left were generated by Catholics in solidarity with the liberation struggles of the poor in the Third World. Let us first look at l'Entraide missionnaire,[12] an organization founded in the early fifties by a group of missionary congregations to provide support for missionary projects overseas and to continue education for missionaries at home. In the late sixties, influenced by Latin American liberation theology and the radicalization of Québec society, l'Entraide modified its understanding of its task and began to look upon the Church's mission in the light of "the preferential option for the poor." Seen from this perspective, preaching the Gospel implied a commitment to the emancipation of the oppressed.

In 1969 l'Entraide was assigned a full-time executive director, thereby allowing the organization to broaden its concern for the poor countries of the Third World. In 1970 it produced a critical report on Canada's foreign policy in regard to Latin America. The new orientation, not surprisingly, produced many conflicts in the religious congregations that supported l'Entraide and in the wider Québec Church. In the early seventies l'Entraide went through several reorganizations and several debates regarding "the ideology" it was adopting in its missionary education.

In those years conflicts of this kind were universal in missionary organizations in all parts of the Church. Should Christians preach the Good News, as the old missionaries had done, as God's gracious act to save and sanctify those who believed? Or should Christians preach the Gospel, as the new missionaries were beginning to do, as God's gracious act to save human beings from the evil powers that diminish them, and to empower them to struggle against these oppressive structures? In the seventies, as mentioned at the beginning of the chapter, the second view was accepted by several ecclesiastical bodies. Pope Paul VI's message *Evangelii nuntiandi* of 1974 — though not free of all ambiguity — affirmed that the Church's mission was to proclaim the name of Jesus and to promote the liberation from oppression promised by him.[13]

The famous Latin American theologian Gustavo Gutierrez was the guest speaker at the 1975 annual congress of l'Entraide on the topic, "L'évangile: outil d'oppression ou de libération?" In dialogue with Latin American liberation theology, l'Entraide developed its own critique of capitalism as an economic system that enriched the centre at the expense of the periphery and hence widened the gap between rich and poor countries, and the gap between rich and poor within these countries. Recognizing the close connection between what was happening in the Third World and what was happening in Québec and Canada, l'Entraide began to speak out in public in relation not only to Canada's foreign policy but also to the marginalization of the poor and unemployed at home.

Because of these radical public statements, l'Entraide was repeatedly accused within the Québec Church of going beyond Catholic social teaching and following instead a reprehensible Marxist ideology. Yet l'Entraide did not think of itself as Marxist; it was critical of capitalism and supported a socialist vision, but the theoretical orientation it followed was defined not by Marxism but by "the preferential option for the poor," which includes such topics as solidarity with the people marginalized in their own society for whatever reason, whether it be class, race, gender, culture, religion, sickness or old age.

L'Entraide missionnaire was, and still is, one of the most important institutions for raising the consciousness of the Catholic community. It continues to publish its bulletins, its dossiers, and its letters of protest or encouragement in the changing political context. The great Québec Catholic educational event was, and still is, the annual Congress organized by l'Entraide every September, providing for several hundred participants, with lectures and panel discussions, workshops on topics dealing justice at home and abroad, and forms of public worship that integrate the love of God with solidarity among the poor. The topic of the 1991 Congress was solidarity with Native peoples.

Another, much larger Catholic institution concerned with the Third World is the Canadian Organization for Development and Peace (Développement et paix in Québec), founded by the Canadian bishops in 1967 out of the new understanding of love, solidarity and liberation derived from the Second Vatican Council, liberation theology and subsequent ecclesiastical teaching. The aim of Development and Peace, according to the bishops, was "to come to the aid of the poor and oppressed in the world and to support them in their struggle for justice."[14] Part of the function of Development and Peace was to educate the Catholic community in Canada regarding the misery in the Third World, the causes of the underdevelopment of these regions, and the oppressive domination exercised by the present economic system and its international financial institutions. Since the political climate in the Québec of the seventies differed from that of English-speaking Canada, the francophone section of Development and Peace tended to offer a more radical analysis of underdevelopment and a more radical critique of world capitalism than did the anglophone section. Because of the consciousness-raising activity of Développement et Paix, I include it in this account of the Catholic left in Québec.

In Québec as in the rest of Canada, this educational activity was carried on by local committees attached to dioceses or parishes, guided by facilitators, some of whom worked full-time for Development and Peace. In Québec these facilitators were in constant contact with the head office in Montréal. They were provided with information regarding the overseas projects of the organization and, more importantly, they became informed participants in discussions that sought to analyse the historical situation of various Third World countries and the ways in which the developed North was implicated in their plight. This learning process enabled the facilitators to promote in their groups a Catholic sense of international solidarity that did not remain abstract but prompted an analytical approach, preferential solidarity and a critical stance toward the political and economic policies of their own country. To this day Développement et paix fulfils an important consciousness-raising function in Québec.

THE CATHOLIC LEFT AND POPULAR ACTION FOR CHANGE IN QUÉBEC

The previous account of the left-wing organizations created one or two decades ago — CPMO, Vie ouvrière, Politisés chrétiens, l'Autre parole, l'Entraide missionaire, and Développement et paix — reveals that with the exception of the PC, these groups continue to be active. While they were influenced by the Marxist culture present in the Québec of the seventies, apart from the PC they were not Marxist organizations. They developed their own social analysis based on preferential solidarity with the popular sector in Québec and the oppressed masses in the Third World. The principal engagement of these organizations lay, and still lies, in the field of popular education. They also exercise pressure in society and mobilize protest actions against repressive measures, but their continuous activity is educational: it is to raise people's consciousness, to criticize the dominant capitalist ethos and the prejudices of society, and to promote a culture of solidarity. Yet, as we shall see, recent developments have also prompted practical involvement in support of popular groups and their projects for improving their social conditions.

First, however, we should note some other Catholic institutions that also engage in popular education. Le Centre Saint-Pierre in down-town Montréal, an Oblate foundation, is an important adult education centre. It provides evening courses on the Christian life and the relevance of the Gospel for society from a perspective defined, for the most part, by the preferential option for the poor. Le Centre justice et foi, a Jesuit institution, also exercises an educational function: it sponsors the monthly review, Relations, with an editorial policy that reflects the option for the poor, and organizes panel discussions and workshops on controversial topics that uphold a radical commitment to justice. The same Centre also engages in advocacy regarding matters dealing with refugees, immigrants and other minorities. Also, in English-speaking Montréal the Social Justice Committee, originally a Catholic institution but now ecumenical, holds regular public sessions that analyse oppression in Third World countries and reveal the damage done by North American imperialism.

Two other small institutions that are deeply engaged in consciousness-raising, require a slightly fuller description. Le Comité chrétien in support of human rights in Latin America was founded in 1976, to a large extent through the effort of refugees from Chile who had come to Québec after the coup d'état. The aim of the committee was twofold: it defended human rights in Latin America through letters of protest addressed to Latin American governments that had violated human rights, and through pleas addressed to the Canadian government asking it to respond boldly to these situations; it also raised the awareness of Québecers in regard to the conditions of oppression in Latin America. The great achievement of the committee is the organization of a big annual demonstration on the 24th of March, called "*l'évènement Romero*," that commemorates the assassination of Archbishop Oscar Romero in 1980 by right-wing forces in El Salvador supported by the US. Oscar Romero demonstrations now take place in many Québec cities; in Montréal the well-organized demonstration regularly includes as many as fifteen hundred marchers.

Another consciousness-raising group is la Théologie contextuelle, founded in 1955, a circle of about twenty men and women, most of whom work as helpers, facilitators and educators among the unemployed, welfare recipients, the working poor, immigrant groups and refugees. A few of the members are professional theologians. The purpose of this circle is the development of "contextual theology." This means putting in context the three principles mentioned at the beginning of this chapter, derived from Latin American liberation theology and eventually accepted by several authoritative ecclesiastical statements: to make a preferential option for the poor, to produce a social analysis of the situation that afflicts them, and to become engaged in the raising of consciousness. The task the contextual theology circle has chosen for itself is to offer correctives to the dominant academic theology that tends to explore the meaning of the Christian message in abstract terms, without reference to the concrete suffering of the poor and the structures that produce this suffering.

Over the years the contextual theology circle has chosen to deal with a variety of questions. One question was what the Catholic religion meant to people in the popular sector. After listening to these people, the circle realized that for the majority the inherited Catholic religion was a set of ideas and practices that had nothing to do with their real problems. For many the Church was associated with an establishment that remained indifferent to their poverty and exclusion; only for a few was the Gospel a religious message that gave them dignity, strength, and the will to improve their situation in solidarity with others. After hearing these voices the circle was able to identify the ideological distortions that have crept into Christian preaching and Christian piety and that prevent people from using their inherited religious tradition as a source of strength for social struggle. The circle was also able to analyse the ideological elements in the secular culture that make people feel that social change is impossible and give them a sense of total powerlessness.

The circle has produced a document, based on the experiences and reactions of people in the popular sector, that criticizes the unemployment and welfare legislation of the Québec government. The document was later submitted to the parliamentary commission. It also brought out a document dealing with the increasing precariousness of employment and the hopelessness engendered in people who cannot find a steady job but work only temporarily or part-time. This document, submitted to the Québec bishops, was used by them as the basis for a pastoral letter protesting the deteriorating conditions of employment.

This account of the Catholic groups and voices that reflect the preferential option for the poor and seek to raise the consciousness of society remains incomplete. A more detailed account would have to include groups situated in the outlying regions of Québec, the social justice committees of religious orders and of certain dioceses, and the names of many individual courageous lay persons, sisters, priests and bishops.

A recent development, beginning in the outlying regions of Québec, has revealed a new face of the Catholic left. In these regions the neoliberal policies of the federal and provincial governments are leading to economic decline, rising unemployment, and the emigration of the young. The people in these regions fear that their social and cultural stability is being threatened; they feel deserted by the governments, the political parties, the corporations and the business and professional elites of Québec and Canada. In response to this, the local churches have begun to exercise a significant leadership in analysing the situation, collaborating with other groups to organize consciousness-raising public assemblies and supporting cooperative endeavours to devise alternative, small-scale economic initiatives to protect the social stability of these regions.[15]

In 1984 the diocese of Gatineau-Hull initiated this procedure by appointing a commission to study the economic crisis and increasing poverty in the region. The report, entitled "Bienheureux, les pauvres? Réflexions et prises de position sur la misère dans l'Outaouais Québécois," set the tone for several subsequent interventions. In 1985 Gérard Drainville, the bishop of Amos in the north-west region, published a challenging report entitled "Espoirs et défis de l'agriculture dans le Québec d'aujourd'hui." Later the same diocese collaborated with popular groups and local organizations to set up an action committee called the Comité régional d'intervention to promote regional development. Similarly, in the region Saguenay-Lac Saint-Jean the diocese of Chicoutimi initiated a three year programme (1988-1991) to analyse local conditions, to articulate the causes of poverty and social decline, and — in the third year — to collaborate with local groups to devise alternative models of economic development. The meeting inaugurating the third year of the programme was attended by five hundred people from the region. In 1989 a similar project, Pour un plan de développement: de la pyramide á la table ronde," was initiated by the diocese of Trois-Rivières. In collaboration with local organizations this project also hopes to move into action.

In 1990 the diocese of Rimouski participated in a large meeting organized by popular groups that sought to mobilize the people of the region, and to stimulate new ideas for supporting companies in trouble and for initiating alternative ventures. In April 1991 the bishop of Gaspé,

Bertrand Blanchet, published a paper "La Gaspésie a-t-elle un avenir?" as his contribution to the ideas to be discussed at a large regional meeting in May of the same year, and the diocese of Gaspé tried to mobilize the local parishes to make their contribution to the regional endeavour.

In all these instances, we note, bishops and diocesan committees do not behave as actors with authority: they behave as collaborators with popular groups and local organizations in solidarity with the poor and marginalized. Their involvement goes beyond popular education and consciousness raising and includes joint action.

A similar Catholic involvement has occurred in the low-income (popular) neighbourhoods of the large cities. Here Christian activists, employed by church institutions or secular agencies, work with local groups to enhance the sense of community and solidarity and to generate self-help projects and small economic ventures for the benefit of the neighbourhood. In Montréal la Table de concertation justice et foi brings together the Christian networks that serve in various low-income neighbourhoods of the city. The emphasis here is on collaboration with popular groups and labour organizations. In Québec City le Centre d'action populaire en milieu ouvrier (CAPMO) is the organization that brings together Christians activists in low-income neighbourhoods and supports them in struggles and endeavours jointly undertaken with other popular groups and labour organizations. In Hull, the parish of Notre-Dame produced a document, "l'Option apostolique," that outlined a pastoral approach reflecting preferential solidarity with the unemployed and encouraging collaboration with other popular groups.

These new practices of the Catholic left have also resulted in their support of the (pan-Canadian) Working Committee on Social Solidarity, involving representatives of many popular groups — workers, women, welfare recipients, immigrants — that in 1987 produced a joint declaration, "A Time to Stand Together: A Time for Social Solidarity," proposing social and economic policy directions at odds with the government's neoliberal political programme. In Québec the above-mentioned church groups support "Solidarité Populaire Québec" and its alternative vision of society, and cooperate with the present Commission populaire itinérante that is holding hearings in various parts of the country on the topic of "le Québec on veut batir!"

We can conclude from all this that today the Catholic left in Québec, while much smaller than it was in the seventies, continues to display considerable vitality. Its main contribution is still in the field of popular education and the promotion of a culture of solidarity, but in recent years it has also become active in solidarity with other popular groups. It must be admitted that despite its dedication, the Catholic left is a minority movement in the Church. The great majority of Catholics who attend Sunday mass in their respective parishes are only vaguely aware of the progressive documents published by their bishops and have never heard of the left-wing Catholic organizations discussed in this chapter. The middle-class ethos has successfully shaped their perception of the Christian message. However, activists of all tendencies, progressive or not, are almost by definition minorities; their influence and example do not depend on their numbers.

THE SIGNIFICANCE OF THE LEFT CATHOLIC THOUGHT FOR A NEW SOCIALIST PROJECT

These Catholic organizations are broadly guided by the same social philosophy or social theology. They are not Marxist, they do not define oppression in purely economic terms, they resist any determinist social theory, and they distrust the positivistic approach in social science that hopes to uncover the laws according to which society supposedly operates. They define their position through the preferential option for the poor: they extend their solidarity to all groups and classes that suffer exclusion from the economic, political and cultural life of society. They support the liberation struggles of women, of workers, of the unemployed, of aboriginal peoples, of visible minorities and other marginalized communities.

At the same time, these Catholic organizations recognize that the social analyses made by these different groups or classes are likely to be non-identical. These collectivities — whether workers, the unemployed, women, or aboriginal peoples — assign priority to the oppression under which they suffer, and while they take into account the oppression of others and search for connecting links, they are likely to arrive at social analyses that differ, however slightly, from one another. The Catholic left, if I interpret the participants correctly, reject the idea that people have to be in perfect agreement on social analysis before they can act together, and they tend to entertain a pluralistic understanding of the left. Following what in liberation theology is called "the primacy of practice," they are inclined to hold that joint solidary action among various marginalized groups tends to modify the way in which they look upon society, and that joint action is therefore able to narrow the gap between their divergent social analyses. Joint practice wherever possible precedes agreement on theory.

This attitude, together with its ethical-cultural stance makes the Catholic left very open to cooperation in the formation of a new, plural socialist project. In the past, the economic left was insensitive to this dimension; Marxists were, on the whole, unwilling to engage in systematic reflection on cultural and ethical issues. Thinkers like Antonio Gramsci were exceptions. Today, those who remain faithful to the socialist ideal believe that this indifference to the ethical-cultural factor was a mistake.

Without a culturally-mediated ethical sense of solidarity, the general population will not support the labour movement or socialist political parties. A purely utilitarian ethic does not provide sufficient motivation for the prolonged struggle for social justice, especially if the full fruits of the struggle will be enjoyed only by future generations. Why should people make sacrifices? Sacrifices can be justified in utilitarian terms only if they contribute to the well-being of the people by whom sacrifices must be made. But in many situations solidarity with the victims of society transcends self-interest.

In Marxist theory of the Second International variety, the collective self-interest of the working class, conceived as an objective factor, was supposed to account for the willingness of workers to engage in the class struggle, even if they did not expect to reap the benefits in their own lifetimes. Their sacrifices, according to this sort of Marxism, were not prompted by an ethical commitment. However, material class interest so conceived provides no impetus for the labour movement to act in solidarity with aboriginal people in Canada, or oppressed peasants in Latin America. Here solidarity surely transcends material self-interest, be it individual or collective.

The preferential solidarity repeatedly mentioned in this chapter is of this kind. It has to be motivated by an ethics of ends, not of means; and it must be sustained by the virtues of love and justice. Of course, many people are committed to these values without ever articulating them. Workers in labour unions and socialist parties have sustained burdensome struggles under difficult circumstances without ever asking themselves why they made these personal sacrifices. They are heirs to an ethical tradition which, if they are secular, they may even be unable to articulate. I am inclined to believe that in actual fact these workers have experienced moral outrage at all conditions of oppression; they have inherited a passion for justice derived from religion, from a deeply lodged memory of a God who is intolerant of oppression and exploitation.

In the present culture, however, religious memories have faded. Market and consumer values have become omnipresent. Where, then, will people find the moral resources for preferential solidarity with the poor and oppressed? What are the powerful symbols that will empower people to transcend utilitarian values? This is a question contemporary socialists must ask themselves. One reason why a wave of right-wing reaction is presently sweeping through the Western world is, in my opinion, that people are frightened by the recognition that favouring a just and sustainable society on the world scale demands a high price, and a strong measure of self-limitation. A fear such as this can only be overcome by a moral vision.

It seems to me that the great world religions are the major social sources for an ethic of solidarity and self-limitation. Some high-minded individuals may turn to Kant's categorical imperative, but the excessive rationalism of the Kantian ethic prevents it from being widely embraced. I recognize, of course, that the world religions are an ambiguous heritage: they all contain elements that legitimate privilege, injustice, and cruelty. At the same time they also bear within them, sometimes deeply hidden, the message that people belong to one another, that they are — as the Bible says — their brothers' and sisters' keepers, and that compassion and solidarity belong to the very nature of human being. The young Marx drew upon this tradition when he called the human being "a species-being" (Gattungswesen): by this he meant that we differ from animals because unlike them we are prompted by our very nature to promote the well-being of the entire human species — a position rarely advocated by philosophical arguments. If socialism is to become a mass movement it will have to draw upon the promise of solidarity contained in the ancient religious traditions.

NOTES

1. While in Ontario the Christian left is an ecumenical movement including Protestants and Catholics, in Québec, formerly a Catholic culture, the Christian left is a Catholic movement.
2. Paul VI, *Octogesima adveniens*, n. 31, see *Proclaiming Justice and Peace*, ed. Michael Walsh and Brian Davies, Mystic, CT: Twenty-Third Publication, 1991, p. 257.
3. For the impact of the Quiet Revolution on the Church, see Gregory Baum, *The Church in Québec*, Montreal: Novalis, 1991, pp. 15-47.
4. Cf. Gregory Baum, "Toward a Canadian Catholic Social Theory," *Theology and Society*, New York: Paulist Press, 1987, pp. 66-87.
5. The five volumes of the Dumont Report were published by Fides, Montreal, in 1971 and 1972. For an analysis of the Report, see *The Church in Québec*, pp. 52-65.
6. Fernand Dumont et alii, *L'Église du Québec, un héritage*, un projet, appendice II, Montreal: Fides, 1971, p. 316.
7. The Report on Cap-Rouge, *Vie ouvrière*, January 1975, especially p. 34.
8. Since the CP did not survive the eighties, I shall in this chapter only mention events connected with the CP that reveal the ideological conflict in the Catholic left.
9. Gregory Baum, "Politisés chrétiens: A Christian-Marxist Network in Québec, 1974-982," *Studies in Political Economy*, Summer 1990, pp. 7-28, also published in *The Church in Québec*, pp. 67-89.
10. See the reports of Raymond Levac, *Vie ouvrière*, June-July 1979, pp. 329-332, 368-373.
11. For a brief a history of l'Autre parole, see Monique Dumais, Louise Melancon, Marie-Andrée Roy, "Dix ans déjá,' *l'Autre parole*, June 1986, pp. 4-6.
12. For information on l'Entraide missionnaires I have relied on the booklet, *Une histoire d'avenirs*, produced and published by this organization in 1987.
13. For the text, see *Proclaiming Justice and Peace*, pp. 296-297.
14. For information on Development and Peace, I have relied on the brochure, "Principes de base et orientations," produced by the francophone section of Development and Peace in 1984.
15. This recent development in the churches is presented and analysed in a paper by Guy Paiement, "La solidarité avec les personnes démunies," presented to la Société canadienne de théologie at the October 1991 conference and to be published in the proceedings of the conference in the series 'Héritage et projet' put out by Fides in Montreal. Guy Paiement is an activist, thinker and author, initiator of La table de concertation justice et foi in Montreal, whose articles appear in many Québec reviews.

REFERENCES

Baum, Gregory. "Toward a Canadian Catholic Social Theory," *Theology and Society*. New York: Paulist Press, 1987. pp. 66-87.

Baum, Gregory. "Politisés chrétiens: A Christian-Marxist Network in Québec, 1974-1982," *Studies in Political Economy*. Summer 1990. pp. 67-89.

Baum, Gregory. *The Church in Québec*. Montréal: Novalis, 1991.

Dumais, Monique; Louise Melacon and Marie-Andrée Roy. "Dix ans déjá," *l'Autre parole*, June 1986.

Dumont, Fernand et alii. *L'Église du Québec, un héritage, un projet*, appendice II, Montréal: Fides, 1971.

Vie Ouvrière. January, 1975.

Vie Ouvrière. June-July, 1979.

Vie Ouvrière. May-June, 1991.

Vie Ouvrière. July-August, 1991.

Vie Ouvrière. September-October, 1991.

Vie Ouvrière. November-December, 1991.

Walsh, Michael and Brian Davies (eds). *Proclaiming Justice and Peace*. Mystic, CT: Twenty-Third Publication, 1991.

THE CHRISTIAN LEFT IN ONTARIO: REFLECTIONS ON THE CURRENT JUNCTURE OF THE INTERCHURCH COALITIONS

"The Christian Left" includes a broad range of people who claim some allegiance to and receive inspiration from the Christian gospel and Churches, and who support social change in the interests of those who are marginalized and disaffected by the current socio-economic status quo. One of its expressions consists of twelve interchurch coalitions which may be described as the centrepiece of the Christian Left in Ontario and English-speaking Canada.

Christians have played a part in all the major social struggles of the last decade — peace, feminism, environmentalism, rights for aboriginals and people of colour, labour disputes, Third World solidarity, gay and lesbian rights and the farming crisis. There was even a group called "Christians in the NDP" who tried to integrate Christian convictions with a left-leaning political party. The 1980s and early 1990s have witnessed a burgeoning of social movements that have become a new locus for political activity. Progressive Christians have not been absent from the building of these movements,[1] even though the religious inspiration that propelled them into the public arena might not have been openly or clearly articulated.

The interchurch coalitions deserve special attention because they are the most institutionalized manifestation of progressive Christians working for social change. They receive most of their funding from the Churches, their Boards are staffed by Church appointees, and their mandates are derived from the Churches' collective desire to promote justice concerns at home and abroad. Many Church members might not know of their existence, which has prompted one writer to express amazement at the level of ignorance concerning the coalitions at the congregational level in comparison to their international reputation.[2] Nevertheless, they have made a significant contribution both to Church life and to social movements in Canada. Their combined annual budgets total $2.5 to $3 million annually

($6 million if the funds distributed overseas by the Inter-Church Fund for International Development are included), which is a considerable investment of Church resources. Although a few university theses on particular coalitions, and a sprinkling of articles have been written about them,[3] their significance deserves more recognition than the little academic and journalistic attention they have received.

The interchurch coalitions are in the middle of a very serious review of their structures and mandates, and this chapter hopes both to contribute to this re-structuring process, and to introduce new people to these important institutions. After examining the history of the coalitions, and describing their areas of work, we will move into an analysis of the challenges they face in the neoconservative 1990s.

HISTORY OF THE COALITION

The coalitions were not created all at once, but arose in response to particular issues facing Canadian Churches and society, as specific individuals within the Churches lobbied on behalf of particular causes. As a result, each of the coalitions has its own particular origin and evolution. The oldest, GATT-FLY (now known as the Ecumenical Coalition for Economic Justice (ECEJ)) began in 1972, while the youngest coalition, the Inter-Church Coalition on Africa, dates from 1982.

It is possible to speak in general terms of the birth of the coalitions having occured at a particularly auspicious moment in the lives of the Canadian Churches. Given the different social and ecclesial circumstances, such groups could not have been created in the 1950s or earlier. The 1950s was a period of denominational divisiveness and separation. As Roger Hutchinson says, "Protestant-Catholic co-operation gradually emerged against the background of suspicion and isolation."[4] It was the ecclesial and social climate that developed in the 1960s to the 1980s that made the coalition possible.

The longer roots of the coalitions, however, reach back into the Depression years and beyond. The mainline Protestant Churches had a long tradition of ecumenical cooperation that involved many common projects before, during and after the two World Wars. The "social gospel" activity of the inter-war years combined a spirit of ecumenism amongst Protestant Churches with a desire for justice in the social arena. Christians were active in trade union struggles and farmer's organizations, most notably in western Canada, in the peace movement and in urban poverty struggles. One of the fruits of this "social passion" was Christian participation in the creation of the Co-operative Commonwealth Federation (CCF) in 1933.[5] This social gospel activity subsided, however, with World War II.

Until the 1960s, the Roman Catholic Church and the Mennonite Churches were much more isolationist in their social policies. Roman Catholics were by and large wary of movements and political parties that included socialist ideas and that encouraged mixing with non-Catholics, who they imagined might threaten their faith. There were some efforts at co-op and credit union organizing in the 1930s in predominantly Catholic areas like Antigonish and Cape Breton in Nova Scotia; but the Catholic tendency in English Canada, where Catholics were in the minority, was to look after their own and try to preserve a Catholic faith in what was perceived to be a hostile Protestant environment.[6]

During this period, the Mennonite Churches in Canada were also very concerned about mixing with both Protestants and Catholics in whatever social programs were initiated. Redemption for them meant becoming a separate, holy people removed from a warring, fractured society. The Mennonites remained the "quiet in the land" until World War II when, as conscientious objectors, they undertook public service in lieu of joining the military. This experience of social service allowed them to break out of their isolation in the years after World War II, and the creation and rapid growth of the Mennonite Central Committee (Canada) gave institutional expression to this shift.[7]

The social and ecclesial context of the 1960s and 1970s also provided a stimulus to ecumenical social justice organizing; it supported a move away from isolationist tendencies within the Roman Catholic and Mennonite Churches and spurred a renewed social gospel vision on the part of the Protestant Churches. One of the many factors explaining this shift was the zeal and new analyses of missionaries who, after returning from overseas appointments, challenged home Churches in unprecedented ways. For the Roman Catholic Churches in the 1950s, Pope Pius XII had given a mandate to the Churches of the North to support the Churches of the South by providing ten percent of their personnel for overseas mission work. Meanwhile, the protestant Churches, still strong in missionary endeavours, began to re-think their mission work as a result of being thrown out of China after the 1948 revolution. Their encounter with partners from the Third World in World Council of Churches' forums, further stimulated a global awareness. The Mennonite Central Committee saw dramatic increases in the number of overseas volunteers.

Many of the missionaries and overseas workers were not politicized and certainly not radical when they originally undertook their assignments. In theological terms, they went overseas with the idea that they were going to "bring Christ to the heathen" rather than to discover the God that was already present in the people.

A conversion did occur in the countries of the South. Frequently, the Canadian missionaries were converted to a new vision of Christian mission work. Foreign Church personnel very often went to the poorest areas of the host country. Their direct experience of dire poverty, human rights violations, militarism, and transnational corporations working in the Third World raised new questions about the structure of the global economy and Canada's role in it. They continued to pursue these questions upon their return to Canada. Many of the first organizers of the interchurch coalitions had significant overseas experience.[8]

In the Roman Catholic tradition, Vatican II (1962-65) and its aftermath were significant turning points in Church policies on a number of fronts. Initiated by the charismatic Pope John XXIII, Vatican II was a Council that brought together the bishops from around the world to chart the future direction of the Church. The documents of the Council, in particular the "Decree on Ecumenism," and the "Constitution on the Church in the Modern World," stimulated a vision of the Church that incorporated strong ecumenical co-operation and Catholic involvement in social issues of the day.[9] Protestant observers were present at the Council, as were Roman Catholic observers at various World Council of Churches gatherings. Further papal social teaching, in particular Pope Paul VI's "On the Development of Peoples" and the World Synod of Bishops' "Justice in the World," had a progressive edge to them. In Canada, the newly established Canadian Conference of Catholic Bishops also began to publish Labour Day statements on a variety of social themes.

The Latin American Roman Catholic bishops took the process a step further. Meeting in Medellin in 1968, they called attention to the underdeveloped nature of their continent and called on the Church to struggle against the causes of poverty and injustice. This was a radical turning point in the alliance of many bishops and clergy with the ruling classes of Latin America. The subsequent Latin American bishops' conference in Puebla, Mexico in 1979, further affirmed these developments by calling on all sectors of the Church to adopt the "preferential option for the poor."[10]

These bishops' conferences spoke on behalf of a growing Church movement that was challenging local and international structures of injustice. Their religious framework was articulated by a "liberation theology" whose proponents were very much linked to popular social movements across Latin America. Third World liberation theologians also issued strong appeals and challenges to Northern Churches and Christians to become active on public policy issues affecting Third World development.

Within Canada, the 1960s witnessed a number of co-operative efforts amongst the Canadian Churches that would not have been possible a decade earlier. In 1965, a Working Conference on the Implications of a Health Charter for Canadians was co-sponsored by ten churches as well as ten other voluntary agencies. In 1968, twelve churches working with the federal and some provincial governments co-sponsored a conference entitled "Christian Conscience and Poverty" which focused on domestic poverty. The follow-up to the conference was the establishment of a "Coalition for Development" that focused on tax reform, aboriginal people, world development and support for local citizens' groups. While this coalition did not survive, it did provide a forum for leaders in the Churches and voluntary organizations to meet one another and establish a basis for communication and co-operation that could be relied upon in future years as the coalitions were emerging.[11]

With the end of the Vietnam War in the early 1970s, people's sensibilities concerning their capacity to effect progressive social change reached new heights. A social movement had been able to stop a major war undertaken by a world superpower, and several Christians and Churches had participated in this anti-imperialist struggle. Once the war ended, expectations rose that other pressing local and global issues could be dealt with through citizen advocacy.

THE TWELVE INTERCHURCH COALITIONS

Each coalition has its own particular history to tell, and its own learning experiences to share; together, they can compile their information and organize for progressive social change. The distinct features of each coalition need to be recorded and examined more systematically, and to this end this chapter will give a short synopsis of their history, vision and strategies, and the contributions they have made.

In response to the on-going poverty and human rights violations in the Third World, a number of coalitions were formed. The Inter-Church Committee for Human Rights in Latin America (ICCHRLA), formed in 1977, which focuses on Latin America and the Caribbean, grew out of an earlier more ad hoc ecumenical Church group, the Inter-Church Committee on Chile (ICCR), established in direct response to the Pinochet coup in Chile in September 1973. The ICCR, acting in response to friends and Church partners under siege in Chile, sought to defend human rights and denounce the brutal repression that followed the military junta's seizure of power. As refugees began appearing at Canada's doorsteps, the ICCR urged the Canadian government to accept them.

Emerging from this experience, the ICCHRLA was created to assist the Canadian Churches in responding to issues throughout Latin America. The work expanded rapidly as conditions in the region deteriorated in the late 1970s and 1980s. Today it includes supporting persons and groups in Latin American countries that defend human rights, intervening on behalf of victims of human rights abuses, and monitoring Canadian foreign policy in relation to countries that are persistent human rights violators. The ICCHRLA also organizes visits by Canadian Church leaders to Latin America and by Latin Americans who have witnessed human rights abuses to Canada in order to disseminate information and analysis to Church organizations, governments, and international bodies.

The Inter-Church Coalition on Africa (ICCAF) was formed in 1982 to work in partnership with the Churches of Africa. Their prime concern has been to educate Canadians about the realities of Africa, and, to this end, it has organized fact-finding missions and exchanged visits. In recent years, much attention has been focused on apartheid, and on the impoverishment of Sub-Saharan African countries.

The Canada-Asia Working Group (CAWG) was formed in 1978 to monitor human rights and social justice issues in the vast continent of Asia. It has made links not only with Church groups abroad, but also with organizations and unions of peasants, workers, women, and tribal people.

Of particular concern in the 1980s were developments in the Philippines, Korea, East Timor and Sri Lanka. In addition to providing analysis on developments in these countries, CAWG seeks to promote solidarity through linking Canadian and Asian popular organizations working on similar social justice issues.

China is a country which prior to the 1948 revolution had received many Christian missionaries who often arrived with attitudes that the Churches would now call religious imperialist. One of the goals of the current Canada-China Programme, established in 1976, has been to help the Canadian Churches to rethink the role of Christian missionaries in foreign countries. The Programme has also responded to China's growing participation in the world community. This coalition facilitates special events of common interest to both Canadians and Chinese, especially Christians in both countries, including exchanges and the promotion of various material on China.

Each of the Churches has a programme of assistance for projects in the Third World that promote development. In addition to these organizations, since 1974 the Churches have also funded the Inter-Church Fund for International Development (ICFID) which distributes Church and CIDA monies to support community-based economic, educational and health programs. ICFID also provides a forum in which Church agencies can develop common analyses of international issues, discuss policies, and coordinate efforts.

Each of the Third World coalitions listed above relates to the research and advocacy arms of Christian denominations at a head office level. For the most part, they do not have a mandate to develop a grassroots constituency. The Inter-Church Committee on World Development (commonly known as Ten Days for World Development) was formed in 1973 to promote the idea that authentic development in the Third World demands justice more than charity.[12] The Ten Days program addresses itself to changing political and economic structures, both within Canada and internationally, that cause oppression and poverty abroad. Over two hundred local committees across Canada undertake study and action programs on themes such as human rights in Central America, Canada's aid policy, and the Third World debt crisis. The Ten Days major action period is in late January when these local committees, with the assistance of a team of visitors from around the world, offer local Churches and community organizations a wealth of information and action possibilities.

Project Ploughshares, which deals with militarism, has since its inception in 1976 also developed a grassroots constituency of about forty-five groups across Canada. Its research on Canadian military policies, disarmament and development, the arms trade, and nuclear arms is directed towards promoting peace and finding alternative defence policies. Local groups also undertake their own programs of action and advocacy. Project Ploughshares is one of the largest peace groups in Canada, with over twelve thousand financial supporters and a sponsorship that extends beyond the Churches to include other community and development agencies. Canada's Peace Churches, the Mennonites and the religious Society of Friends, have shown particular leadership in Project Ploughshares.

There are two coalitions that focus on the economic policies of government and business. The first is the Ecumenical Coalition On Economic Justice (ECEJ)[13] that was born out of an evaluation of the Canadian government's role at the second United Nations Committee on Trade and Development (UNCTAD) meetings in 1972. The original goals of GATT-FLY, as it was called then, were to do research for the Churches on Canada's economic and trade relationships with the developing world, and to lobby the Canadian government to adjust its policies and international agreements in a way that would allow for more favourable conditions in Third World countries. In the course of its work, ECEJ recognized that there were severe limits to the power that community groups had in influencing government policy. It switched its strategy away from government lobbying to one that gave priority to working with popular groups in Canada and abroad. The coalition now works on economic analysis, education and action with unions, farmers' groups, aboriginal organizations, and women's associations. ECEJ's most recent area of education and advocacy has been with the Action Canada Network around the Free Trade deal with the United States and Mexico, and the debt crisis within Canada and the Third World.

The second such coalition, the Task Force on Churches and Corporate Responsibility (TCCR),[14] formed in 1974, acts as a watchdog for Canadian corporate practices at home and abroad. In its early years, the TCCR promoted economic boycotts of repressive regimes in Chile and South Africa. A frequently used tactic of the TCCR has been to have a member Church purchase token shares in a corporation thereby permitting the shareholder to address the Annual Shareholders' Meeting. TCCR guidelines identify areas in which the policies and practices of public corporations are evaluated. For the TCCR, ethical investment and good corporate citizenship include responsible use of world resources, respect for human rights, and positive assessments of employment practices, advertising, the impact of corporate behaviour on the economy, and connections with the military. In its recent work on Third World Debt, the TCCR lobbied the directors of the banks to establish policies and practices that would ease the burden on these countries.

The Inter-Church Committee for Refugees (ICCR) was established in 1980 in response to the Churches' increasing involvement in refugee concerns at local, national and international levels. Its goals are to support the work of the Churches in the resettlement of refugees. On the political front, ICCR works to develop common Church positions and to lobby the government on Canadian and international refugee policies and programs. With monitoring, publicity and advocacy on the world refugee situation, ICCR seeks to promote policies that attack the root causes that create refugees in the world's crisis areas.

The Interchurch Committee for the Promotion of Justice in Canada (PLURA), formed in 1974, grew out of a common concern to address the causes of poverty in Canada. PLURA makes financial and other resources available for grassroots action programs carried out by groups of low-income persons in Canada. The objectives of the coalition are to empower the poor and to educate the general public on issues relating to poverty, and also to promote changes in social, economic and political reality. Unlike most of the other coalitions, PLURA only operates on a provincial level and has no national staff person coordinating or managing requests for support, or working at a national, more political level.

Finally, Project North, the pre-cursor to the Aboriginal Rights Coalition (ARC), was formed in 1975 in response to the concern of northern aboriginal organizations regarding the non-recognition of aboriginal rights and large scale resource development in the north. The change of name occurred in 1989 when ARC was re-organized to include aboriginal organizations and local committees within its decision-making structures. A key goal in this re-organization was to promote a non-paternalistic manner of Church participation in aboriginal struggles. Education and advocacy on the just settlement of aboriginal land claims, cutbacks to aboriginal programs and related military and environmental concerns are some of the issues in which ARC is involved.

The ecumenical interchurch coalitions collectively have been unique actors in the various struggles for liberation, justice and peace over the past two decades. They have a wealth of information concerning their diverse structures and mandates, and how social change can be effected. With a high level of ecumenical cooperation, Christian denominations have been encouraged to leave aside doctrinal differences and to find a common ground on which people could act. That common ground has been a critique of the socio-economic status quo from the perspective of the poor and the oppressed. The terms "preferential option for the poor" and "peace, justice and the integrity of creation" have expressed this common ground in theological terms.

The coalitions have trained a significant number of committed and highly skilled activists who are able to promote issues of social justice within the Churches and to the larger Canadian public. There are now solidarity networks of Christians committed to social change across Canada and in the Third World. Church leaders have themselves been educated on a large number of specific issues as they have been called to comment on various government policies. The coalitions have provided a growing body of research and analysis that has affected Church institutions and members, as well as other organizations.

The interchurch coalitions have operated as officially sanctioned instruments of the Churches. Their money comes from head office Church budgets; their boards are staffed with denominational representatives, and the policy and action recommendations make their way back into denominational structures. While it is certainly true that many people in the pews might not know of their existence, the coalitions are within the heart of the Church at an ecumenical and denominational level. Although they often function as a gad-fly relative to Church structures and policies, they do so at a very high level. These coalitions are not groups that are on the fringes of the Church; their connections with institutional Church structures have been a distinguishing characteristic of their work.

CURRENT STRUGGLES AND FUTURE CHALLENGES[15]

The current juncture in the history of the work accomplished by the Canadian Churches on social issues requires careful analysis and action. The 1990s is clearly a different era: Canadian society, the global economy and the Churches themselves have changed since the 1970s and 1980s when the coalitions were initially created and developed. The coalitions and the sponsoring Churches began, in 1990-1991, through the Commission on Justice and Peace of the Canadian Council of Churches, to undertake a comprehensive analysis of this new context and an evaluation of how they will proceed with their social mandate. This will determine priorities and perspectives in the years to come. The struggles and challenges before them are considerable.

Certainly the central struggle that faces the coalitions in this decade, one that has its parallel in other progressive circles as well, is how to work for social change in a neoconservative era. The coalitions were founded in a more liberal period when optimism for social change favouring poor and disadvantaged groups was high. The dominant mood was one of a progressive ecumenism at work in the world, healing its hurt and divisiveness.

The 1990s, however, began with a firmly entrenched neoconservative ideology. The Free Trade Agreement, attacks on social programs, and new wars in the Third World demonstrate the aggressiveness of Canadian and global elites to re-establish hegemony. This ideological shift to the right has its reflection in Church structures as well. The Church is not ideologically neutral in these debates on international and national questions; reactionary movements are also organizing within Church structures. The United Church has experienced a serious loss of its funding base as conservative sectors, organizing around the issue of ordaining self-proclaimed gays and lesbians, have been able to challenge a variety of progressive positions that the Church has taken. Within the Roman Catholic Church, the Vatican's strategy has been to replace retiring bishops with conservative appointees thereby diluting episcopal support for Catholic social justice initiatives. An example of this is the reorganization of the structures of the Canadian Catholic Conference of Bishops in 1990 to weaken the advocacy mandate of its Social Affairs Commission.

All the mainline Christian Churches are also in a funding crisis. Ecumenism, particularly social justice ecumenism around issues that are controversial and disturb wealthier Church contributors, is increasingly being seen as a luxury in the face of the very survival of the denomination itself. Have the Churches fallen victim to self-censorship out of fear of a conservative backlash? How bold can any initiative afford to be? In theological terms, how can the Churches and coalitions be prophetic in a neoconservative era? What reforms need to occur *within* the churches to enhance the space that permits progressive public policy work?

A second area of challenge and struggle is the overall balance between the issues with which the coalitions are concerned and the relative lack of cross-fertilization between the coalitions themselves. Historically, most of the coalitions began with a concern for the Third World. The key locus for building a more just world was seen to be abroad, where poverty and injustice were most visible. Since that time, however, some of the coalitions, most notably the ECEJ, have shifted towards domestic concerns because the globalization of political-economic issues has been realized. The work of promoting "justice at home," however, has shaken the powers that be more than the international work. The backlash from the corporate world for the CCCB's "Ethical Reflections on the Economy" in 1983, and the ECEJ's leadership in the anti-Free Trade struggle of the Action Canada Network (then the Pro-Canada Network), was heard loudly and clearly in the offices of the coalitions and Church headquarters.

The issues before the Churches and coalitions are now several: can there be any real "solidarity" with Third World partners without working on Canadian issues or on the Canadian end of Third World issues? In the overall coalition work, what should the proportional balance between domestic and international work be? Knowing that "domestic" work will be controversial and conflictual, what strategies are needed to manage the ensuing conflicts? Linked with this is a growing concern over emerging social issues which are not being sufficiently addressed by the Churches: violence and discrimination directed towards women, the feminization of poverty, environmental degradation, the farm crisis in the West and the devastation experienced by fishing communities in the East, the Middle East, and gay and lesbian issues. The question for the Churches interested in promoting these issues ecumenically will be how to do so in a period of tighter budgets and neoconservative thinking. One of the many questions which need to be asked is whether coalitions should be merged to allow for new coalitions to form.

Because each coalition deals with a specific issue of injustice and oppression, the overall vision and direction is vague. The challenge ahead involves finding how to deepen the analysis of each coalition so that its strategies in a particular area of injustice will contribute to the building of an overall vision.

The Churches and coalitions must now focus on a way to structure their traditional "concern for the poor" in the future. Taking care of the sick and addressing the needs of those who are suffering have been major concerns of the Christian tradition in Canada. The coalition experience, however, moved the Churches beyond traditional charity (building hospitals, schools, etc.) to justice-oriented work with the poor. The term "option for the poor" captured a new sensibility: the Churches were now going to focus on the social, political, and economic structures that oppress people, but a charity-approach to deal with social issues is again on the rise in the 1990s. The cultural drift is towards encouraging volunteerism in projects such as food drives, rather than a structured analysis of the causes of global and domestic hunger. A local Church has much more success organizing a food drive than supporting a campaign to establish a guaranteed annual income. As a result, the question being asked by the Churches and the coalitions is how to deepen and advance a justice-based commitment to the poor in the context of a Canadian Church where the poor are often not present or are invisible. Who is the coalition's constituency: the poor on whose side they struggle, or the Church members who pay the bills but whose interests sometimes conflict with those of the poor?

A means of developing a grassroots constituency for the coalitions requires further reflection in the years to come. Historically, with the exception of the Ten Days and Project Ploughshares, the interchurch coalitions were not set up to have their own grassroots networks; they were to act as think-tanks and social advocates at official levels. Nearly all the coalitions are headquartered in southern Ontario and their resources are generally unilingual. The original assumption was that the individual Churches, through their denominational and regional structures, would follow up the research of the coalitions.

What has occurred, however, is a "hit and miss" pattern of information and action plans making their way back to the people in the pews. Denominations, at times even at head office levels, do not feel plugged into the life of some of the coalitions. The interchurch coalitions are, in fact, the Church's best-kept secret: there is now a pool of competent people working on key issues of our time that many church-goers know almost nothing about.

Should the Churches allow the coalitions to develop grassroots groups within, related to, or outside the Churches? Or should most of them continue as research and advocacy arms operating at official levels of the Church, thereby leaving it to the Churches at denominational levels to do the outreach work to people in the pews? Some voices within the coalition family are arguing that it ought to develop pedagogical and pastoral strategies at the base, as well as to continue its research and lobbying. Many groups throughout Canada are anxious to have the coalitions decentralize their work. Should some of the coalitions establish their offices in other parts of the country?

A further challenge for Church coalitions in the future is how to relate to the broader "social movements." Should coalitions continue to be "ecumenical," that is, to work primarily with Church people, or should they be moving toward an issue-based "solidarity coalition" model?

Historically, who would have thought in the 1950s and 1960s that Protestant and Roman Catholics would be working together in coalitions in the 1970s and 1980s? The coalition model of the last twenty years was that of the "ecumenical Church in the world." But the last twenty years has also witnessed the emergence of a variety of secular community organizations whose structural organization and militancy continue to grow. There is a hesitancy, however, to form alliances and new structures with non-Church groups based on the assumption that in periods of scarce resources, Churches should draw inward. The challenge for Christians in an age of secularization is whether they can adapt to see themselves as salt or spice in the movement for social change, rather than as the main ingredient.

The theological underpinning of Christian involvement in social justice is becoming more important in English Canada. The original genius of the creation of the interchurch coalitions was to overlook traditional divisive theological issues (over church authority, the sacraments, etc.), to allow for work in areas of common social concern. Roman Catholics and Protestants might not have been able to agree on the role and authority of the Pope, for example, but they were able to agree on the importance of working against Pinochet's regime in Chile. Theological issues and the religious motivations inspiring denominational involvement were left aside so that common work could move ahead. Working ecumenically on issues of social justice has instead produced new experiences and new understandings of what it means to be a Christian and what the role of the Church might be in a modern, secular society. But, the coalitions have done very little reflection on the theological relevance of their work.

The liberation theologians emerging from the Third World have been sharper to integrate theological reflection into social analysis and action. They recognize that as people see the world through different eyes and as they act to change the world, their understanding of religious faith also changes. Theological reflection is crucial to their self-understanding and motivation.

In Canada, the neoconservative era has also deepened the wedge between faith and justice work. Progressive people in and on the margins of the Churches are searching for the theological insight into the meaning of their struggles. In the Third World, there are "contextual theology" centres that try to do this. Who will articulate the theological significance of this work in Canada? Where will it be done? How can Christians working for justice be assisted in articulating their theology?

VISIONING DURING A TIME OF *KAIROS*

The word *kairos* is a Greek term that is used in Christian theology to refer to a "crisis time," a time when monumental changes are occurring. Certainly Canada, and indeed, the global political economic landscape is undergoing a "Kairos" moment in the early 1990s. The Canadian Churches, and in particular social justice work, are also in the midst of potentially profound changes. A desire to update and to renew a progressive Church agenda is being met with pressure to dilute the critical perspective of the coalitions.

At the same time, the challenge and inspiration that is coming from a chorus of voices from around the world representing hope and pain is rising: Third World peoples whose fate seems to worsen with each new victory of corporate capitalism; gays and lesbians, people of colour and indigenous people in Canada and abroad whose basic human rights are still being abrogated; workers, fisherpeople, farmers and peasants who have yet to find a place in the New International Order; women who are experiencing the violence of a patriarchal system in many ways; and the environment itself whose silent cry has yet to be heard in many circles.

The progressive wing of the Church is in search of a vision that can motivate and orient the Church's response to these issues in the 1990s. The coalitions were formed in the 1970s when there was a positive climate of opinion, strong leadership and a progressive ecumenical vision. The "social gospel" period of the 1920s and 1930s was a time in Canadian history when another quickening of events produced a Christian passion for social justice. Today, a vision of the future path no longer exists: progressives are somewhat fractured in the Churches because of the existence of neoconservative groups and forces, and because of internal differences over how to handle many of the questions raised above. They increasingly see this period as a time of "wandering in the wilderness," when "resistance" is paramount rather than a time to develop ideas about "social progress." The time is being used to pause and take stock, to focus on asking good questions, and to re-energize by drinking from the wells that will sustain Christians involved in social transformation over the long haul.

NOTES

1. See Dennis Howlett, "Social Movement Coalitions: New Possibilities for Social Change," *Canadian Dimension*, (November/December 1989), p. 41-47.
2. Eric Weingartner, "Canada's Interchurch coalitions," *The Presbyterian Record* (June, 1991), p.29.
3. The bulk of this written material has been referred to in this paper. The biographical details follow in the footnotes.
4. Roger Hutchinson, "Ecumenical Witness in Canada: Social Action Coalitions," *International Review of Mission*, vol. LXXI, no. 283, (1982), p. 344.
5. See Richard Allen, *The Social Passion*, (Toronto: University of Toronto Press, 1973), for an historical analysis of this movement within the Protestant Churches.
6. See Gregory Baum, *Catholics and Canadian Socialism*, (Toronto: James Lorimer and Co, 1980), where he outlines some of the historical roots of progressive Catholics in the 1930s and 1940s.
7. See Joe Mihevc, "The Politicization of the Mennonite Peace Witness in the Twentieth Century," (Ph.D thesis: University of St. Michael's College, 1988), Part Three.
8. For example, Frances Arbour, the first director of the ICCHRLA, writes of the politicization that occurred when she worked as a missionary in Mexico, and its impact on her commitment to human rights advocacy work in Canada. See Frances Arbour, "Canada: The Inter-church Committee on Human Rights in Latin

America," in *Doing Theology in a Divided World,* ed. Virginia Fabella and Sergio Torres, (Maryknoll: Orbis Books, 1985), p. 45-50.

9. The Teachings of Vatican II, (Westminster, Maryland: The Newman Press, 1966), p. 179-210 and 439-556.

10. For documentation and commentary, see: [On Medellin] John Drury (trans.), *Between Honesty and Hope,* (Maryknoll: Orbis Books, 1970) and John Eagleson and Philip Scharper (ed.), *Puebla and Beyond,* (Maryknoll: Orbis Books, 1979).

11. Roger Hutchinson, "Ecumenical Witness in Canada: Social Action Coalitions," p. 344-7.

12. For a comprehensive overview of the work of Ten Days for World Development, see: Rebecca S. Voight Larson, "Ten Days for World Development: A Case Study in Development Education," (Ph.D thesis: University of Calgary, May 1988).

13. There are two theses that have been written on the ECEJ: Dale Hildebrand, "The Inter-church Coalition GATT-FLY, Theological Praxis, and the Option for the Poor: Towards a Canadian Contextual Theology," (M.A. thesis: University of St. Michael's College, 1987), and Brian Ruttan, "The Interchurch Project Gatt-fly 1972-1980: A Reconstruction," (Ph.D. thesis: University of St. Michael's College, 1986).

14. On the Task Force on Churches and Corporate Responsibility, see: Tim Ryan, "The Legitimacy of the Large Modern Business Corporation and the Roman Catholic Social Teaching Tradition," (Ph.D. thesis: University of St. Michael's College, 1983).

15. The following section relies on notes and files of the Commission on Justice and Peace of the Canadian Council of Churches, 1990-91, as it undertook a re-visioning process for the coalitions.

REFERENCES

Allen, Richard. *The Social Passion.* Toronto: University of Toronto Press, 1973.

Arbour, Frances. "Canada: The Inter-church Committee on Human Rights in Latin America," *Doing Theology in a Divided World.* ed. Virginia Fabella and Sergio Torres, Maryknoll: Orbis Books, 1985. p. 45-50.

Baum, Gregory. *Catholics and Canadian Socialism.* Toronto: James Lorimer and Co, 1980.

Drury, John. *Between Honesty and Hope.* (trans.) Maryknoll: Orbis Books, 1970.

Eagleson, John and Philip Scharper (ed.) *Puebla and Beyond.* Maryknoll: Orbis Books, 1979.

Hildebrand, Dale. "The Inter-church Coalition Gatt-fly, Theological Praxis, and the Option for the Poor: Towards a Canadian Contextual Theology," (M.A. thesis: University of St. Michael's College, 1987).

Howlett, Dennis. "Social Movement Coalitions: New Possibilities for Social Change," *Canadian Dimension.* (November/December 1989), p. 41-47.

Hutchinson, Roger. "Ecumenical Witness in Canada: Social Action Coalitions," *International Review of Mission.* vol. LXXI, no. 283.

Mihevc, Joe. "The Politicization of the Mennonite Peace Witness in the Twentieth Century," (Ph.D thesis: University of St. Michael's College, 1988).

Ruttan, Brian. "The Interchurch Project Gatt-fly 1972-1980: A Reconstruction," (Ph.D. thesis: University of St. Michael's College, 1986).

Ryan, Tim. "The Legitimacy of the Large Modern Business Corporation and the Roman Catholic Social Teaching Tradition," (Ph.D. thesis: University of St. Michael's College, 1983).

The Teachings of Vatican II. Westminster, Maryland: The Newman Press, 1966.

Voight Larson, Rebecca S. "Ten Days for World Development: A Case Study in Development Education," (Ph.D thesis: University of Calgary, May 1988).

Weingartner, Eric. "Canada's Interchurch Coalitions," *The Presbyterian Record.* (June, 1991).

Chapter 11

Michael McConkey

Toronto's Neighbourhood Association Movement, in Light of the Artificial Negativity Thesis

Two of the most influential social movements of the past few decades have been the ecology and citizens' movements. From a perspective of social movements rooted in the arena of the city, it is interesting that influential voices in each of these movements have emphasized the neighbourhood as the foundation for building radical social change.[1]

It is argued that, in a modern megalopolis, only the neighbourhood provides the human scale for public life that is necessary to recreate the classical forms and sensibilities of democracy, and hence cultivate the qualities of genuine citizenship in self-empowered, autonomous communities. And at least one major study of neighbourhoods as revolutionary foci can point to a modern example of neighbourhood associations playing a major role in radical political and social change.[2] From the perspective of Toronto, this is particularly interesting because, going back to the late 1960s, this city has had an intriguing history of grassroots politics grounded in neighbourhood associations.

There are some in this city, though, who might suggest that the previously colourful and dynamic history of neighbourhood associations in Toronto is done a disservice by implying any continuity between it and the present state of such associations which are latter portrayed as reactionary and xenophobic. I am inclined to think, however, that this view says more about the critics' unexamined commitment to our dominant ideology — albeit in a mild form. To get a grasp on these issues, before examining the specifics of Toronto's neighbourhood associations and their history, it will be necessary to set the discussion in a theoretical context.

The artificial negativity thesis, developed by a group of neo-Adornian theorists working around the journal *Telos*, offers a helpful context for examining the subject matter of this chapter. The *Telos* group begin where the first generation of critical theorists, known as the Frankfurt School, left off. In the oppressive atmosphere of World War II, the Cold War and U.S. plastic cultural conformism, the first generation wrote of a world where the dialectic of enlightenment had caused the eclipse of reason, in reason's name. The ethical fabric of social life had been undermined by a technocracy that reduced all issues to questions of efficient and effective management. If the end of ideology thesis was valid, it was not because domination and exploitation had been transcended, but because they had become so entirely systematized that one could barely distinguish them from administration. The human world had been degraded to the level of a totally administered society where human ends were determined by technical means, and technical means were rationalized by the privileged knowledge of experts. All space for critical judgment was smothered, and the citizen reduced to the level of a shadowy one dimensional man.[3]

The artificial negativity theorists accept this analysis as far as it goes. However, they argue that even as the Frankfurt School was publishing its famous books advancing this analysis, the analysis itself was rapidly becoming obsolescent. The State-corporate bureaucratic rationality that managed the totally administered society and its one dimensional people was already coming into crisis. Bureaucratic rationality can only act effectively to rationalize society if it has some bearings by which it can be guided. In the totally administered society, the very efficiency of bureaucratic rationality prevents its further effectiveness by denying the peoples' right to voice the frustrations that they feel about their society — including, no doubt, its hyper-rationalizing character. If such frustration is kept out of visible manifestation, due to the bureaucracy's permanent rationalizing of all possible venues of appearance, frustration could ferment undetected, threatening bureaucratic rationality. Without some means to take its bearings on this emergent opposition, the bureaucracy cannot do its job. A second dialectic of reason was developing. As the enlightenment version of rationality, with its promise of human freedom, unfolded into the domination and exploitation of bureaucratic rationality, this new form of reason was developing into a rationality crisis that threatened its self-maintenance as domination and exploitation.

The solution to this rationality crisis has been the development of artificial negativity. By artificially cultivating its own opposition, the bureaucracy could control it, while simultaneously creating a forum for voices of frustration and discontent — hence giving the bureaucracy the bearings it requires to act effectively. The actual funding of oppositional organizations, and the institutionalization of diversity through "affirmative action" (broadly defined), have been the main routes toward creating this artificial negativity.

The problem is that even in attempting to artificially create opposition, the rationalizing bureaucracy cannot help creating conditions that continue to rationalize. This is true not only in that the organizations that are funded, and the institutions into which the diversity is incorporated, are, or must become, counter-bureaucracies — a reflection of what they are supposed to be negating! Even more fundamental is the problem that the very nature of the strategy works against the emergence of the genuine (even if artificially generated) opposition that the rationalizing bureaucracy originally sought to engender.

Control of funding keeps organizations tame, subduing their positions down to the scale and tone necessary for receiving further funding. Affirmative action, even as it institutionalizes diversity and mitigates traditional discrimination, actually weakens potentially organic opposition by incorporating its most articulate voices into the established order *with a vested professional interest in the very inequalities that contributed to their institutional achievement.* Bureaucratic rationality, once it reaches its rationalizing zenith, is thus forever caught in the spiral of a rationality crisis — trying to artificially create negativity, only to have the very instrument of creation turn out to be another rationalizing mechanism.

According to the theorists of the artificial negativity thesis, this crisis presents a unique opportunity. Bureaucratic rationality's out-of-control rationalization continually pushes it further and further in the search for artificial negativity, to the point where it could be in serious danger of actually contributing to a re-opening of the public sphere that it had previously closed down. Hence, it could give rise to the emergence of genuinely organic opposition which will not be a mere appendage of the rationalizing bureaucracy, but one that can offer a self-conscious, systematic opposition to bureaucratic rationality itself. Herein may lie the seeds of a new radical politics for the age of bureaucratic rationality.[4]

While this latter, potentially positive dimension of the artificial negativity thesis will not play a great role in the study that follows, it will be worth bearing in mind at the conclusion.

THE FIRST PHASE: 1960s – 1970s

While neighbourhood associations have probably had a long history in Toronto, it was in the later 1960s that they were suddenly thrust into the historical limelight of the city's politics.[5] These associations, which were to become the subject of much public scrutiny by the early 1970s, had a wide range of orientations, operations and objectives.[6]

The one factor that did galvanize them, though, was a growing discontent with the policies of the long-standing pro-development city council. This council, long dominated by a group known disparagingly as "the old guard," by the mid-1960s was caught up in a major reconstruction of the city of Toronto in line with the newly emerging consumption needs of monopoly capitalism.[7]

This reconstruction included massive "urban renewal" of poorer neighbourhoods ringing the downtown core, and a startling series of proposed expressways, charted to cut through some of the more affluent neighbourhoods, connecting the core with the rapidly expanding suburbs. It was upon these hotly contested terrains that the neighbourhood association movement of the 1960s – 1970s eventually emerged. The history of this movement's emergence begins with the "urban renewal" of east end and semi-ghetto neighbourhoods, described here by Michael Goldrick:

> one important aspect of the function of Toronto's city government in expanding central growth and protecting property values was to 'clean up the slums.' Regent Park was the first project of this nature, and a number of subsequent urban renewal schemes were on the books. In one, Don Mount, working-class residents were turfed out, displaced and processed in a way which provoked the first real resistance to urban renewal. Other neighbourhoods like Don Vale, Kensington, and the most celebrated, Trefann Court, after witnessing the process in earlier projects brought renewal to a halt.[8]

It is true that the struggle around Trefann Court proved to be the central one in the fight by these neighbourhoods against the old guard's urban renewal strategies. And this was not, as the more cynical might suggest, because work in the Trefann Court neighbourhood launched the career of John Sewell, Toronto's most famous reform politician.[9] Nor was it only because the relative, if tentative, success of the Trefann Court challenge helped momentarily to turn the tide against the urban renewal strategy. More fundamental than even this was that it was in the Trefann Court struggle that people first began talking seriously about reorganizing the power relations between the neighbourhoods and city hall.[10] This was the beginning of a brief period in the history of Toronto when notions of radical democracy and decentralisation, championed by many neighbourhood associations, seemed as though they might genuinely be on the public agenda.

Another central moment in the rise of the neighbourhood association movement was the battle to stop the Spadina Expressway, planned to cut through some the more tranquil neighbourhoods of west end Toronto. This battle became the catalyst for the rapid spread of neighbourhood associations across the city. The story of the struggle to stop Spadina is a long and complex one that involved a gradual swelling of neighbourhood opposition throughout the late 1950s and the 1960s, culminating in guerilla street theatre, protest parades along the planned route and an ever increasing confrontation with an implacable municipal administration. The climax was the apparently sham hearings of a vitriolic Metro Transformation Committee.[11]

Like the Trefann Court struggle, the Stop Spadina movement finally succeeded in its immediate aims; and in its insistence on not merely refusing the expressway, but also on calling into question the entire issue of the city's transportation policy, it had an impact far beyond its specific victory. For our purposes, however, what is of even greater interest than these accomplishments is the diverse neighbourhood association movement that this struggle set in motion.[12]

It was the unique character of these new associations that distinguished them as a movement, and made "citizen power" the watchword of both the new associations, and the older ones who were given a new lease on life. An insistence on decentralization of urban planning decisions, and a shift of emphasis from property rights to personal rights — resulting, for example, in the change of many "ratepayers associations" — into "residents' associations," are some of the most important differences that marked the new movement.

Another significant difference was that the new neighbourhood association movement involved the first successful attempt at broad coalition building among Toronto-area neighbourhood associations. The most conspicuous among these was the Confederation of Resident and Ratepayer Associations (CORRA). Founded in 1969, in response to the Spadina struggle, by 1972 CORRA had a total of thirty six member groups. Power in CORRA was firmly placed in the hands of the associations' delegates, and while its primary focus was on city-wide issues, it also fought particular neighbourhood issues when asked for help by local groups. Following the important municipal election of 1972, CORRA tried to take a longer-range perspective, and in 1973 it came up with a proposal for major decentralization in Toronto. Their plan was organized around a prior unification of the various component parts of Metro Toronto, which were then to be broken down into what would be a couple of dozen mini-cities of 100,000 population a piece. Each part would subsequently be divided into very small wards of approximately 20,000 population each.[13]

Another interesting model of coalition building, though quite different in many ways, was the RCO/GRO. Organized in 1969, the Riverdale Community Organization (RCO) was a loose assembly of local groups concerned with the quality of neighbourhood life in Riverdale. In 1972, by way of a community convention, the RCO was re-constituted as the Greater Riverdale Organization (GRO). The RCO/GRO was a smaller, but closer, coalition than CORRA, formed mostly out of small scale associations. Its more important difference, however, was its much more explicit and militant attitude towards power relations with city hall. In the estimation of the Bureau of Municipal Research, the RCO/GRO "set out to organize the people of the area into small groups in order to build a mass-based community power block. The aim was to organize the people so they could win control over their own neighbourhoods, with the ultimate goal of challenging the existing power structure."[14]

This more militant approach to neighbourhood organizing led the RCO/GRO to have a much more tense relationship with the politician-reformers who emerged in the 1969 Toronto municipal election, and who appeared to triumph in the 1972 election. Indeed, the RCO/GRO kept its distance from the fateful '72 election. This was in stark contrast to CORRA, which proved to be perhaps the single most decisive influence in that watershed election.

Under the banner "CO '72" (Community Organizing, 1972,) CORRA set out to organize support for reform candidates across the city's neighbourhoods. These reform candidates themselves had emerged from neighbourhood struggles with developers and city hall. They called for a complete rethinking of city council's uncritical proclivity for rampant development. But more importantly, these reform candidates, and CO '72 that organized locally for them, represented an effort to put city hall back in the hands of local people living in their communities. Or at least this was the widely held perception.

The election in 1972 of a near-majority of reformers on city council, along with a quasi-reform mayor, and its troubled aftermath, is a subject that has been much discussed elsewhere.[15] Here it suffices to say that history proved the initial flush of enthusiasm to have been exceedingly premature. Not only did the reformers divide into a hard-line and not-so-hard-line faction, but even the presumed hard-liners perceptibly moved away from the more radical agenda that they originally seemed to champion.

Consequently, the 1972 election did not turn out to be the watershed in achieving neighbourhood power in city politics that many first perceived it to be. This fact, however, should not lead us to underestimate the significance of this election, for it is clear that the decline of the neighbourhood association movement's days of militancy dates from 1972. The reasons suggested to explain this fact are many, but it is particularly interesting to consider where they relate to the theoretical context provided by the artificial negativity thesis.

Some of the explanations are obvious ones that have to do more with personal psychology than social theory. For instance, there was a certain sigh of relief in some corners — a sense that vigilance could finally be relaxed, now that the citizens' own representatives were nearly a majority on the council. This, combined with a widespread sense of fatigue after so many years of continual organization and activity, persuaded many to quietly recede from public life back into the worlds of personal and family relations.

Another point, raised with particular vigour by Michael Goldrick, is that a general view of the neighbourhood associations as a movement clouds over class distinctions. In his estimation, the middle class neighbourhoods achieved their ameliorative agenda with the reform election, reconstructing Toronto city government on liberal values of pluralism, and protecting the integrity of the local environment. The working class associations, were, however, seen by Goldrick as intent on restructuring city power relations, so the reform election — along with its demobilizing of the middle class neighbourhood associations — left them dissatisfied and isolated.[16]

One can hardly deny the importance of class in the neighbourhood association movement. Indeed, any serious history of this Toronto movement which, incidentally, still remains to be written will have to give considerable thought to the issue of ethnicity and gender, as well as class, both of which are almost completely neglected in the existing literature. Yet Goldrick acknowledges that the RCO/GRO's approach was piece-meal, despite its militant and radical rhetoric, and it is even arguable that the "middle class" CORRA's proposal for Metro Toronto to be constructed as a confederation of mini-cities might have contained the kernel of a more radical vision than that of RCO/GRO. Class does not serve well as an overall explanation for who was demobilizing by the 1972 election, or how and why they were doing it.

From the perspective of artificial negativity, a more intriguing explanation is suggested by the Bureau of Municipal Research: "the election of many of the movement's leaders to City Council deprives ratepayers and citizen groups of some of their best organizers; many other 'activists' were co-opted into the governing system — to serve as aldermanic assistants or on boards and task forces."[17]

In terms of the artificial negativity thesis, the dominant order attempts to bureaucratically rationalize itself by constituting its own opposition, by which to guide its rationalizing bearings. In the process, the opposition becomes but an extension of the bureaucracy it is supposed to be opposing. First, the "radicals" of civil society become the "reformers" of city hall. This is the more obvious and dramatic manifestation, but ultimately it only implicates a dozen-odd people. More important are the more than thirty local planning groups with citizen participation established after the 1972 election. Furthermore, after the elections, citizens sat on a number of municipal organizations: for example, the Planning Board, the Toronto Parking Authority, the Toronto Harbour Commission, the Conservative Authority, and the Toronto Transit Commission. Here, and in the staffing of aldermanic offices, we begin to see a really significant number of "activists" being skimmed off the neighbourhood association movement and "co-opted" as the *internal opposition* of the municipal bureaucracies.

This effect of artificial negativity probably provides the best explanation for the interlude of the late 1970s and the 1980s, in which the neighbourhood association movement seemed to dry up. The best insight into the significance of this interlude can be gathered by examining the evolution of the Bureau of Municipal Research's view regarding the movement, and the latter's place in city politics.

AN INTERLUDE: 1970s – 1980s

The idea has circulated that the Bureau of Municipal Research (BMR) constituted a rare instance of independent and thoughtful research in municipal matters.[18] Perhaps I am missing something here, for although I admit that my knowledge of the Bureau's work does not go much beyond this issue, I am at a complete loss to see this interpretation. BMR membership included a list of who's who in corporate Canada along with their professional service industry of lawyers, consultants and others, a variety of governments — mostly municipal, mostly in southern Ontario — and three labour groups. Although this hardly constitutes a representative list of groups who might be concerned about municipal issues, it does, however, represent who could pay. And given who was paying, one could be forgiven for suspecting that the research produced might be such as to serve the interests of the corporate-municipal bureaucracy's agenda. Indeed, viewed through the lens of artificial negativity, this is precisely what we find with respect to the BMR's treatment of the neighbourhood association movement.

The BMR's first approach to the matter was a study published in 1970.[19] This was an early response to a movement that was just beginning to blossom. Indeed, the research for the study was conducted prior to both the emergence of the influential neighbourhood association confederations and reformism's ground-breaking 1969 election. Though formally a private research institute, the BMR was serving its corporate-government clients as a reconnaissance-branch of the rationalizing bureaucracy; it was keeping them abreast of the latest upsurge of popular resistance.

In this early phase, when the neighbourhood association movement seemed to have explosive potential for militant opposition and radical reconstruction, the BMR adopted a distinct framework of analysis that kept the greatest potential for militancy in theoretical manacles. In this early study, the BMR presented an abstraction called "the City," represented as the agent of the urban common good, which in turn was a concept informed by higher education and higher income. "The City" was contrasted with "the neighbourhoods," based only on narrow self-interest.[20]

This dichotomy was situated in the "liberal democratic theory of politics." "This theory contends, among other things, that citizens should be involved in government, and that this involvement should be grounded in effective communication between the rulers and the ruled."[21] Considering this analysis, it was hardly surprising that the BMR concluded that, while the neighbourhoods should participate in local government, their role should be limited to that of the "junior partner."[22] It is important to note, however, that the BMR supported the neighbourhoods in having this role, albeit junior, in local government. In addition, the BMR did make a point of examining the attitude of the old guard in trying to shut the neighbourhood associations out of effective participation.[23]

If this appears to be merely staking out a moderate middle ground, the BMR might well have been pleased. From the perspective of the artificial negativity thesis, though, something a little more complex appears to be involved. This whole process of incorporating the neighbourhood associations into decision-making, but not allowing them any autonomy, is an expression of artificial negativity. In legitimizing neighbourhood associations as an oppositional "input factor" for the regulatory-planning perspective of "the City," negativity is artificially created; but denying that opposition effective autonomy and continually reducing its dimension to that of occasionally manifesting self-interest denies it the kind of presence that would allow the emergence of an organic opposition. By supporting — as, by the way, the establishment Toronto newspapers did — the fight against arrogant politicians and planners who treat concerned citizens with disdain, the BMR line helped to streamline municipal government and prevent the profound legitimacy crisis that could ensue if such abuse continued. This is one of the roles played by the opposition in artificial negativity: to alert the bureaucracy to irrationalities, allowing them to be rationalized before leading to a serious legitimacy crisis. It is when groups like CORRA or RCO/GRO, in their different ways, go beyond this feedback role and demand actual control that this strategy becomes risky.

This explains how the Toronto newspapers, which initially supported the reform movement following the 1972 reform election, with the rationalizing process in motion, could later turn around and condemn the neighbourhood association movement for its "excesses." [24] The line between an artificial opposition priming the bureaucracy's rationality, and an organic opposition radically challenging the bureaucracy, needed to be firmly drawn. An awareness of this fine balance informs the BMR's 1970 study.

Its next major foray into this territory was produced in the completely changed political atmosphere of 1975. The old guard had been successfully rationalized in the 1969 and 1972 elections, and by 1975, for the reasons discussed above, the neighbourhood association movement seemed to be in decline — or at least, its more radical and militant elements. In this less threatening atmosphere, the BMR seems to have been more willing to acknowledge the sound historical basis for reflecting upon more radical notions of democracy, but it again strictly limited the application of its own analysis to the status quo. [25] Despite the more liberal tone of the second study, the same essential thrust won out: the neighbourhood associations must be given a hearing, but always as the junior partner, deferring to the elected representatives. Indeed, aside from its more temperate tone, and a useful historical overview of the neighbourhood association movement, the second foray differed little from the first. There was, however, one notable difference, reflecting things to come.

The first study strongly urged government not to fund neighbourhood associations: they "cannot function as a form of grass roots participation if they are creations of the local government. If the groups are either the creation of local government or have their operations subsidized by local government, their political autonomy is sacrificed." [26] The crisis that was erupting at a dizzying pace in 1969-70 put a premium on avoiding delegitimizing practices and relationships.

By the more secure days of 1975, however, with the sense of crisis past, the BMR was comfortable proposing a more conventional relationship of artificial negativity: consolidating the bureaucracy's control over its artificial negativity, and ensuring the latter's institutional entrenchment. Now they recommended strategic funding of neighbourhood associations, financial aid to help establish such groups, nominal funding of capital expenses for office set-up, and funding of special projects.[27] While the neighbourhood associations were still not to have any control over the purse-strings, they were to be kept financially afloat insofar as they served as the artificial opposition for the bureaucracy's rational fine-tuning.

This latter approach was more attuned to the standard practices of bureaucratic rationality and artificial negativity. This awareness was reflected in the policy of the Canadian federal government, which since the mid-1960s has always been highly attuned to the needs of artificial negativity, in the years that followed the decline of the neighbourhood association movement's militancy. For instance, the Neighbourhood Improvement Program of the 1970s had citizen participation legislated as a part of its process.[28] Perhaps not coincidentally, in September 1971, Toronto City Council adopted a joint-departmental report advocating a program, also called the Neighbourhood Improvement Program, and which also inserted citizen participation into the process.[29]

Harold Chorney has discussed the intensity of the urban planning profession's concern with artificially creating community in urban neighbourhoods during these years.[30] Though the latter part of the 1970s was perhaps marked by the possibility that a neighbourhood-centred politics was again gaining momentum in Toronto, John Sewell's mayoral election in 1978 exposed this hope to be a mere illusion. While Sewell's early involvement with the struggle of the Trefann Court neighbourhood may have found him aligned with an authentically radical position, already by the beginning of the 1970s he had abandoned this approach in favour of a conventional reformism with all its bureaucratic implications. In addition, Sewell's defeat in the 1980 election, and Art Eggleton's long term as mayor, led to a decade of thorough ideological, political and economic retrenchment. In the 1980s, the developers moved back into city hall; by 1985 the first food banks opened, and the notions of neighbourhood democracy and citizen power seemed a distant memory.

Much of the discourse at a conference on Neighbourhood Planning in November 1984 was reflective of this period. Here, the faithful in attendance were rewarded with such treats as Progressive Conservative liberal-feminist Jane Pepino slamming the reformers for "today's" lack of affordable housing; and consultant Frank Lewinberg's paper, which documented the accelerating growth of isolation and anonymity in Toronto urban life. Rather than connect these tendencies to the rending of the city's social fabric through crime, substance abuse and mental illness, however, Lewinberg cheerily proposed that city planners adapt the housing stock in a manner calculated to entrench this drift to pathological alienation.[31]

The years 1984 to 1988 were widely perceived as a developers' romp gone madly out of control. And, then, in 1988, another alleged reformist city council was elected, and the election itself was the product of organizational support coming from Reform Toronto. Unlike the decentralized, grassroots CO '72, though, Reform Toronto had no particular connection to the neighbourhood association movement, and the 1988 election seems to have had no significant impact upon the state of that movement.

From the late 1980s, and into the early 1990s, however, there did seem to be a resurgent neighbourhood association movement, but one coming from a position that appeared, to its potential allies on the left to be extremely different from that of the first wave of the 1960s-70s. This new neighbourhood association movement, if indeed one was emerging, challenged the cherished assumptions about the public good held dear by the traditional Canadian left — assumptions that gained a powerful new base of life with the surprise election of Ontario's first NDP government in 1990.

THE NEW MOVEMENT: WHITHER THE LEFT?

Contrary to the impression one might get from dwelling upon the battle memoirs of the reform and activist '72ers, neighbourhood associations did not disappear in the mid-1970s. In 1991, a city of Toronto publication indicated that there were over a hundred such associations.[32] Furthermore, while a questionnaire sent out to the neighbourhood associations revealed a decrease in emphasis on issues of decentralized decision-making and neighbourhood power — though by no means a complete absence of such an emphasis — a commitment both to ameliorating city life through neighbourhood activism, and to the elevating of individual citizenship through local political activity, remained influential currents in the neighbourhood associations.

In addition, as the neighbourhood association officers who took the initiative to telephone me in response to the questionnaire more often than not sought to emphasize, a new vitality has been re-entering the neighbourhood associations, giving many of their members a renewed sense of involvement in a movement. Illustrative of this was the particularly strong expression of the president of an east end neighbourhood association who had previously been involved in the founding of CORRA. To her, there was a striking similarity between the prevailing mood and focus then and in 1991.

Such a view was not shared by all on the "left" in Toronto politics. There was a rapidly spreading impression that neighbourhood associations in Toronto were emerging as one of the main obstacles to the construction of welfare State housing, in a city with an indisputable housing crisis. The associations were increasingly characterized as reactionary, parochial and xenophobic: the NIMBY (Not In My Backyard) syndrome as the dark side of populism.

While the general public's impression of the neighbourhood associations' opposition to welfare State housing was, no doubt, exaggerated and oversimplified, in essence it was accurate. Many neighbourhood associations were playing a major role in obstructing the construction of such housing in their communities.[33] The left's reaction, however, was somewhat problematic. It seems to stem from deeply harboured social democratic assumptions that welfare State housing, and its function in a just and egalitarian society, are unambiguously good — an assumption even shared by many who are not social democrats.[34]

When viewed through the lens of the artificial negativity thesis, all this may be seen as quite questionable. Those on the left who supported the neighbourhood associations in the earlier days, with their explicit calls for decentralization of power and radical democracy, seemed to appreciate that significant social change depended upon the autonomy of self-empowered communities. This is in danger of being forgotten by today's left critics of the neighbourhood associations. Indeed, it is surely not too original a notion to suggest that the welfare State cultivates a client mentality, a heteronomous consciousness which stands in direct contradiction with the autonomous consciousness of self-empowerment represented by the neighbourhood associations — at least in principle.[35] Welfare State housing offers the bureaucracy a valuable instrument of rationalization. It may solve the housing problems of some members of the socioeconomic underclass, but it also — and in the long run more importantly — enables the bureaucracy to effectively manage that underclass.

Viewed in this light, the early 1990s neighbourhood association movement does not appear so dramatically different; it was rather part of the Toronto left which was failing to hold a consistent position. When the neighbourhood associations opposed the bureaucratic rationality of the expressway and urban renewal engineers, they were popular heroes. But when they oppose the bureaucratic rationality of welfare State housing's social engineers, they are reactionary populists. The infrastructural engineers and the social engineers, however, only differ in their object of operation, not in their mode of operation, nor its assumptions. The neighbourhood associations have consistently acted to defend their communities from both forms of bureaucratic rationality, whenever it has sought to encroach on the neighbourhood. Theirs has been a consistent, if untheorized, position.[36] And, if consistently pursued in all neighbourhoods, it would indeed rather quickly plunge the bureaucracy into a severe legitimacy crisis. In this context, the neighbourhood associations threaten to transcend their assigned role as artificial negativity, and become an organic opposition to bureaucratic rationality.

Left out in the cold amid all this (quite literally) are the potential tenants of the welfare State housing projects. If the neighbourhood associations' defense of their communities against bureaucratic rationality stunts the bureaucracy's ability to cultivate a client mentality in these potential tenants, it still leaves the latter with no — or only a miserable — roof over their heads, and many of them are children. Yet the only way for these people to develop an autonomous consciousness capable of finding long term solutions, not only for their housing needs, but for all their socially-determined problems, is through the self-empowerment of collective struggle. This requires a wide range of factors to be operating in their favour. One of the most important will be having the political and physical space to build such solutions. If the neighbourhood associations' opposition to welfare State housing is not, as many on the left contend, just a self-satisfied and bigoted abandonment of the socio-economic underclass, but a principled rejection of the community-destructive character of bureaucratic rationality's social engineering ethos — however much this rejection may be based on inadequate understanding, or be poorly articulated — then these same neighbourhoods must also open themselves up to the underclass's efforts at self-empowerment. Indeed, the neighbourhoods and their associations must help to cultivate such initiatives.

Like those before them who opposed the Spadina Expressway, not just by a knee-jerk refusal but by the demand for a complete rethinking of transportation policy, the neighbourhood associations must help develop a social agenda that poses a positive solution to poverty and homelessness, in a democratic society of autonomous communities and neighbourhoods. Only by sharing their neighbourhoods, which they have so valiantly defended from the designs of bureaucrats, can there be a peaceful and just resolution of social and economic inequality, prejudice and oppression, which does not continue to feed the welfare State and its bureaucratic rationality.

This could be a central plank in the political agenda of the 1990s in Toronto. If the left shares in creating this agenda, joining the neighbourhood associations in a creative spirit, and contributes to the building of neighbourhood initiatives that open space for the underclass's self-empowerment — and, indeed, puts this issue explicitly front and centre in all debate about social-welfare housing — it may yet play a constructive role. However, a left whose only response to the neighbourhood association movement's struggle against social welfare-housing is to derisively dismiss it with standard leftist excuses of class exclusivity and false consciousness will have no constructive role to play. The choice is a critical one.

NOTES

1. Robert Fisher, *Let the People Decide: A History of Neighbourhood Organizing in America* (Boston: Hall, 1984); Milton Kotler, Neighbourhood Government; Murray Bookchin, *The Rise of Urbanization and the Decline of Citizenship* (San Francisco: Sierra Club Books, 1987); Murray Bookchin, *Urbanization Without Cities*, (Montreal: Black Rose Books, 1992), Readings in Libertarian Municipalism, (eds.) M. Bookchin and J. Biehl (Burlington, Vt.: Social Ecology Project, 1991).
2. Manuel Castells, *The City and the Grassroots* (Berkeley, Calif.: University of California Press, 1983), part 5.
3. For an introduction into this rich tradition of critical theory: *The Essential Frankfurt School Reader*, (eds.) Andrew Arato & Eike Gebhardt (New York: Continuum, 1982); Max Horkheimer & Theodor W. Adorno, *Dialectic of Enlightenment*, trans. John Cumming, (New York: Continuum, 1986 [orig. 1944]); Max Horkheimer, Eclipse of Reason (New York Continuum, 1974 [orig. 1947]); and Herbert Marcuse, *One Dimensional Man* (Boston: Beacon Press, 1964).
4. On artificial negativity, see Paul Piccone, General Introduction, *The Essential Frankfurt School Reader* op.cit.; "The Changing Function of Critical Theory," New

German Critique, 12, Fall 1977; and "The Crisis of One-Dimensionality," *Telos*, 35, Spring 1978; and also Tim Luke, "Culture and Politics in the Age of Artificial Negativity," *Telos*, 35, Spring 1978.

5. On the early history of the neighbourhood associations, at this point usually restricted to ratepayers, c.f. Jim Lemon, "Toronto: Is it a Model for Urban Life and Citizen Participation," *Community Participation and the Spatial Order of the City*, (ed.) D. Ley (Vancouver: Tantalus Research, 1974), p. 47.

6. Insights into some of the more prominent associations of the period, including the Rosedale Ratepayers' Association, the Great Riverdale Organization, the Confederation of Residents and Ratepayers Associations, and the Trefann Court Residents' Association, can be sampled in *Citizen Participation: Views and Alternatives*, (eds.) F.J. Frisken and H.P.M. Homenuck (Toronto: York University, Urban Studies Program, 1972).

7. A good discussion of these issues can be found in Michael Goldrick, "The Anatomy of Urban Reform in Toronto," *The City and Radical Social Change* (ed.) D. Roussopoulos (Montreal: Black Rose, 1982). pp. 262-67.

8. Goldrick, p. 268.

9. Trefann Court was part of Toronto's legendary Cabbage Town district. It was one of the first to resist urban renewal, in the mid-1960s, demanding a resident-guided process that would ensure the security of their community. Finally, Toronto city council supported their claim on 1969. And in 1971 Trefann Court won its case in having redevelopment funded in compliance with their own plan for the neighbourhood. Ironically, though, their community improvement plan has fuelled gentrification in the neighbourhood. Apparently, control over the planning process alone was not a radical enough claim. For John Sewell's account of his earlier years organizing in the Trefann Court neighbourhood, and how this led directly to his first election campaign, c.f., *Up against City Hall* (Toronto: James Lewis and Samuel, 1972).

10. On the emerging radical localism of the Trefann Court community, c.f. Graham Fraser, *Fighting Back: Urban Renewal in Trefann Court* (Toronto: Hakkert, 1972). pp. 255-63.

11. The roots of the Spadina Expressway dispute can be traced back to 1948, and various degrees of opposition took shape in the late 50s and early 60s. It was only in 1969, though, that a concerted campaign was undertaken. The fierce struggle over the expressway was finally defused in June 1971 — despite a certain length of it being built — when the new Ontario Premier Bill Davis took the pragmatic step of siding with the popular opposition, against Metropolitan Toronto. Lemon, pp. 45-46.

12. Lemon, p. 48.

13. On CORRA generally, c.f., Lemon, pp. 48-49. On the mini-cities scheme particularly, c.f. Jim Lemon, "CORRA: Its views on power in local communities," City Hall, July 27, 1973, pp. 106-07. (Future references to Lemon in these notes continue to refer to the former source.)

14. Bureau of Municipal Research (hereafter, BMR) "Citizen Participation in Metro Toronto: Climate for Cooperation ?" *Civic Affairs*, January 1975, p. 19. Two students of the period, who were also personally involved with these events, generally concur with this assessment of the RCO/GRO's objectives, though the one writing from the greater temporal distance on the period concludes that the association's tactical approach proved ultimately to be too piece-meal and short term, failing to focus attention beyond the immediate cause of people's problems. Lemon, p. 50 and Goldrick, p. 270. It is the latter who offers the critique. The best source on the RCO/GRO is the work of its principle organizer, Don Keating: *The Power to Make it Happen* (Toronto: Greentree, 1977); *The Greater Riverdale Organization: Reflections on the Project as a Model for Community Development* (Toronto: Office of Community Consultation, Ministry of Community and Social Services, 1974); and "Looking Back at Community Organizing," *City Magazine*, 3(6), July 1978, pp. 36-43.

15. Goldrick discusses the fragmentation of the '72ers, pp. 274 ff. The drift of the hardliners from radicalism to conventional reformism is charted in the career

evolution of their most prominent member: Bill Freeman, "John Sewell and the New Urban Reformers Come to Power," *The City and Radical Social Change*, (ed.) D. Roussopoulos (Montreal: Black Rose, 1982) Also of interest for this period, J. Caufield, *The Tiny Perfect Major* (Toronto: James Lorimer and Co., 1974).

16. Goldrick, pp. 279-80.
17. BMR, p. 21.
18. Rob Ferguson, "The Demise of the Bureau of Municipal Research," *City Magazine*, 7(1), Fall 1984.
19. BMR, "Neighbourhood Participation in Local Government," Civic Affairs, January 1970. This was a study responding directly to the sense of crisis stirred by the neighbourhood association movement, arguing that neighbourhood groups should be made part of local government's consultative process, but disabused of any ideas about neighbourhood self-government. The neighbourhoods were to be junior partners to the City, with its more expansive and integrated perpsective.
20. Ibid, pp. 6-9.
21. Ibid, p. 5.
22. Ibid, pp. 13-14.
23. Ibid, p. 11.
24. "A Matter of Proportion," Toronto Globe, August 16, 1974; and "Citizen Protest is Good — Up to a Point," Toronto Star, August 16, 1974.
25. BMR, "Citizen Participation... p. 7.
26. BMR, "Neighbourhood... p. 13.
27. BMR, "Citizen Participation... p. 57.
28. David Ley, "The Neighbourhood Movement in a Canadian City," *Urban Resources*, 1(3), Winter 1984, p. 24.
29. *City Council Minutes*, Toronto, 1971, vol.2, pp. 283ff, and 1972, vol.2, pp. 239ff.
30. Harold Chorney, "A Critical Theory of Urban Public Policy," City Magazine, 6(2), October 1983, pp. 27-32. In fact, Chorney's argument, here, very much reflects the artificial negativity thesis: not only does he argue that planners had to "artificially engender community spirit," but he also points out that this artificial engendering carries the very real danger of re-cultivating a kind of urban-based radical politics that had been eradicated decades earlier. On this latter point, see also Harold Chorney, "Amnesia, Integration and Repression: The Roots of Canadian Urban Political Culture," *Urbanization and Urban Planning in Capitalist Society* (eds.) M. Dear and A.J. Scott (London: Methuen, 1981).
31. *Toronto Neighbourhoods: The Next Ten Years, Papers Delivered at the Neighbourhood Planning Conference*, Toronto, November 16-17, 1984. (Toronto: City of Toronto Planning and Development Department, June, 1985). pp. 2 and 36-37, respectively.
32. "Residents and Ratepayers Association Alpha-Listing for the Date Ending 07/24/91," available from the Information Desk, City Hall, Toronto.
33. Kate Lazier, "Social Housing Bashed," *Now*, October 10-16, 1991, p. 19.
34. I use the term "welfare State housing" because I believe it is more accurate, and it allows me to avoid the conventional phrase "social housing" which partakes of the standard social democratic assumption in its conceptual collapsing of society into the (welfare) State.
35. These ideas have been explored by John McKnight, "Regenerating Community," *Social Policy*, 17(3), Winter 1987; and "Professionalized Service and Disabling Help," *Disabling Professions* (London: Marion Boyars, 1977). Also, in the latter, see the introductory essay, of the same title, by Ivan Illich.
36. It cannot be denied that the complex nature of these positions have opened the neighbourhood associations to some bigoted discourse in denouncing welfare State housing. I know of no evidence, however, that this discourse is not just the misguided and desperate groping for articulation of opposition to a serious threat to the community amid a profoundly anti-intellectual culture which gives most people few analytical or critical skills with regard to complicated social issues.

REFERENCES

"A Matter of Proportion," *Toronto Globe and Mail.* August 16, 1974.

"Citizen Protest is Good — Up to a Point," *Toronto Star.* August 16, 1974.

Arato, Andrew and Eike Gebhardt (eds.) *The Essential Frankfurt School Reader.* New York: Continuum, 1982.

Bookchin, M. and J. Biehl (eds.) *Readings in Libertarian Municipalism.* Burlington, Vt.: Social Ecology Project, 1991.

Bookchin, Murray. *The Rise of Urbanization and the Decline of Citizenship.* San Francisco: Sierra Club Books, 1987.

Bookchin, Murray. *Urbanization Without Cities: The Rise and Decline of Citizenship.* Montreal: Black Rose Books, 1992.

Bureau of Municipal Research. "Neighbourhood Participation in Local Government," *Civic Affairs.* January 1970.

Bureau of Municipal Research. "Citizen Participation in Metro Toronto: Climate for Cooperation ?" *Civic Affairs.* January 1975.

Castells, Manuel. *The City and the Grassroots.* Berkeley, Calif.: University of California Press, 1983.

Caufield, J. *The Tiny Perfect Major.* Toronto: James Lorimer and Company, 1974.

Chorney, Harold. "Amnesia, Integration and Repression: The Roots of Canadian Urban Political Culture," *Urbanization and Urban Planning in Capitalist Society.* M. Dear and A.J. Scott (eds.) London: Methuen, 1981.

Chorney, Harold. "A Critical Theory of Urban Public Policy," *City Magazine.* 6(2), October 1983. pp. 27-32.

City Council Minutes. Toronto, 1971, vol.2, pp. 283ff.

City Council Minutes. Toronto, 1972, vol.2, pp. 239ff.

Ferguson, Rob. "The Demise of the Bureau of Municipal Research," *City Magazine.* 7(1), Fall 1984.

Fisher, Robert. *Let the People Decide: A History of Neighbourhood Organizing in America.* Boston: Hall, 1984.

Fraser, Graham. *Fighting Back: Urban Renewal in Trefann Court.* Toronto: Hakkert, 1972.

Freeman, Bill. "John Sewell and the New Urban Reformers Come to Power," *The City and Radical Social Change.* D. Roussopoulos (ed.) Montreal: Black Rose Books, 1982.

Frisken, F.J. and H.P.M. Homenuck (eds.) *Citizen Participation: Views and Alternatives.* Toronto: York University, Urban Studies Program, 1972.

Goldrick, Michael. "The Anatomy of Urban Reform in Toronto," *The City and Radical Social Change.* D. Roussopoulos (ed.) Montreal: Black Rose Books, 1982.

Horkheimer, Max and Theodor W. Adorno. *Dialectic of Enlightenment.* (trans. John Cumming) New York: Continuum, 1986 [orig. 1944].

Horkheirmer, Max. *Eclipse of Reason.* New York: Continuum, 1974. [orig. 1947].

Keating, Don. "Looking Back at Community Organizing," *City Magazine.* 3(6), July 1978. pp. 36-43.

Keating, Don. *The Greater Riverdale Organization: Reflections on the Project as a Model for Community Development.* Toronto: Office of Community Consultation, Ministry of Community and Social Services, 1974.

Keating, Don. *The Power to Make it Happen.* Toronto: Greentree, 1977.

Kotler, Milton. *Neighbourhood Government.* Indianapolis: Bob Merril, 1969.

Lazier, Kate. "Social Housing Bashed," *Now.* October 10-16, 1991.

Lemon, Jim. "CORRA: Its views on power in local communities," *City Hall.* July 27, 1973.

Lemon, Jim. "Toronto: Is it a Model for Urban Life and Citizen Participation," *Community Participation and the Spatial Order of the City.* D. Ley (ed.) Vancouver: Tantalus Research, 1974.

Ley, David. "The Neighbourhood Movement in a Canadian City," *Urban Resources.* 1(3), Winter 1984.

Luke, Tim. "Culture and Politics in the Age of Artificial Negativity," *Telos.* 35, Spring 1978.

Marcuse, Herbert. *One Dimensional Man.* Boston: Beacon Press, 1964.

McKnight, John. "Professionalized Service and Disabling Help," *Disabling Professions.* London: Marion Boyars, 1977.

McKnight, John. "Regenerating Community," *Social Policy.* 17(3), Winter 1987.

Piccone, Paul. "The Crisis of One-Dimensionality," *Telos.* 35, Spring 1978.

Piccone, Paul. "The Changing Function of Critical Theory," *New German Critique.* 12, Fall 1977.

Sewell, John. *Up Against City Hall.* Toronto: James Lewis and Samuel, 1972.

Toronto Neighbourhoods: *The Next Ten Years,* Papers Delivered at the Neighbourhood Planning Conference, Toronto, November 16-17, 1984. (Toronto: City of Toronto Planning and Development Department, June, 1985). pp. 2 and 36-37, respectively.

Chapter 12

Henri Lustiger-Thaler

POLITICAL CULTURE AND THE POLITICS OF BRICOLAGE: THE CASE OF MONTRÉAL

The new social movements literature has drawn our attention to the fact that the relationship between grassroots groups and political parties has come undone. One effect of this has been a protracted search on the part of the State for efficient self-monitoring mechanisms within civil society. The aim is to create a controlled kind of politics, regulating its implosion into areas of social life. In so doing, the modern State has a unique role in depoliticizing conflict as part of a process of political maintenance and stability, predicated on social regulation.

When, moreover, politics are in general seen as untrustworthy, the State seeks to "normalize" the noninstitutional (non-party) expressions of opinion represented by the new social movements. Examples abound of the attribution of carefully constructed statuses to once fairly marginalized political concerns; at the same time, those that can not easily be accorded such status are placed beyond the pale of the conventional political sphere, progressively isolated from the general public, and stigmatized as "single issue" concerns. Indeed, even before this strategic articulation of community politics with State apparatuses (through public consultation, joint commissions, round-tables, etc.), social movements, through their desire for status, often bought into a process of rationalization which was clearly removed from their control. This "buying in" occurred within the context of an increasing fiscal, social, political and increasingly ecological "crisis of crisis management."[1] It also reflects, in a more complex fashion, the State's decreasing ability fully to manage its own legitimation and distributive functions. The modern State relies more and more on community initiatives to deal with innovation, initiatives which it then undermines through its own bureaucratic procedures, which in turn deepens the crisis. The State-social movement relationship that emerges out of these processes takes on a logic that I refer to, in the urban context, as a "politics of bricolage."[2]

In this new kind of urban politics, technocrats adopt a guise of accountability whilst actually creating possibilities for the State to determine the political choices which people make in a variety of formerly "private" concerns. These choices, filtered through State bureaucracies, are not meant to transform the deeper logic of the State system, but only to deal with its immediate reproductive concerns. The critical relationship between democracy and vested power becomes decoupled, and an abstract representational "democracy" occupies an increasingly disjointed centre stage.

What does this relationship between the new politics and the crisis-prone structures of State institutions mean? As a formal system is challenged by new social and political demands, hegemonic forms of political culture have emerged to shape the claims of social movements in support of what is deemed to be the only workable democracy.[3] In this representational process, citizens are liberally accorded *expression*, rather than power. The actual demands of particular citizens are silenced, while "citizens" (in general) appear to be "listened to," an obliging trope for political expediency.

THE POLITICAL ECONOMY OF CITIES

Whilst the State and the technocratic designs of New Class interests are central to the types of political-cultural mutations described above, the restructuring effects of capital also require attention.[4] The recent work of David Harvey is relevant here.[5] For Harvey, the postmodern turn has not broken in the slightest the growth imperative of capital. He inquires whether the momentous changes which have occurred in Western societies since the 1972 recession indicate a postcapitalist society or only the latest transformation within capitalism itself, reflected in a cultural movement, postmodernism. In his analysis, new growth strategies have emerged as a response to the latest periodic crisis of capital. They have spawned the phenomena of sub-contracting, service production and neo-entrepreneurialist ideologies, which neatly fit the postmodern penchant for a "pluralizing" of realities. These have in turn reproduced the relocations, deskilling and speed-ups which characterize modern globalization and the realization of value. As the Fordist-Keynesian compromise wilted under recurring bouts of inflation and recession, corporatist forms of mediation gave way to flexible short-term growth strategies, linked to the increased autonomy of finance capital. This has undone fragile and momentary neo-corporatist settlements between organized labour, capital and the State. As production is spread across the globe through deregulation, a heightened individualism emerges as a political credo. People feel less secure about the capacity of traditional organizations on the left to represent their interests while disparity between classes actually becomes more accentuated through the growth of an urban underclass.[6]

Cities, the locus for much of this activity, are experiencing the full effects of the contradiction between globalization and localization. A political measure of this is a decline in the democratic appeal and legitimacy of municipal institutions, an example of B. Jessop's admonition that the capitalist economy and its democratic shell have begun to part company.[7] Deepening Jessop's analysis, M. Gottdiener argues that the local State, in particular, may not be as necessary to capital as we have been led to believe, with local regulation now being carried out by capital itself.[8] Referring to American cities, Gottdiener contends that the retreat of the welfare State, through local privatization, means that capital has accepted the responsibility for uneven urban development and what it holds in store for the urban labour force.

This extends to a new propensity for workers to willingly privatize their consumption through arranging with employers the cost of health care and privatized school schemes, rather than pushing for a socialization of labour's costs of reproduction. In Québec and Montréal, as the provincial and local States rid themselves of the cost sharing through privatization, capital has increasingly inserted itself (through sub-contracting service delivery) into areas of public provision that were once ostensibly under democratic control. Privatization thus becomes a complex political process, reinforced by local political cultures, wherein significant resources and decision making authority are delegated to private business interests.[9]

In this shift from public responsibility to private sector initiative, regulation through joint capital and State ventures has become a central feature of modern urban economies. In the case of Montréal, this includes the pursuit of a high-tech aero-spatial sector, whilst comparatively paltry sums are invested in local employment development plans or in combating the city's growing list of social despairs. As public provision becomes scarcer, urban movements mobilize on a variety of issues. These emerge as attempts to "rearticulate" the public and the private through forms of politics based on consumption, and increasingly once more on production. What these movements are pitted against, however, is not merely these condensed urban expressions of the globalization of capital and its "postmodern disjointedness," but also the normalizing "flexible politics" outlined above, which confront their demands with a discourse that conflates "decentralization" with "efficiency" and cost reduction.[10]

FROM POLITICAL ECONOMY TO POLITICAL CULTURE: THE CASE OF MONTRÉAL

Modern cities exist in a global economy based on periodic crises in profitability, and marked by a constant search for disciplined local labour pools. As First World economies such as Canada seek international competitiveness by relying on the low end of the non-unionized wage scale, the quality of life in the city drops correspondingly. Montréal is an urban centre in visible decline, saddled with an aging industrial infrastructure and an expanding cheap labour service sector.[11] The abandonment of fixed capital in manufacturing plants, offices, etc., throughout the seventies and eighties, followed a now classic North American pattern of dein-dustrialization. The process of restructuring, however, occurred at a slower and more politically unusual pace in Montréal due to the unique conjuncture of political forces at work.

Job creation has historically had a low priority for city administrators. Plant closures became commonplace in Montréal, particularly from 1961 to 1981, as traditional industries disappeared in favour of capital-intensive sectors. Industries which have returned, since the early eighties, have been attracted to the more favourable conditions in the new "outer cities" or self-sufficient suburbs surrounding the island. This form of capital restructuring has its counterpart in the growth of the local State and local capital interests. The shift in the structure of capital investment laid the groundwork for the emergence of a powerful developer's lobby group that found a voice at City Hall, in the last years of the Civic Party regime, and in the subsequent Montréal Citizens Movement administration.

The Quiet Revolution also played an important part in creating the political and social context in which Montréal now finds itself. Prior to the sixties, municipal administrations in Montréal were composed exclusively of property owners. Universal suffrage came as late as 1968. A political culture of "administering the city," rather than the city as a political arena, has deep roots. The Civic Action League, created in 1954 (which ruled until 1986 under Jean Drapeau) was made up mostly of small businessmen. These inauspicious beginnings are ensconced within the city's Charter, which specifically refers to an administering body rather than a political entity.

Hence from the early seventies onwards reform of the Municipal Charter became a significant issue. This reform arrived slowly, for a number of reasons. Principally, the modernization of the Québec State and its educational, health and public service systems was given priority over reforming municipal structures, however dysfunctional they were for the longer term interests of the provincial State. But also, throughout the sixties and seventies municipal elites and their acolytes had little interest in seeing their fiefdoms rocked by modernizers. The most significant urban reforms came as a response to the crisis produced by the demise of the provincial Keynesian welfare State in the early seventies. To properly manage these contradictions within the increased complexity of the Québec State system localities became an attractive terrain for provincial strategies. The reforms which were to structure local power in Montréal grew out of a process of provincial crisis management. This was aided by a regionalist politics, of the mid to late seventies, in which a social democratic model of State building was actively pursued by the Parti Québecois.

Provincial reforms in the late seventies (particularly Bill 105 regarding democratic procedure at City Hall) were a sort of basic map of the shape and contours of the emerging local State. Policies of decentralization regarding land-use planning and tax reform were a watershed.[12] Local governments could now decide upon the services needed in their constituencies, and how to find the monies to underwrite them. This reform had two effects; a) it unburdened the provincial State from equalizing municipal services throughout Québec (by according fiscal responsibility to municipalities); b) it created a basis for the development of a specifically urban politics and urban social movements.[13]

THE MONTRÉAL CITIZENS MOVEMENT: FROM A NEW SOCIAL MOVEMENT BASE TO URBAN GATE-KEEPERS

The creation of the Montréal Citizens Movement(MCM) in 1974 has had a major effect on the way politics is carried out in Montréal. The MCM came out of a period of political mobilization which has been described as the summit of citizen militancy. Against a background of archaic practices at City Hall, wherein an elected mayor presided with almost no accountability, much was stirring in the neighbourhoods. Citizens' committees emerging from Saint Henri, Little Burgundy, Mercier, Saint Jacques, Milton Park and other economically depressed inner-city regions acquired significant expertise and visibility in the sixties, addressing issues such as health and housing. The first linking of these activities with municipal politics occurred through the CSN's political action committees (CAP), created in 1968. In 1970 the CAPs formed an urban political party called the Front d'action politique (FRAP). The enactment of the War Measures Act by the Federal State during the FLQ crisis put an abrupt end to this party.[14]

The next progressive political initiative in Montréal was the MCM, founded in May 1974. It developed principally from the Montréal Inter-Trade Union Council (composed of ex-FRAP members and members of Montréal-based unions) and the Progressive Urban Movement (PUM), a coalition of left anglophone intellectuals and community organizers. The Parti Québecois, as well as the flagging Québec NDP, joined in this new political initiative in the winter preceding the official founding of the MCM.

The MCM manifesto of 1974 was written very much in the spirit of the community groups which animated the membership. Emphasis was placed upon the importance of establishing neighbourhood councils with a wide mandate for decision-making. Other points in the manifesto proposed radical alternatives to problems of housing, transportation, leisure, health and local employment. The manifesto put forward a decided challenge to the then ruling party, through its focus on decentralization. Stephen Schecter has presented a compelling analysis of the party at its inception, pointing to its many political anomalies; but in spite of these contradictions the MCM won 45.3% of the popular vote in 1974, capturing 18 out of 45 seats.[15] The surprisingly high number of elected MCM councillors created a situation wherein these elected members were stronger in City Council than their real base in the neighbourhoods. The relationship between "parliamentary" and "extra-parliamentary" struggle, one which the MCM prided itself on, was confounded by this rapidly acquired representative weight.

The extra-parliamentary side of the MCM suffered as a result. Where extra-parliamentary action was pursued, the inexperience of the youth wing of the MCM was all too evident. The ultimate contradiction of the party, however, lay in its fundamental orientation. This manifested itself in an inability to define a clear line of political development, hampering whatever progress was possible through extra-parliamentary action. Indeed, the socialist bias of the activists in the MCM was becoming more and more difficult to articulate as they felt increasingly uncomfortable in seeking popular mobilization for a party whose leadership displayed a growing social democratic and 'New Class' orientation.

If the seventies offered a helpful ideological terrain for the MCM, the eighties, after successive gains and losses at the ballot box, did so considerably less. As the possibility of assuming power became a reality, the MCM leadership turned to nurturing an image of itself as a stable and pragmatic opposition party. This meant watering down, to the point of becoming unrecognisable, its remaining left proclivities. The strategy of the party during this period was to establish a high degree of legitimacy amongst influential circles within the business sector, whilst maintaining their links with community groups.

The issue of local economic development was a viable and opportune vehicle for establishing a new rapport with several key community groups that had been ignored by the Civic Party. Alienation from the corridors of City Hall was, however, also felt by developer lobby groups. This changed in the last few years of Civic Party rule, but only on an ad hoc basis. Developers continually expressed the need for more consultation with the Executive Committee on such matters as land planning and site locations. The distrust that Jean Drapeau, who was the Mayor at that time, harboured for the developers' lobby gave the MCM some golden opportunities to pursue alliances with them.

The most telling change in the MCM (prefiguring its conduct in power) was the distance it created between its populist party program and its practices in the period leading up to the 1986 elections. The rhetoric of democratization was central to the task of reorganizing City Hall to fit the plans of the new administration; a plethora of mechanisms (standing commissions, District Advisory Committees) was set up which would facilitate the broad consultative process that the MCM placed at the core of its new participatory design. In reality, however, the discourse of democracy became a screen for a merging of power centres around the Executive Committee. Rather than promoting more transparency in city government, the MCM became the purveyor of a centralist doctrine of rule.

The newly elected party in 1986 initially received a good deal of critical support from grassroots groups, the left and even the mainstream press in Montréal. The MCM's honeymoon lasted into the following year. Jean François Léonard and Jacques Léveillée assessed the performance of the party in terms of the remarkable impact it had on changing alliances in municipal politics generally, and urban social movements in particular. They argued that with the Civic Party in disarray, there was now little opposition, with the exception of groups concentrated around housing issues, particularly the then developing Overdale fiasco.[16] This underscored an emerging new "pragmatic" ideology amongst some community groups. The new pragmatists included the emerging community development corporations, quality of life associations and even locally based unions. The strategy of the pragmatists was to participate in the unfolding game, filling the public spaces opened by the new promise of "consultation."

Since that assessment, much has occurred between the grassroots groups and the city. The new pragmatism underscored a more profound transformation within community groups themselves, as they took on an increasing service role within the context of declining service provision by local and provincial State apparatuses. The client relationship which developed between grassroots groups and the city, after 1986, parallels the 'clientelizing' by community groups of their own grassroots constituents. Due to the increased scarcity of services, a good many community groups in Montréal are increasingly caught up in a logic of "delivering the goods." In several cases this has overshadowed the social or political vocation that was animated their original raison-d'être.[17] Aside from the general disorganization of left political opposition, this sea-change in the internal rationale of grassroots groups also helps explain the cautious hand played by urban social movements in the 1990 municipal election. This election saw the MCM returned to power in another landslide victory.

NEW POLITICS, OLD POLITICS AND THE URBAN FACTOR

The process of building a new oppositional political voice in Montréal took many turns. Dissent within the MCM itself was the first real source of an emerging opposition.[18] Due to a failed attempt to form a coalition of interests, two opposition parties emerged on the left: the Democratic Coalition of Montréal (DCM), formed in 1989, and the first green municipal party in Canada, Ecology Montréal (EM), which was formally established in April 1990. The DCM consisted of four dissident councillors who rejected the centralist trend in the MCM and demanded openness at City Hall, in effect advocating a return to the principles which had originally animated the MCM. Ecology Montréal was formed by a mixed group of social ecologists and ecofeminists determined to keep urban environmental issues and their social consequences on centre stage during the election period. From the outset EM was very much of a "reluctant party,"[19] concerned with establishing a new set of ethical and "green" guidelines for engaging in municipal politics. Many activists in Ecology Montréal were in one way or another linked to federal and provincial Green Party networks.[20]

Relations between the DCM and EM were strained from the start, given the experience of the councillors and the relative inexperience of the ecology party members. Both parties, however, also emerged in a political climate that was generally unreceptive to oppositional politics. There was the lingering sense, amongst many individuals and urban movements, that the MCM had not yet exhausted its democratic potential, or at the very least that it was more in the interest of grassroots groups to be on the inside than the outside. This was evident in the lack of success that the DCM had in attracting the remaining left within the MCM. In "progressive districts," with histories of militant community organization, coalitions of popular groups demanded that their MCM councillor remain loyal to the party.

The dynamic within EM was of a different nature. The party was concerned with developing an ecological way of pursuing politics. With some exceptions, its activists largely avoided considerations of a broader left program. Indeed, it was not even clear that the larger Québec environmental movement(s) supported the EM initiative. Certainly one element that did not help was the simple fact that EM was overwhelmingly anglophone, and many of its activists had little contact with francophone environmental organizations. Indeed, the "old politics" of linguistic divisiveness peculiar to Québec was hardly absent from the "new politics" in Montréal. Meanwhile, grassroots groups and urban social movements generally kept a fair distance from both of the two new left of centre parties.

The November 1990 election period plainly mirrored this fragmented political scene, wherein the DCM represented a voice on the social democratic/left, EM a collection of ecological principles (of a left temperament), while urban social movements were locked into a wait-and-see strategy.[21] Added to this urban realpolitik was the groundswell of democratic discourse that the MCM was able to muster in support of its position in most debates. The discourse of democracy and decentralization that the MCM had historically nurtured was now worth its weight in gold, as it surreptitiously became the calling card of their new political and technocratic interests. The MCM clearly appealed to a wider political spectrum than all the other parties combined. Its hegemonic positioning effectively marginalized these other parties into appearing to be single issue organizations, or simply parties proposing an unworkable form of politics. Through these means, the MCM was able to immobilize a genuine movement of protest, whilst securing its own public perception as pragmatic urban democrats.

In order not to split the opposition vote, a nonaggression pact was signed by the two left of centre parties. It was largely successful in equally dividing fifty one districts between them. The DCM and EM also included in their pact a promise not to run against the remaining two left candidates within the MCM. The 1990 election results saw three DCM candidates return to City Hall.[22] No one was elected from EM, although two candidates took 19.5% and 23% of the popular vote in their respective districts. All this unfolded in a general public climate that produced the lowest voter turnout in twenty-five years.[23]

The elections accorded the MCM the opportunity to further refine its hold on centre ground, largely due to the fragmented organization of the opposing political discourses. Its advocacy of citizen "participation" quietly coded the call for decentralization with power as an unrealistic endeavour. The practice of the MCM accords well with what the Frankfurt School theorist, Leo Lowenthal, has described as "psychoanalysis in reverse:" that is, it instils a public pathology that confirms individuals as incapable of governing their own affairs.[24] This type of paternalism is implied in a negative representation of the political options offered by the opposition, a representation on which the MCM depends for its own claim to be practising "democracy." Indeed, if the fragmented discourse of the opposition had not existed, the MCM might have needed to create it politically and nurture it socially. The MCM has in this regard become expert in departicularizing the specificity of diverse urban struggles. Examples of these practices are the politically selective funding of community projects, the running of high profile Black candidates, and the recent MCM discourse on poverty. This process is more than simply cooptive image-management: it involves a skilful use of contemporary political culture in the form of a politics of bricolage, wherein the reigning party's strategy is flexibly adapted to the discursive matrix of the varieties of representations and conflicts of the moment. Bricolage politics in this sense rests on a general acknowledgment, by a wide spectrum of actors, of the virtual absence of a political centre; a condition which social movements have been instrumental in creating. The various demands are deflected or absorbed by being reduced to matters of technocratic routine, or alternatively marginalized beyond the pale of the political, nurturing identity politics in civil society.

Since the election, the MCM has further entrenched its New Class political interests, creating a technocracy that remains remarkably aloof from the city's current social and economic decline. The party's unwillingness to confront the provincial State on the controversial Ryan reforms of 1991 (which effectively cut transfer payments to municipalities by $367 million) reappeared in the administration's attack on the pension funds of its own blue collar workers in labour negotiations in 1991. At a time of increasing hardships for Montréalers, the bureaucracy of the Montréal Urban Community (MUC) and the costs of the MCM administration continue to grow only in proportion to the parade of despair outside local food banks. Much to the chagrin of many an activist that once canvassed for the MCM, a party that ten years earlier espoused a philosophy of grassroots democracy had by 1991 become little more than a vehicle of (would-be) administrative efficiency.

BUILDING A CRITICAL PUBLIC SPHERE: RECLAIMING COMMUNITY POLITICS

The fragmentation of the left in Montréal has thus nourished New Class interests. These interests represent issues in ways which aim at decoupling them from their bases in social movements. In this process the lines differentiating the valid concerns of groups from those of the new urban gatekeepers become blurred. Political reform becomes transmuted into a vapid brand of cultural reform; citizens are accorded "expression," through public mechanisms, rather than power. Instead of having to deal with the political claims of different groups, these demands are neutralized through mechanisms that purport to give "universal access."

This was well exemplified by the MCM's running of a high-profile Black community activist in a 1991 by-election, while its own record on minority rights (particularly regarding the Black community) had been pitifully timid; during the by-election the MCM emerged as the party concerned with electing the first Black councillor to City Hall. As Russell Berman has noted, New Class political interests, operating in the name of "the people," adopt a rhetoric of citizenship that separates representation from real political status.[25]

But at the beginning of the 1990s there was enough occurring in the Montréal political scene to suggest that a new conception of agency in urban social movements might be emerging. The MCM was having unprecedented difficulty controlling its technocratic bias, as the city continued to decline socially, economically and, most recently, demographically. An everyday sense of crisis lingers in Montréal as unemployment rises, services decline, and political solutions seem virtually unattainable. The city is caricatured as ineffective. Due to this, urban social movements are now more successful in building oppositional positions based on local ties which are less easily coopted.

Left of centre parties are themselves at a sort of turning-point. The DCM has been slowly gathering its forces in traditional communities with an eye on the 1994 municipal election. In a by-election in the west-end district of Notre Dame de Grace in November 1991, a community activist known for her work in anti-poverty groups won easily with 44% of the popular vote. The MCM candidate did poorly.[26] The ecological party was at this time in a process of internal reorganization, with a view to refining its analysis of urban life. With the DCM expanding its interests towards environmental concerns, the basis for a real merger between the DCM and EM had never been so promising. Such a coalition, along with the support of ethno-cultural communities, the local labour movement (which lost its remaining illusions about the MCM in the 1991 negotiations with municipal blue-collar workers), the new cultural politics, and traditional neighbourhoods, could well breach the armour of the MCM.

In the early 1990s grassroot groups were also redefining their strategies in an effort to reclaim some of the autonomy taken from them during the first few years of the MCM rule. The MCM had begun a process of neighbourhood reorganization through the creation of nine new administrative districts. The ostensible rationale behind this reorganization was to create a more effective delivery of services. Instead, the result has been a dismantling of communities through the combination of neighbourhoods with vastly different social and economic priorities, rendering urban poverty and unemployment even more politically invisible. This has most affected neighbourhoods which had been developing the community expertise to address just such issues, against enormous labour market odds.

There were two notable effects: a) a growing community perception of an undermining of their neighbourhoods, and their "new politics," for example, the grassroots groups which had emerged to represent them on social issues; b) radicalization of the service delivery function of existing groups, through the appearance of a new set of political circumstances which exposed the bureaucratic nature of New Class policies. Through this technocratic attempt to undermine community sentiment, coupled with the ineffective political voice given to the new geographical districts (in the form of District Advisory Committees), it has become clear that the "decentralization" strategy of the MCM involves unacceptable constraints on local initiatives.[27] An increasing number of groups have opted to work in their traditional communities, establishing their own social priorities, rather than follow the technocratic designs of City Hall. Service delivery itself, in this sense, has become repoliticized and actually closer to its real social vocation as a prefigurative model of a broader municipal redistributative network based on a democratic "politics of need" rather than yet new forms of political clientelism. This emerging, if still fragile, discourse on empowerment represents a new challenge to the hegemonic political culture and its centralist proclivities, through its focus on locality.

* * *

Given the politically subaltern nature of municipalities, decentralization within the local State clearly implies demarcating greater levels of autonomy from provincial State structures, thus generating new local decision-making capacities. Most grassroots groups now engaged in the politics of urban poverty are essentially dealing with redistributive issues, which are currently locked in provincial State containers. The political impasses they confront are largely due to the invoking of administrative limits by local and provincial bureaucracies. Challenging this understanding of urban life offers a way both to decentralise both democracy and to refocus attention on the deeply political dimension of cities, as a precursor to a broader debate on participatory democracy.

Indeed, in 1992 urban social movements and progressive urban political parties in Montréal appear to be on the verge of some substantial realignments. Hopefully these transformations can provide the basis for a new and critical public sphere. As the recent political history of Montréal has shown, this would require a substantial strategic reevaluation by a wide spectrum of progressive urban forces (the "many socialisms"), in which still unresolved older struggles find common cause alongside the new politics: an ambitious response to the politics of bricolage.

NOTES

1. C. Offe, "Crisis of crisis management: elements of a political theory" in J. Keene (ed.) *Contradictions of the Welfare State*. Cambridge: The MIT Press, 1984.
2. "Bricolage" (literally, "fixing" or "patchwork") politics belongs to the social pattern of what has come to be understood as the "postmodern." The political shearing of the left's meta-narrative has had the effect of legitimating all values in a political system. Fragmentation and massness become kindred spirits in these disassembling practices, as groups collapse into subgroups, their code of self-recognition becoming so culturally specific as to be politically non-communicable. Politics here is no longer associated with a generalized political sphere attached to rights and obligations, but with a class of values. The new middle class life-style politics and territorially bounded mobilizations (the NIMBY phenomenon) are the empirical bench-marks of this sea-change within contemporary social struggle. In the case of Montréal, the politics of bricolage refers to the discursive framework of the participative liberal politics of New Class political interests, wherein the democratic potential of the city is exchanged for the summun bonum of linguistic competency and representation.
3. The operative understanding of political culture used in this text is informed by several variables. These include, the historical practices of local government and the *local* State, New Class interests, the 'difference' of the new social movements, *left* and alternative green parties, and a subsidiary but too often neglected feature in new social movements analysis, the recursive effects of flexible capital restructuring.
4. The notion of the New Class was first clearly enunciated by Alvin W, Gouldner. Gouldner argued that the New Class, due to their cultural capital, were experts at political decoding and diagnosis. Their cultural capital aspires to unite both power and goodness, having access to an instrumental rationality and a Jacobian moralism. See A.W. Gouldner, *The Future of Intellectuals and the Rise of the New Class*, New York: Continuum, 1979. The usage of "New Class interests," in this text, refers specifically to the primacy of politics, power and culture as mediated by linguistically competent agents. These agents, in the name of socio-economic rationality, have instrumentalized the state to introduce new modes of social domination. They are a knowledge-manipulating political stratum. In a sense, the theoretical revival of the New Class comes on the heels of the general sociological inadequacy of "new middle class" theories, in their largely failed attempts to bridge diverse economic and political interests. A New Class perspective, by focusing on political processes, direct analysis towards cultural forms of representation. This allows a more critical discourse about the very nature of democracy, thus far absent in discussions of the "new middle classes." For an update of Gouldner's original notion, see T. Luke, "Community and Ecology" in *Telos*, no. 88, summer, 1991.
5. D. Harvey, *The Condition of Post-Modernity*, Oxford: Basil Blackwell, 1989. See also the critique of Harvey's work by Doreen Massey in "Flexible Sexism," *Society and Space*, vol. 9, no. 1, 1991.
6. The growth of the urban underclass remains in this regard an unstated political problem. Paradoxically, it parallels the growth of New Class interests. If the New Class can be characterized in terms of their political credentials, the underclass can be analyzed in terms of their lack of political rights and their eroding grasp on the fundamentals of modern citizenship. See Barbara Schmitter-Heisler, "A Compara-

tive perspective on the underclass: questions of urban poverty, race and citizenship." in *Theory and Society,* vol. 20/4, 1991.

7.   B. Jessop, "Capitalism and democracy; the best possible political shell?," in G. Littlejohn (ed.) *Power and the State,* London: Croom Helm, 1984.

8.   M. Gottdiener, "The two tiered theory of the state: resolving the question of the determination for the local state," in E.S. Greenberg and T.F. Mayer (eds.), *Changes in the State: Causes and Consequences,* London: Sage Publications, 1990.

9.   For a solid discussion on this topic see Richard C. Hula, "New forms of urban public service: privatization and local political culture" paper presented at the meeting of the ISA in Madrid Spain, July 9-13, 1990.

10.   This notion is developed in Margit Mayer, "The post-Fordist City," in *Socialist Review,* vol. 21, no.1. Jan-March, 1991.

11.   The stagnation of the Montréal economy, whilst most evident in the last twenty years, has been a constant feature since the fifties. Some of the major postwar contributing factors were: trade liberalization policies; the effects of the Auto Pact for the general Québec economy; the rationalization of industry drawn to Southwestern Ontario by the American "shadow effect"; the enactment by Federal authorities of the Borden Line, (which effectively stopped the development of a petrochemical industry in Montréal); the loss of British markets due to the Common Market (one of Montréal's oldest and most secure overseas export venues); the expanding Toronto air transport industry; and most importantly the demographic mobility of finance capital itself.

12.   P. Hamel and L. Jalbert, "Local power in Canada: stakes and challenges in the structuring of the state," in C. Pickvance and E.Preteceille (eds.), *State Restructuring and Local Power: A Comparative Perspective,* London: Pinter Publications, 1991.

13.   A. Baccigalupo. *Les administrations municipales québecois des origins a nos jours,* 2 vols. Montréal: Les editions Agence d'Arc Inc., 1984.

14.   This was accomplished through accusations and innuendos of complicity with the Front de libération de Québec (FLQ).

15.   S. Schecter, *The Politics of Urban Liberation,* Montréal: Black Rose Books, 1978.

16.   The Overdale affair, (a case of tenants struggling against eviction and unsatisfactory relocation policies) raised serious contradictions within a party intent on holding onto its one-time perception as a tenants rights advocate. J.-F. Léonard and J. Lévéillée, "Bilan du RCM: à la recherche de l'opposition perdue," in *Le Devoir,* Nov. 12, 1987.

17.   There are exceptions to this general rule in housing groups and particular local economic development corporations.

18.   During this period, urban social movements were by and large adjusting to the new terms of participation accorded to them by City Hall Long-time community activists were being actively pursued to sit on councils adjudicating technical matters of local concern.

19.   See V. Lyon's article,"The reluctant party: ideology versus organization in Canada's Green Movement," *Alternatives /2,* 1989.

20.   For a full discussion of alternative political parties during this period see H. Lustiger-Thaler, "New social movement discourses: the unsolved democracy" in W. Carroll, (ed.), *Contemporary Social Movements in Theory and Practice,* Toronto: Garamond Press, 1992.

21.   In effect, urban social movements had the most to lose, at least strategically, through a partisan move.

22.   It was clear, for most political analysts, that the DCM wins were tied to the good reputations of individual councillors, rather than their party's political program.

23.   One MCM councillor seriously argued that the low voter turnout was an indication of the satisfaction of the general Montréal populace with the programs of the party.

24.   L. Lowenthal, *False Prophets,* New Brunswick: Transactions Books, 1987.

25.   R. Berman, "Popular culture and populist culture," *Telos,* no. 87, 1991.

26.   Both the two parties to the right of the MCM did relatively well, each respectively winning 22% and 23% percent of the popular vote. With the probable merger of

these two parties for the 1994 elections, there is a real possibility of a reinvigorated municipal Right in Montréal. The EM candidate barely won 1% of the vote. The party was badly prepared for the race due to internal discord. While future trends cannot be predicted from by-election results, a protest vote was clearly sent to City Hall by the citizens of N.D.G.

27. The District Advisory Committees have no political mandate and deal with minor details of local planning.

REFERENCES

Baccigalupo, A. *Les administrations municipales québecois des origins a nos jours*. 2 vols. Montréal: Les editions Agence d'Arc Inc., 1984.

Berman, R. "Popular culture and populist culture," *Telos*. No. 87, 1991.

Gouldner, A.W. *The Future of Intellectuals and the Rise of the New Class*, New York: Continuum, 1979.

Greenberg, E.S. and T.F. Mayer (eds.) *Changes in the State: Causes and Consequences*. London: Sage Publications, 1990.

Hamel, P. and L. Jalbert, "Local power in Canada: stakes and challenges in the structuring of the State," in C. Pickvance and E. Preteceille (eds.), *State Restructuring and Local Power: A Comparative Perspective*. London: Pinter Publications, 1991.

Harvey, D. The Condition of Post-Modernity. Oxford: Basil Blackwell, 1989.

Hula, Richard C. "New forms of urban public service: privatization and local political culture" paper presented at the meeting of the ISA in Madrid Spain, July 9-13, 1990.

Jessop, B. "Capitalism and democracy; the best possible political shell?," in G. Littlejohn (ed.) *Power and the State*. London: Croom Helm, 1984.

Léonard, J.-F. and J. Lévéillée, "Bilan du RCM: à la recherche de l'opposition perdue." *Le Devoir*, Nov. 12, 1987.

Lowenthal, L. *False Prophets*. New Brunswick: Transactions Books, 1987.

Luke, T. "Community and Ecology," *Telos*, no. 88, summer, 1991.

Lustiger-Thaler, H. "New social movement discourses: the unsolved democracy" in W. Carroll, (ed.), *Contemporary Social Movements in Theory and Practice*. Toronto: Garamond Press, 1992.

Lyon, V. "The reluctant party: ideology versus organization in Canada's Green Movement," *Alternatives*. /2, 1989.

Massey, Doreen "Flexible Sexism," *Society and Space*. vol. 9, no. 1, 1991.

Mayer, Margit "The post-Fordist City," *Socialist Review*. vol. 21, no.1. Jan-March, 1991.

Offe, C. "Crisis of crisis management: elements of a political theory" in J. Keene (ed.) *Contradictions of the Welfare State*. Cambridge: The MIT Press, 1984.

Schecter, S. *The Politics of Urban Liberation*. Montréal: Black Rose Books, 1978.

Schmitter-Heisler, Barbara "A Comparative perspective on the underclass: questions of urban poverty, race and citizenship," *Theory and Society*. vol. 20/4, 1991.

Chapter 13

Louis Favreau

THE "BACKYARD REVOLUTION" IN QUÉBEC: PEOPLE AND COMMUNITY IN A LIBERAL DEMOCRACY*

The time has come to review what has been happening in the popular movement of Québec. Important shifts have occurred in the orientation of this movement that have raised significant political and strategic questions. The results of a three-year survey (1985-1988) regarding the popular movement in Québec suggest some answers to these questions. The findings reveal that although the movement is undergoing significant changes in many areas, it is not, as is often suggested, in decline. Rather, it is undergoing a social and cultural transformation.[1]

A TURN TO THE RIGHT OR NEW FORMS OF POLITICIZATION?

Between 1950 and 1965, community recreational organizations existed alongside traditional political parties in Québec. In working-class neighbourhoods, social clubs fulfilled the function of charities. From 1965 to 1980, however, these organizations became more socially-oriented; typical examples of this transformation were the neighbourhoods of Hochelaga-Maisonneuve, Petite-Patrie and Centre-Sud in Montréal. The leadership of these organizations was, however, increasingly at odds with the emerging younger, culturally-oriented and more political leadership of community and alternative radio stations, community pressure groups and women's support groups.

The 1980s witnessed a general crisis of social and political "militancy," which in turn led to a process of rapprochement between popular organizations and the more traditional charitable "mutual aid" organizations, by means of initiatives such as "coordinating round-tables" (*tables de*

---

* This article was translated by Daniel Salée

concertation). This rapprochement was partly due to changes within the political left which, historically, had considerable influence on the practices of the popular and community movements. New non-sectarian attitudes have fostered greater collaboration between groups which, only a short while back, often thought of each other as enemies. Action is now more clearly focused on objectives shaped by hard day-to-day realities. Unemployment among youth and women, for example, is a central concern shared by most popular groups. Similarly, the renewed importance of culture and humanistic values provides all these community organizations with a shared identity. The current vacuum at the level of party politics makes "rapprochement" and social experimentation elsewhere much easier.

This new attitude does not imply a "depoliticization" of the popular movements. In fact, all that is changing is the *form* of politicization: popular groups no longer reject the more conventional mechanisms of political democracy, and it is now acceptable to lobby political decision-makers at provincial and municipal levels in order to promote community-oriented issues.

At the same time, the popular movements' goal of radically transforming society was considerably toned down in the 1980s. It now seems less important to fight for grand social principles and political ideals than it is to meet more prosaic — but more realistic — objectives, rooted in the experience of everyday life. Action is no longer defined or planned in terms of a right-left dichotomy; it is more concerned with what will work and what will deliver the goods. The popular movements are shedding their negative image for a more constructive, self-confident appearance. They remain progressive in their orientation, but the avant-garde socialist political organization of the 1970s is no longer seen as the path to social transformation. The will to "break the system," as Louis Laberge, President of the FTQ (Federation des travailleurs et travailleuses du Québec) put it in 1973, is no longer part of the progressive agenda. The result of this shift in attitude is, however, a certain naïvité, and the occasional inability to analyze power relations correctly.

While popular groups are rarely conservative, some do favour, in practice, a greater degree of integration into the system. For example, the staff of the Services externes de main d'oeuvre (SEMO), may have adopted the feminist discourse on the importance of women's autonomy, but women on welfare, whom these officers work to reinsert into the labour market, often find themselves trapped in low-paid, demeaning and precarious job situations, and left alone to the administrative dictates of government-sponsored "re-skilling" programs. Similarly, the staff of the Corporations de développement économique communautaire (CDEC) also tend to express their objectives in the context of what is possible within the constraints of the dominant socio-economic system. To them, social change hinges primarily on employment, and to achieve this goal they uncritically promote peaceful coexistence with the private sector.

By and large, popular groups are still motivated by the ideal of social progress, but their all too often limited means and resources force them to compromise on their principles. Hence La Puce Communautaire, for example, a community computer business in the Hochelaga-Maisonneuve district of Montréal, continues to cater to its primary target clientele by making computers accessible to local women and community groups, but it also tries to attract more "profitable" clients from among small and medium size firms. Similarly, the various Groupes de ressources techniques (GRT) have, over time, turned into cooperative housing consultants, thus blurring the line between militant advocacy and professionalization.

Popular groups are thus not exactly experiencing a turn to the right, but an increasing number are finding a home at the centre of the political spectrum. From an ultra-left perspective, there is no doubt that most of the popular groups examined in the survey are now far removed from the "revolutionary" positions of the past. Today's popular groups are not interested in a radical social break under the leadership of a working-class political party. The point is no longer to topple the bourgeois State and smash the capitalist system, but rather to try and rectify the often miserable conditions of existence of an overly-large segment of the population. Popular groups are aware that the system has failed to resolve the crisis of unemployment. Their present aim, more modest but perhaps more realistic, is to achieve a different, community-based type of economic development.

In many ways, today's militants shun any particular model of intervention and community action. This is not to say that they cannot lead political battles or even win important victories. The Centre communautaire Christophe-Colomb in the Petite Patrie neighbourhood in Montréal is a case in point. With the help of various community groups and immigrant support groups, the Centre has succeeded in securing access to local schools for its activities in spite of the resistance of the Montréal Catholic School Board and the private sector. Similarly, the Société populaire d'habitation de Rosemont secured 50,000 signatures on a petition calling for the transformation of certain municipal sites into subsidized housing, rather than into office or manufacturing space as originally intended by the city authorities.

Poor financing and inadequate credentials are the main problems facing popular groups. As a result, their very existence is in constant jeopardy and, for some groups, lobbying is their last and only resort. Others get together to create so-called "tables de concertation et d'action" (roundtables for coordination and action), and try to get what they can by applying pressure on supportive city councillors. They adopt an incremental, muddling-through approach, that betrays a marked absence of models and practices of social change. Yet, if their political aims are not always clear, or are even non-existent, the undeniable concern of such groups for social justice makes them nonetheless important for the communities they serve.

Rather than speak of decline, therefore, it seems more appropriate, especially in light of the recent increase in community initiatives, to speak of the remarkable resilience of the popular movement. The popular movement in Québec is at a crossroads, and can be more aptly understood as currently undergoing an incubation period, during which new ideas are germinating and taking shape, ideas which will later be widely accepted by the social class these groups represent. Day care centres are a good example of this process: today women do not bear any stigma for taking their children to a day care centre, whether they work outside the home or not. More generally, even if they only operate on a local scale, community groups are dynamic social sites in which new forms of socialization, new ideas, new social relations and challenges to the dominant social order are emerging.

THE POPULAR MOVEMENT: DECLINE OR RENEWAL?

There is a real sense in which the part-advocacy, part-social service organizations and groups constitute, and feel part of, a single "popular movement." In the twenty-five year history of this movement in Montréal (to take a major example), it has barely become institutionalized: its activities and decision-making process are highly decentralized; it essentially operates at the neighbourhood level. In addition, full-time workers in the community sector are poorly paid and their working conditions are often precarious;[2] their control over their organizations is generally limited, and group members' sense of involvement is weakening. Finally, non-statutory and irregular financing by the State also makes institutionalization difficult.

One gets an even clearer sense of the lack of institutionalization of the Québec popular movement by comparing it with popular movements in other countries. In France, for example, the movement is well structured into a confederation, and is strongly inspired, in both its ideology and its organization, by the labour movement. In English Canada, the popular movement tends to exist more on the basis of various "sectors:" each sector is organized nationally, but has few local or regional roots, and lobbying is the preferred course of action. Consumers associations or the Canadian Abortion Rights Action League are typical examples. Interestingly, the U.S. popular movement, referred to as the "backyard revolution," is more similar to Québec's experience.[3]

In the case of Québec, another major question posed by the shifts discussed above is whether the movement is losing its community-oriented character to the benefit of the middle class that now generally controls its decision-making. At first glance, the middle class composition of the full-time workers of today's popular groups might lead one to believe that this is indeed the case. However a more nuanced appreciation of the current situation is in order. On the one hand, Québec's popular groups remain unequivocally rooted in the underprivileged strata of society, and their work is clearly aimed at upgrading the socio-economic lot of the poor and the marginalized. On the other hand, it may be argued that in recent years they have been content to play a supplementary role, merely filling in for the State in areas where the State fails to provide adequate or specific services. For all these reasons, critics maintain that the popular movement in Québec is now on the defensive, spreading itself too thin, much too service-oriented, and all too keen on seeking partnerships with the private sector; lobbying seems to be its only concern, to the detriment of real political militancy.

While it is difficult to draw any generalized conclusions at this stage, there are some positive trends emerging. First, while the social and political radicalism of the past decades is indeed on the wane, groups that are trying to link up with the women's movement (e.g. Women's centres such as Centre-Sud's Centre d'education et d'action des femmes (CEAF) or Hochelaga-Maisonneuve's La Marie-Debout) are developing and expanding despite the initial reluctance of militant feminists. Secondly, in spite of the claims of some authors to the contrary,[4] the idea of "the local community" — the neighbourhood — is stronger than ever. Youth centres, women's centres, disarmament and peace groups and others all operate out of given neighbourhoods. For these groups, the local community, an *underprivileged* neighbourhood, is becoming a definite reality, existing within a geographically and culturally defined territory, and operating on the basis of well-organized local support structures.

Groups concerned with housing, for example, have existed for a long time; but here too the approach is now to focus on the local community. Plans are drawn up by "quartiers," which suits the Montréal Citizen's Movement (MCM) and the Democratic Coalition at City Hall, but may also have long-term implications which are more radical.

Québec's popular movement continues to evolve. It was not previously, nor is it today a mass movement with mass organizations, a large membership, and much public visibility. It is still largely made up of small groups continuously transforming themselves. Yet its leadership is now stable and relatively experienced: it is not uncommon to find people among the leadership with 5, 10, 15 and even 20 years of experience in community organizations; and whether they are paid professionals or volunteers, they are generally drawn from the neighbourhoods they serve. This contradicts the argument made by Jacques T. Godbout that these people are potential bureaucrats whose increasingly remote management role alienates them from the needs of their constituents.[5] Our own findings point rather to the economic precariousness in which these organizers and administrators have to live. Even if they tend to become more professional in outlook, they reflect the concerns of their constituents.

Although the popular movement may be little known to the wider public, it is playing a significant role in the transformation of attitudes within society. Like the ecology movement, it is spreading the idea of "the community" and of ways in which a better quality of life can be achieved.

DOES THE POPULAR MOVEMENT ORIGINATE FROM A SOCIAL MOVEMENT?

The popular movement is a social movement to the extent that it exists, at least partially, as a collective challenge to political and cultural domination.[6] Popular groups take up this challenge when they display the ability to mobilize human and material resources around collective issues, bringing together often heterogeneous forces within a given community, initiating democratic social change and implementing strategies for solving new social problems.

For the past twenty-five years, the popular movement in Québec has struggled against the legitimacy of the dominant social system. Joining forces with the union movement, the women's movement and the peace movement, it grew out of battles for the improvement of the quality of life of the underprivileged and a persistent search for solutions and services to alleviate the plight of the poor and the marginalized.

In fact, elements of the marginalized and the salaried middle class have led to a number of significant social innovations. In the field of culture, for example, they have led to the creation of community radio stations and theatre groups, and to the establishment of centres of popular education and training. In the field of politics, they have contributed to the creation of grassroots political organizations and parties (e.g. Front d'action politique (FRAP), the MCM, the Democratic Coalition in Montréal, and the Rassemblement populaire in Québec City); and also to a greater awareness of third world politics, and of the importance of international solidarity (e.g. the establishment of solidarity groups with Chile, El Salvador, the Philippines and Nicaragua, as well as various organizations for international cooperation). In the social field, they have stimulated the expansion of social rights in health, education, housing, consumer protection, social assistance, and support for youth and women. Finally, in the economic field, they have helped to foster the establishment of community and cooperative enterprises.

Even today, examples abound of the popular movement's capacity for initiating social change. Its resilience is remarkable. The Centre d'éducation et d'action des femmes (in Montréal's Centre-Sud) grew progressively from a baby-sitting service to an action centre for women without abandoning its original objectives. Similarly, the "Chic Resto Pop" (a community restaurant) evolved from a social rights militancy approach to a support group and an employment resource centre for young welfare recipients, while simultaneously establishing itself as a business. Although it has integrated consultants and experts into its operations, it has never shifted from its collective management, nor has it become a charitable institution.

We are in fact witnessing a qualitative evolution within the popular movement, particularly among community support groups. Volunteers in these groups have adopted more collective and more socially relevant forms of intervention, which are particularly visible in housing. Economic intervention reflects new forms of personal and collective motivation which may well lead to the establishment of "social enterprises." Left-oriented popular groups have also changed their approach: rigid political lines have been abandoned for a greater concern for the local community, the quality of life and the environment, as well as for more pragmatism.

THE EVOLUTION OF THE POPULAR MOVEMENT

Until recently, analysis of Québec's popular movement has emphasized either the trend towards its integration[7] and professionalization[8] or the emergence of new values and its subversive capacities.[9]

Benoît Lévesque and Paul R. Bélanger have produced what we feel is the most stimulating reflection on the popular movement to date.[10] Their analysis rests on both the cultural and the political-economic dimensions of the movement: they argue that the popular movement went through three major periods of development, from militancy to becoming a pool of public services. From 1963 to 1968, emerging citizens' committees practised what Bélanger and Lévesque refer to as a "syndicalism" (direct action) around collective consumption issues. Then, from 1969 to 1976, the movement became more radical and challenged the policies of the welfare State. Finally, since 1976, it has been characterized by the rise of service-oriented groups. The new prominence of these groups within the popular movement is, according to Lévesque and Bélanger, the result of a compromise between

> the will to democracy and empowerment on the one hand, and the increasing tendency of the state to withdraw itself from the social sphere on the other hand. Governmental policies undermine the democratic aspirations of services users and workers by channelling them towards alternative services rather than widening the social basis of public services.[11]

While popular groups are fields of experiment in democracy and participation, State policies and the bourgeoisie restrict them to narrow spheres of activity. They are increasingly limited to the role of subordinate, service-providing outlets; mere subcontractors of the State, providing services which the State no longer has an interest in providing. Lévesque and Bélanger argue that popular groups are in fact locked in a "double movement" which forces them to oscillate uncomfortably between subversion (as part of an alternative social movement), and a mere extension of the State.

While the analysis presented by Lévesque and Bélanger is relevant, their attempt to periodize the development of the popular movement in this way is questionable. The so-called passage of the popular movement from militancy to service roles was simply never experienced by a wide variety of popular organizations. Popular clinics, popular education centres, food banks, Associations coopératives d'économie familiale (ACEF) all appeared in the first period of the movement's history and were designed from the outset as service-providing organizations, not as political pressure groups.

Similarly, during the so-called service-oriented period that is said to have begun in 1976, many groups, such as housing committees, pursued unequivocally political activities. Since 1985, one can find, in Québec's major urban centres, various popular groups which have been directly active on the political scene, struggling for progressive measures. Finally, it is not uncommon to find groups which have existed — and continue to exist — both as service outlets and as political pressure groups (e.g. Au bas de l'échelle, (at the bottom of the ladder) Association communautaire d'économie familiale (ACEF), Association pour la défense des droits sociaux (ADDS), l'Organisation populaire des droits sociaux (OPDS), etc.). It is certainly true that in their early development, most popular groups are militant, and that in later phases their survival is often dependent on their ability to offer high quality services. However, it is also clear that the popular movement in Québec has spawned highly versatile groups and organizations throughout its history.

This reality has been recognized by Françoise Romaine-Ouellette in her study of the women's movement in Québec.[12] According to her, popular groups and organizations can be best understood as fulfilling one or all three general functions or categories of action: *socialization* (support activities, recreation, education); *services* (the establishment of community resource centres); and *democratic pressure* (political militancy, the promotion of social and individual rights). Some groups may decide to emphasize one category of action over another, depending on their circumstances and on the general conjuncture; others may even combine two, or all three, categories of action.

Lévesque and Bélanger's analysis also fails to provide answers to more specific questions. Why, for example, did most food banks disappear in urban centres? How can the new local dynamic of popular groups with regard to municipal politics be explained? Why are many groups opposed to each other on the question of the reform of Québec's health and social services system?

Part of the problem is that Lévesque and Bélanger focus on those areas of intervention which are linked to the State-sponsored social service sector. By virtue of this choice, they have omitted youth and women's groups as well as the movement of resistance against urban development. Yet these are an integral part of the current ferment in the popular movement in Québec, and what is presently occurring in those groups is indicative of the direction many groups are now taking.

A more accurate portrayal of the situation experienced by the popular movement should, therefore, include the following realities: first, certain forms of mobilisation are no longer appropriate; the radical militancy of the 1970's makes no sense in times of political and ideological sclerosis. Second, community and popular groups, associations and organizations of all kinds are multiplying as a result of the increased presence of a salaried middle class in many fields of activity (e.g. community information).

POPULAR MOVEMENTS, SOCIAL MOVEMENTS AND DEMOCRACY IN QUÉBEC IN THE 1990s

Since the first half of the 1980's, trade unions and the popular movement have undergone a significant ideological and political shift. Both have been lured by various forms of "concertation" and social partnership. But paradoxically, both have proven remarkably resilient in the face of the major issues of the decade. Unions have had to deal with a crisis of militancy and have shown a greater openness to feminism and peace activism. They have also found a middle road between private and public interests. The popular movement, on the other hand, has displayed an extraordinary vitality since the mid-1980s, both in socio-economic terms (labour cooperatives, community economic development corporations) and in the socio-cultural field (especially a proliferation of local information networks).

In some ways, the demands of the popular movement, its formal democratic structures, and its collective action directed against the powers that be, lead one to conclude that it shares the main features and objectives of the trade union movement. In other ways, however, the popular movement is closer to the new social movements. It shares the same concern for the quality of life and the environment; it advocates the decentralization of action and equality in the organization of labour. It also emphasizes the need for political and cultural autonomy.

The perceived "decline" of the popular movement and its ideology is largely due to its expansion beyond informal networks and collectives. In a way, the popular movement has been improved by reaching out: in its new manifestations it is more visible, as it is increasingly integrated into larger community organizations such as the Regroupement des centres de femmes, the Regroupement des maisons de jeunes, and the Fédération des coopératives de travail. While joining forces with such organizations may make a popular group appear more institutionalized and less subversive, it also increases its efficiency and its capacity to reach its constituents. This should, instead, be interpreted as a sign of maturity. Today's popular movement is instilled with a previously unknown breadth of perspective and a renewed sense of social responsibility.

The leadership of the popular groups of two decades ago were driven by the dream of changing the world; the possibilities seemed limitless: social and political projects were grandiose and ambitious, and the world was there for the taking. Today's leaders, many of whom were active in popular organizations from the beginning, see things somewhat differently. Rather than invest in abstract political projects, they have adopted a more pragmatic, down-to-earth approach to action. Whereas they previously refused to deploy their professional competence deliberately, so as not to fall into the trap of social integration or competition, today, on the contrary, they are not afraid to apply their expertise to concrete projects. They have come to understand that the professionalization of their activities does not make them any less socially or politically involved. More open to the cultural and affective dimensions of community action, today's leaders have brought a fresher insight to bear on the realization of the ultimate goal, which remains the transformation of democracy.

Despite the economic crisis and the neoliberal offensive of governments, popular groups are not as inward-looking and declining as some observers have hinted. Our data reveals that after a period of despondency, intellectual fatigue and a crisis of militancy, a significant number of popular groups have, since 1985, experienced either a renewal of their activity or new beginnings in new spheres of activity. The history of Québec's popular movement over the past thirty years is thus a remarkable story of resilience and adaptation.

Our survey of some thirty community organizations and over one hundred of their leaders and administrators reveals the existence of several "engines" of collective action, sometimes working in opposition, but more often than not in complementary ways. Belonging to a neighbourhood, being a member of an exploited or underprivileged socio-economic category (welfare recipients, unemployed, tenants), and identifying oneself with a gender or age group, are the foundations upon which groups and organizations have emerged, have made social and cultural gains, and have established a large number of popular institutions that support the social struggles of popular classes.

The former approach to building solidarity through mobilization based largely on agitation, denunciation and direct confrontation with the dominant order, is giving way to new means of expressing solidarity: a willingness to try other forms of interaction. Those who see today's popular movement as a declining and spent social force look at it through the prism of the traditional left for whom the system had to be smashed and rebuilt on new bases. Such a view of things is sociologically unicausal and unilateral. It falsely assumes that society is only governed by the State, as if social movements had little or no influence on the societal process.

A more accurate portrayal of today's popular movement should be based upon an understanding of the particularities of its history. Initially concerned with the living conditions of the popular classes, it has progressively enlarged its field of intervention and its conception of the quality of life. Its orientations and actions are normally defined by the imperatives of social transformation (e.g. the defence of social rights) in the context of "micro relations" of power. This reality is reflected in a three-pronged strategy: a strategy of confrontation involving political militancy and collective action; a strategy of greater independence from the State through the establishment of self- or co-managed services; and a strategy of education and consciousness-raising. Finally, the popular movement has a culture of its own — that is, specific fields of intervention, distinctive structures and *modus operandi*, and a particular way of thinking which emphasizes social and political autonomy and the organization of local communities.

PERSPECTIVES FOR THE 1990s

Is the popular movement condemned to oscillate politically between dreams of an unlikely revolution and social experiments devoid of an overall social project? It is difficult to say at this stage. It seems clear, however, that despite the current trend toward social experimentation and micro-solidarity, popular movements cannot go much further without a more comprehensive social project. The very future of the popular movement hinges on its ability to elaborate and articulate such a project, and this is, indeed, a tall order. As we have pointed out, today's militants are little concerned with models and grand projects of any kind. The softening of political positions and the relative absence of institutionalization both reflect and account for this apparent disaffection.

Yet the gains made over the past 25 years remain and can serve as the foundation for the elaboration of new strategies. A greater degree of autonomy and influence of workers in the management of enterprises and public services, and a greater assertiveness of local communities in their dealings with the State, both confirm the increasing impact the community sector now has on the management of society as well as on the debate about the role of the State. More and more militants of popular organizations are ready to promote a less State-centred social project, without going the way of privatization. Others refuse to leave economic management and job creation in the hands of the State and the private sector, and are working for the establishment of a "social economy." These people are involved in community economic development corporations: there already exist half a dozen in Montréal alone, and about a dozen in the rest of the province.

Yet a basic question remains: should popular organizations in local communities just work to help needy people, or to transform society? The answer given by the present popular movement is a call for the transformation of society.[13] In other words, the popular movement should direct its efforts towards the involvement of the largest possible number of people — and more particularly those who have been left at the margins of society — in social and economic development. The goal is to contribute to the emergence of a new citizenship, to the full realization of a "backyard revolution." This may sound like a pure utopia, but it is a creative utopia that may well generate new social practices.

NOTES

1. This article updates the findings of this survey; the conclusions remain the same. For a detailed analysis see: Louis Fravreau. *Mouvement populaire et intervention communautaire de 1960 à nos jours*. Montreal: les Editions du Fleuve, 1989.
2. On this issue, see Paul R. Bélanger and Benoît Lévesque, "Conditions et division du travail dans les "entreprises" du mouvement populaire" in *Animation et culture en mouvement*, Montréal, Presses de l'Université du Québec, 1987, pp. 82-90.12
3. See Harry C. Boyte, *The Backyard Revolution. Understanding the New Citizen Movement*, Philadelphia, Temple University Press, 1980.
4. See R. Mayer, *La connaissance du milieu et des besoins comme moteur de l'action*. A paper presented to the second annual conference of organizations supported by United Way-Montreal, 1987.
5. Jacques T. Godbout, *La participation contre la démocratie*, Montréal, Saint-Martin, 1983.
6. See Louis Maheu, "Les mouvements de base et la lutte contre l'appropriation étatique du tissu social," *Sociologie et sociétés*, vol 15, no. 1, 1983.
7. See P. Hamel, "Mouvements urbains et nouveaux modes de gestion du social" in *L'inégalite sociale et les mécanismes du pouvoir*, Montréal, Presses du l'Université du Québec, 1985, pp. 241-263. In later works Hamel has somewhat modified his interpretation which is now closer to ours. He now sees the popular movement as a truly social actor in local democracy. See his recent *Action collective et démocratie locale (dans les mouvements urbains montréalais)*, Montréal, Presses de l'Université de Montréal, 1991.
8. Jacques T. Godbout, *La participation contre la démocratie*, Montréal, St-Martin, 1983. Also by Godbout, "La participation politique: leçons des dernières décennies" in J.T. Godbout (ed.), *La participation politique*, Québec, IQRC, 1991, pp. 11-32.
9. G. Gagnon, *Les pratiques émancipatoires en milieu populaire*, Québec, IQRC, 1982. Also by the same author, "Le mouvement autogestionnaire québécois" in G. Gagnon and M. Rioux (eds.), *A propos d'autogestion et d'émancipation*, Québec, IQRC, 1988, pp. 12-140.
10. See their "Mouvement social au Québec: continuité et rupture (1960-1985)" in *Animation et culture en mouvement*, Montréal, Presses de l'Université du Québec, 1987.
11. Ibid., p. 264.
12. F. Romaine-Ouellette, *Les groupes de femmes du Québec en 1985: champs d'intervention, structures et moyens d'action*, Québec, Conseil du statut de la femme, 1985.
13. See L. Doucet and L. Favreau, *Théorie et pratiques en organisation communautaire*, Sillery, Presses de l'Université du Québec, 1991.

REFERENCES

Bélanger, Paul R. and Benoît Lévesque. "Conditions et division du travail dans les "entreprises" du mouvement populaire" *Animation et culture en mouvement*. Montréal: Presses de l'Université du Québec, 1987. pp. 82-90.

Bélanger, Paul R. and Benoît Lévesque. "Mouvement social au Québec: continuité et rupture (1960-1985)," *Animation et culture en mouvement*. Montréal: Presses de l'Université du Québec, 1987.

Boyte, Harry C. *The Backyard Revolution. Understanding the New Citizen Movement*. Philadelphia: Temple University Press, 1980.

Doucet, L. and L. Favreau, *Théorie et pratiques en organisation communautaire*. Sillery, Presses de l'Université du Québec, 1991.

Gagnon, G. "Le mouvement autogestionnaire québécois" *A propos d'autogestion et d'émancipation*. G. Gagnon and M. Rioux (eds.) Québec, IQRC, 1988.

Gagnon, G. *Les pratiques émancipatoires en milieu populaire*. Québec, IQRC, 1982.

Godbout, Jacques T. "La participation politique: leçons des dernières décennies" *La participation politique*. J.T. Godbout (ed.) Québec, IQRC, 1991.

Godbout, Jacques T. *La participation contre la démocratie*. Montréal: St-Martin, 1983.

Godbout, Jacques T. *La participation contre la démocratie*. Montréal: Saint-Martin, 1983.

Hamel, P. "Mouvements urbains et nouveaux modes de gestion du social," *L'inégalite sociale et les mécanismes du pouvoir*. Montréal: Presses du l'Université du Québec, 1985.

Hamel, P. *Action collective et démocratie locale (dans les mouvements urbains montréalais)*. Montréal: Presses de l'Université de Montréal, 1991.

Maheu, Louis. "Les mouvements de base et la lutte contre l'appropriation étatique du tissu social," *Sociologie et sociétés*. vol 15, no. 1, 1983.

Mayer, R. *La connaissance du milieu et des besoins comme moteur de l'action*. A paper presented to the second annual conference of organizations supported by United Way-Montréal, 1987.

Romaine-Ouellette, F. *Les groupes de femmes du Québec en 1985: champs d'intervention, structures et moyens d'action*. Québec, Conseil du statut de la femme, 1985.

Chapter 14

John Clarke

Ontario's Social Movements — the Struggle Intensifies

Popular movements in Ontario currently face unprecedented challenges. Indeed, it must be crystal clear to all but the most dimwitted of functionaries that the segments of society that we represent are under attack as never before. Clearly, any plodding "business as usual" approach to the work and struggles of social movements can only be a recipe for costly defeats.

Much of the situation we face in Ontario is common to the experience of movements across the country and even around the world. The present period is marked by a virulent corporate onslaught; whether they are crowing over the "victory of the market place" in Eastern Europe, bombing air raid shelters in Baghdad or bullying Ontario's NDP Government into fiscal conservatism, the corporate decision makers have decided to change the rules of the game in some very fundamental ways. It is necessary to keep this corporate offensive in mind while discussing Ontario's social movements and the tasks ahead. All social issues are now dealt within the context of a relentless drive to remove all barriers to profit making; nothing can be tolerated that stands in the way of "capital mobility." All mechanisms and initiatives that would impede corporations and their vision of the future have to be smashed. The consequence of this quest for profit can only mean a collision between popular movements and capital.

There are, however, several factors in the Ontario equation that are somewhat distinct. For example, the severity of the economic slump there has been astounding; not only in scope but in the sharpness and rapidity of the decline. Also, a vast transfer of workers into the low wage ghetto has been compounded by over a million people in Ontario being now forced to live on welfare. It is hard to imagine any meaningful discussion of social issues that fails to recognize the implications of one tenth of the population of the province being at the mercy of a system of punitive, sub-poverty government handouts. The ongoing atomization and demoralization of this vast number of people casts its dark shadow over all aspects of the struggle for a progressive political agenda.

The former glory of Ontario as the leading "have" province has been shamelessly used against its poor. The federal Tories place a premium on wiping out social programs there, and traditional cost-sharing arrangements have been dealt a death blow with the 5% cap on the federal contribution to social assistance spending in Ontario. In addition, a large portion of the province's spending on welfare must now be paid without support from Ottawa, and, as a response to mounting caseloads, a 40% increase in the province's welfare budget (to $4.9 billion) was needed in 1991. The Mulroney Government was throttling the poor and unemployed of Ontario, and the provincial NDP Government was, it must be said with regret, far from jumping into the fray on the appropriate side.

A critical aspect has been introduced to the current situation in Ontario, and there is indeed a most encouraging groundswell of popular struggle against the new federal policies. Unfortunately, however, it is in the nature of the Canadian political system that many social programs are delivered by the provinces, and so there can be no viable perspective for social struggle that tries to ignore the provincial government. A major difficulty is thereby posed because, tempting as it would be to zero in on the federal Tory villain and forget the issues of provincial social democratic backsliding, this discussion of Ontario's social movements will have to address the question of how we are (and should be) dealing with the Ontario NDP.

Finally, in terms of the social setting for popular struggles in Ontario, we must take stock of the exceptional level of municipal input into "soft service" provision. In this regard, some of the worst traditions of the English parish relief system have been woven into the fabric of life in Ontario. Basic income maintenance for the unemployed is still delivered locally, through the municipal and county councils, and the result has been a vast and varied patchwork of oppressive welfare regimes that are incredibly resistant to pressure for reform. Housing and child care systems similarly vary from one locality to the next. By the time a rapidly shrinking social spending purse has been handed over to a reactionary rural county, a formula for social retrogression has been put in place. Certainly, as an anti-poverty organizer at the provincial level, a great deal of my time goes into taking on local politicians engaged in the most frenzied efforts to make the poor and unemployed foot the bill for the present recession through program cutbacks. The absence of a centralized delivery of social services is a striking aspect of the Ontario struggle which must be kept in mind.

An evaluation of Ontario's social movements must, therefore, be situated in the context of the strident and multifaceted attack that is being launched on people in communities throughout the province. Of course, it is an extremely dangerous situation but, on the other hand, there is no reason to give in to despair. If people are being squeezed and pushed to the wall, it is equally true that they are organizing in their communities and are fighting back. New forms of struggle are emerging all the time amongst unemployed workers, poor people, tenants and oppressed sectors of the community, that no hostile politician or corporate apologist can afford to overlook. Still, there are limitations that, in my view, beset community organizing.

In 1984, while I was active in the London [Ont.] Union of Unemployed Workers, a sympathetic municipal candidate was visited by a representative of the U.S. Consulate, a charming fellow by the name of Hal Luccius. This man explained that he was gathering information on political and social organizations in Ontario, and that he was especially interested in the local unemployed workers organization. One of the questions Luccius posed was very telling. "How," he asked, "can a union of the unemployed be effective when its members can't shut down any factories?"[1] The question Luccius posed was entirely valid; what is true about organizing the unemployed is true of all social movements. Some sectors of the community are easier to organize than others, and some issues generate political energy more readily than others. Still, as vital a role as social movements can play, I believe we commit a fundamental error if we abandon the perspective that the force capable of really changing this society is the working class. The real power to defeat the corporate onslaught is not to be found in community organizing but in the millions of working men and women organized in their workplaces by trade unions. The way forward for social movements, therefore, depends on how effectively they can forge a link with the power of the organized working class, while, at the same time, encourage within the union movement a far bolder and broader outlook of mobilization and struggle that includes social movements.

In their book *Poor People's Movements: Why they Succeeded, How they Failed* (1977), Piven and Cloward suggest that "(The) capacity to create political crises through disrupting institutions...is the chief resource for political influence possessed by the poor."[2] Under some conditions, the poor or other oppressed groups organized outside the workplace may take the business of "disrupting institutions" a very long way indeed. Certainly, the unemployed agitation of the 1930s shook Canadian society to its roots. Even these epic struggles, however, left a record of the most tenacious militancy and inspiring feats of organized resistance which produced relatively modest results. It was the upsurge of trade unionism following the organizing of the unemployed in the 1930s that achieved far more lasting changes and more solid gains for working people.

The organizing of the jobless during the Great Depression had to be undertaken in a period when mass industrial unionism was still in the future. Still, links between those working and those out of work were forged, and furthermore the agitation of the unemployed did much to pave the way for the remarkable success of trade unions in the late thirties and into the next decade. One of the most exciting aspects of the current environment in Ontario today is the real progress being made towards precisely this alliance between social movements and the labour movement. This alliance has the potential, if it is developed carefully, to strengthen greatly the power of the social movements and, at the same time, to infuse the trade unions with a sense of social struggle that may not immediately emerge from industrial action alone.

However, before closely examining this nascent alliance at the provincial level, a careful reading of how the community organizations have themselves established their own networks within Ontario is essential if we are to evaluate the possibilities for such a partnership with labour. I will focus on the development of the anti-poverty movement, where I am able to speak from personal experience.

THE ANTI-POVERTY MOVEMENT IN ONTARIO

Those working to organize the poor and unemployed are currently confronting very tough odds. The problem goes beyond the lack of a workplace to which we have already referred. There does not even exist a middle class sense of common purpose that might hold together some "single issue" endeavours. Anti-poverty organizing in the recent past *has* produced results, and the prospects for the future are not all bleak; but, still, it is an activity that is swimming against a social and political tide which is unlikely to change. Even in the 1930s, when mass mobilization was achieved, the organizers of the day were aware that they were only holding the line on the democratization of a section of the working class. In his 1936 book, Unemployed Struggles, Wal Hannington of the British National Unemployed Workers Movement, after establishing an exemplary record of resistance to poverty that he had every right to be proud of, sadly concluded that mass unemployment still took a dreadful toll despite all his organization's efforts.[3]

The truth is that oppression never fails to leave its mark on its victims. All progressive community organizing is confronted with this problem and the anti-poverty movement is the sharpest expression of it. The full weight of Poor Law tradition and philanthropic judgements bears down on poor people and holds them back from organized resistance. To be laid off and to collect unemployment insurance is not, generally, seen as a badge of distinction; but the unemployed worker who exhausts those benefits and has to turn to welfare undertakes the modern equivalent of passing through the doors of the workhouse. A stigmatization takes place that (and this is no accident) discourages collective action.

As the recession of the early 1980s struck Ontario, a whole new layer of unemployed workers and jobless youth was thrown into poverty. This, coupled with the worsening situation of those who were already poor, led to a burst of organizing activity. In a wide range of communities, unemployed workers associations and poor peoples groups emerged and, as might be expected, the membership of these bodies was very fluid and the failure rate high. Still, in some key communities, organizations emerged that were able to hold together. The phoney "recovery" of the middle and latter part of the decade failed to reduce the numbers living in poverty;

welfare caseloads mushroomed and hundreds of thousands escaped unemployment only by joining the ranks of the working poor, in part-time,
temporary, casual and non-unionised work. There was, then, no genuine
economic upturn that might have removed the incentive to organize
around poverty. The 1980s witnessed a continuing development of local
groups which increasingly felt the need to pool resources and co-ordinate
activities.

Ontario's poverty edifice is based on the tacit assumption that the poor
can be sealed off from the rest of the working class and shamed into
suffering in silence. Some very powerful interests do alright for themselves
in this situation and find efforts to mobilize the poor or build links with the
broader community to be profoundly dangerous. Employers are rabidly
hostile to agitation for the raising of the minimum wage; they jealously
protect the sub-poverty welfare system as a means of regulating the poor
and disciplining the workforce in general. The widest range of monied
interests, from landlords to cheque cashing companies, have a stake in the
atomized and powerless misery of the poor. As may well be imagined these
political and social interests were far from pleased when, during the 80s, a
challenge to poverty by the poor and their allies was forced, increasingly,
onto the political agenda of Ontario. Local groups were formed that took
up the slogan of the 1930s, "We refuse to Starve in Silence!" Though modest
in number, these democratically structured bodies planted influential roots
in their respective communities.

In London, for example, the Union of Unemployed Workers was able
to articulate clear demands around its local welfare regime and to mobilize
militantly and successfully around them. Mothers and Others Making
Change in Kitchener shocked charity groups in their community by
having the audacity to demand standards of fairness from their local
foodbank. Low Income People Involvement in North Bay stood up and
provided a voice for poor people where it had been assumed that they
should bow their heads and accept whatever was offered.[4]

Example after example could be given of similar local initiatives.
Common to all, however, is a rejection of the "blame the victim" attitude
of the 1980s and a resistance as courageous and determined as that of
workers on a picket line. Support has thereby been generated outside the
ranks of the poor: the 1980s were marked by a growing alliance between
organizations of the poor and supporters in the trade unions, churches
and social agencies. The skills, resources and facilities that such bodies
were able to provide have often been decisive in keeping anti-poverty
groups alive.

Some interaction between local peoples' groups did occur throughout
the 1980s. A rally for jobs was held at the Ontario Legislature as early as
1983 that brought groups in from a number of centres. The London and
Toronto Unions of Unemployed Workers joined forces with Scarborough
Poverty Eliminators in 1986 to wage a successful fight to provide a clothing
allowance for children on welfare. However, it was with the initiation of a

campaign for a 25% increase in social assistance rates that the basis for a provincial movement was laid.

The response of Ontario's Liberal Government to the mounting crisis within the welfare system of the mid 1980s was a tried and tested one: they established a committee to study the problem. In 1986, a series of meetings was held between anti-poverty groups around developing a challenge to the Government's stalling tactics. These ongoing discussions involved organizations in Windsor, Chatham, London, Woodstock, Hamilton, Etobicoke, Toronto, Cobourg, Rancroft, Ottawa and Sudbury. We decided that the key to breaking out of the policy impasse was to demand a badly needed interim increase in welfare rates, and we agreed upon 25% as a serious and far from unreasonable demand, given the sub poverty incomes we were dealing with.

With this common position, we were able to add enormously to our respective local anti-poverty action and begin to coordinate work in the communities. The London Union of Unemployed Workers held a London to Toronto March around the 25% demand, and a petition drive was organized across the province. Although Premier David Peterson at first refused to meet with a delegation from the poor and unemployed on the rate increase call, groups coordinated their efforts to demand such a meeting. In fact this rejection by Peterson mobilized new communities with whom we had had no previous contacts, and the struggle intensified throughout the province. Picket lines went up in many new localities that had not been involved in earlier struggles.

By the spring of 1989, organizational activity intensified in response to the worsening poverty crisis and the clamour for change. In late March, a three-pronged March Against Poverty left Windsor, Sudbury and Ottawa to demand action on hunger, homelessness and poverty from Queen's Park. This was an unprecedented event in that it involved thousands of people and was the largest anti-poverty rally in Ontario since the 1930s. Tangible concessions were forced out of the government but, even more importantly, the basis had been laid for establishing a province-wide coalition.

The Ontario Coalition Against Poverty (OCAP) began to take shape in the early part of 1990, in a context where several other key sectors of the community had already achieved a real level of provincial co-ordination. OCAP found ready-made allies in organizations such as the Ontario Coalition for Better Child Care, the Ontario Coalition for Abortion Clinics, the Co-operative Housing Association of Ontario and the United Tenants of Ontario. As we began to make new links with groups such as these, the importance of further co-ordination became clear.

The then complacent Liberal Government, sensing impending economic downfall and, seemingly confident of a renewed majority, decided to call an election. Their plan for a smug and sleepy campaign in the summer of 1990 backfired, and Ontario's social movements did much to bring this happy development about. Modern parliamentary elections are, of course, leader-centred media events. Social movements, taking stock of this, took the decision to jump into the ring. The anti poverty and environmental movements, joined by provincial employees and teachers, simply hounded Peterson throughout the campaign. The tone was set for the weeks ahead when, at Peterson's press conference to announce the election, a member of Greenpeace was ready to confront him with a tape recording of one of his own empty promises.

Our coalition actively confronted Peterson and his ministers with an ongoing mobilization of the poor. The Premier was personally confronted on twenty-seven occasions right across the province, and also experienced dozens of clashes with Liberal supporters.[5] OCAP's slogan of "Down with the Poverty Premier!" became a household expression by election day. We infiltrated his own nomination meeting in London; he set new standards of arrogance by calling on us to "get a job." The alternative election campaign also saw organizations active on the social front pooling their resources and taking common positions. Under the title of "Adjust Ontario," organizations speaking for tenants, poor people, the disabled and other sectors, drew up a five-point platform of demands and mobilized around them throughout our the campaign.

A definitive pronouncement on the degree to which the actions of Ontario's social movements influenced the election outcome and put the NDP in power is hardly possible; sour grapes or high hopes are too likely to colour the judgement. All that can be said with certainty is that this opposition did play a key role in transforming nebulous disquiet into overt political hostility. The Ontario election was significant in developing a coalition of social movements which took on a common political enemy. At the same time, a broad based grouping of trade union and popular forces known as the Ontario Coalition for Social Justice (OCSJ) was formed to confront the Mulroney government in Ottawa.

The OCSJ, which functions as this province's arm of the Action Canada Network, has been successful in uniting with labour some of the most significant and active social movements in Ontario. Teachers, the women's movement, anti-poverty organizations, students, farmers, truckers, the disabled and aboriginal people have all joined in action with the OCSJ as a result of the anti-free trade fight, which has since taken on much broader dimensions. It has become, in fact, very much a focal point for popular resistance to the Tory agenda in Ontario. The Coalition is probably the most hopeful mechanism for a powerful mobilization of those who are organized outside the workplace in conjunction with the struggles of the trade unions.

The high point of the OCSJ's anti-Tory resistance to date was, undoubtedly, its challenge to that party's policy convention in Toronto in August 1991. An anti-Tory festival was prepared for the week of the Convention, and the anti-poverty contribution to this was to set up a tent city of the homeless called "Mulroneyville." This brought out a whole layer of Toronto's homeless that our movement had previously been unable to reach. The mere act of getting permission to erect the tent community led to a public battle with CN Real Estate (the owner of the site at the base of CN Tower), and spirited discussion at Toronto City Council (which leased the property we sought to use). The resources and support we needed for the week had to be secured, and this led to new or strengthened links with supporters in the broader community. In terms of both advancing our struggle and consolidating ourselves organizationally, "Mulroneyville" was a resounding success.

There was a great deal more to this week of action, however. The first morning of the Tory Convention saw a sunrise ceremony, organized by the Chiefs of Ontario and the Native Women's Resource Centre. Truckers descended on downtown Toronto in an unmistakable display of strength and anger. The Building Trades Council brought thousands of construction workers out to rally at the convention site. The Toronto Disarmament Network and others held a vigil for peace. Tory cutbacks were condemned in actions involving the Ontario Secondary School Teachers Federation, the Ontario Federation of Students, the National Action Committee on the Status of Women, the Ontario Confederation of Faculty Associations, the Ontario Coalition for Better Child Care, the Ontario Farmers Union and a range of others. At a seven thousand strong rally, involving massive contingents from the Canadian Union of Postal Workers and the Public Service Alliance of Canada, only the intervention of mounted police prevented an invasion of the Convention. Very deservedly, the convention of the most hated governing party in modern Canadian history came to look like a fortress under siege. It was a week that developed greatly Ontario's contribution to the anti-Tory fight and paved the way for to challenges on an even larger scale in the future.

If there has been noteworthy success in laying foundations for a concerted anti-Tory fight, the situation at the provincial level is much less encouraging. Following the defeat of the Peterson Liberals in 1990, the NDP came to power in Ontario. They were elected on a platform of significant, though by no means earth-shaking, promises contained in a package known as the "Agenda for the People."[6] Following the election victory, as the economy worsened and the corporate lobby growled ever louder, these promises were at first delayed and then, after a decent interval,consigned officially to the museum of nice ideas.

What has become clear in the Ontario experience is that even mild reform could only be implemented in the face of ferocious opposition from Bay and Wall Streets. The class struggle has always been Bob Rae's weak point and being Premier has not done a lot to improve him in this regard. Unfortunately for him, all his olive branches to the rich and powerful have had little effect; the globalized corporate agenda demands that he fall in line with its neoconservative agenda and nothing less will do. The press has clamoured for fiscal blood and corporate front groups have taken to rallying at the Ontario Legislature. All this has led to a situation where a first year in office that was marked by dithering on the social policy front seems to be giving way to Tory style budget slashing. Keeping the Budget in line is the new fixation of the NDP. The Treasurer has not spoken of a "a line in the sand" yet, but we fear he will.

Despite this appalling state of affairs, the social movements have yet, on the whole, to grapple seriously with the matter of challenging the NDP's shortcomings. Very few groups have been ready to be publicly critical, let alone to mobilize their members. People have been seduced by the illusion that the "consultation process" is on the verge of producing real change. The fact is that very few members of the governing caucus or the cabinet, apart from a handful of political staff, have come out of the social movements, and the hope that these forces can steer the ship where it ought to be going is dying very hard indeed. The result is that many who fought the Tories and Liberals are silently wrestling with their private doubts, while the corporate strategists take to the lawn in front of Queen's Park.

The reasons for such self-destructive inaction are twofold. Firstly, it is suggested (in private) that while Bob Rae may indeed be a major disappointment, his Government must be acknowledged as better than one that would be formed by either of the two big business parties. Those pressing to challenge Government inaction respond to this by observing that the political backsliding of the NDP may well reach a point where the distinction between it and the other parties disappears. In any event, the demands of social movements cannot be placed in a deep freeze to suit anyone's political convenience. Either we are serious about building a better society or our strategy is to simply elect someone "a bit better" and go to sleep for four years.

The second and related position is that any progressive challenge to the NDP at this time will only fuel the corporate attack and land us with "strange bedfellows." Against this, however, advocates of a political challenge see little risk of angry tenants demanding promised rent controls being confused with landlords' lobbyists. When OCAP marched to Queen's Park to demand that the NDP "Keep the Promise on Poverty," or to set up a soup kitchen at the party's convention, no one seemed to think that we were right wingers who wanted to slash social programs. Aids Action Now! was able to occupy the office of the Minister of Health to demand urgent action without being viewed as fundamentalist bigots. When the Ontario Federation of Students marched on the Minister of Colleges and Universities, it was clear that they were out to defend education programs, not to dismantle them.

Social movements must forge ahead with their own agenda; the alternative can only be a provincial regime that aligns itself more and more with corporate politics. The OCAP completely rejects the Government position that the resources to deal with poverty and social problems are simply not there. The resources are potentially there, but can only be accessed by taking on Bay Street. If Bob Rae does not wish to be a hostage to big business, to the Mulroney Government in Ottawa and to the municipal politicians who are eliminating social programs, he must make a commitment to draw on the wealth available in Ontario. This, of course, will meet with much resistance and will require that social movements play a strong role to make this choice for the NDP a very clear one. To do this, however, the movements will have to cease playing the role of the pigs in Orwell's "Animal Farm," who went on countering every criticism with the threat that "Jones (the farmer) might come back."

In the early 1980s, the London Union of Unemployed Workers found itself in a bitter fight with the London city council over its treatment of people on welfare. During a week in which our members had been arrested in the Mayor's Office, and ejected from the Council Chambers, and had pitched tents in the nearby showpiece city park, a letter to the editor was carried by the local newspaper from one of the most reactionary council members. He derided the union as a body that rejected "constructive dialogue" and that actually stood in the way of the reform process. The heading of the letter was "Co-operation vs Confrontation," and it inadvertently went to the heart of the matter. Social movements today must resist the tendency to see themselves as de facto government advisors. The attacks we face have created a situation where that advice falls on deaf ears; it is back to naked struggle whether we like it or not. From a book such as Tom McEwan's The Forge Glows Red (1974) we learn that the Toronto of the 1930s was a place where social and economic rights had no place and where, correspondingly, civil liberties were a dead letter.[7] The police were used systematically to rob the unemployed of any right to assemble peacefully or to organize collectively in their defence. The struggles in Ontario at that time were on a massive scale and were waged in the face of brutal repression. We need to learn those lessons and conduct ourselves accordingly.

The struggles facing social movements will certainly require mass mobilization and solidarity in action between trade unions and the various social movements. Had a large scale March for Jobs on Ottawa been woven into the 1991 PSAC strike and the lead been taken up by the labour and popular movements as whole, a decisive challenge to the Mulroney Government would have been more than possible. Far from feeling a sense of pessimism, there are more than enough grounds for spirited retaliation.

The future of the social movements and the struggles they face must be addressed in the context of the developments in Eastern Europe. The collapse of Eastern Europe, we are told, is the final nail in the coffin for those who have rejected capitalism. Still, based on the experiences of social movements in Ontario over the last decade, it is very clear that we remain on a collision course with capitalism. If we are going to inspire people with hope to mobilize on the scale and in the fashion needed for victory, then surely we cannot limit ourselves to bleating for a few humane revisions. We have to offer working people, the poor, and the unemployed a vision of serious change for the better. The alternative to the corporate agenda is the socialist agenda. If we accept that there is a generalized corporate agenda, dedicated to social retrogression, then the need for a coordinated progressive platform of opposition is easy to see. Apart from the obvious overlap of concerns that do exist between different social movements, there is a great deal of merit in backing each other's causes and working for solidarity in action, even where differences are clear. Real power can be generated by broad fronts that take shape around key demands against common political foes. Social movements in Ontario are becoming ever more receptive to this method of struggle.

NOTES

1.   The "innocent" nature of his work notwithstanding, Luccius confessed to being listed in an East German publication *Who's Who in the C.I.A.* When we got our hands on the East German book that referred to Mr. Luccius and the various "hotspots" in the world he had been active in, we realized that this man indeed had some well informed views on the matter of social struggles.

2.   Piven, Frances Fox and Richard Cloward. *Poor People's Movements: Why they Succeeded, How They Failed.* New York: Pantheon Books, 1977. pp. 70-71.

3.   He also notes that the actual percentage of the jobless active in the struggle never exceeded 10%.
Hannington, Wal. *Unemployed Struggles.* Laurence and Wishart, 1936. Reprint, London, 1979.

4.   In addition to the three communities mentioned above, the 1980s saw unemployed workers or poor peoples organizations formed in at least the following: Windsor, Sarnia, Chatham, Woodstock, St. Thomas, Goderich, Kitchener, Cambridge, Guelph, Hamilton, Welland, Niagara Falls, Toronto, North York, East York, Etobicoke, Scarborough, Whitby, Oshawa, Barrie, Cobourg, Port Hope, Peterborough, Belleville, North Hastings County, North Frontenac County, Kingston, Ottawa, Sudbury, North Bay, Sault Ste. Marie and Thunder Bay.

5.   This lower profile process of chipping away at liberal morale and popularity was many sided. When Ontario Treasurer Robert Nixon came to Peterborough, the United Citizens Organization turned out to hound him. A coalition of Ottawa organizations descended on the campaign headquarters of Dick Patten, MPP. They carried empty grocery bags as a symbol of hunger in their community. When he unwisely chose to be unavailable for a meeting, they left a cake with his staff that had been given to an area food bank months after its expiry date!
    Activity around all candidates' meetings was another major feature of the campaign. In some cases, we visited those that had been arranged by other organizations. The London Union of Unemployed Workers staged a soup kitchen rally outside a meeting held by the local Chamber of Commerce. The North West Ontario Coalition Against Poverty was present at candidates meetings in Thunder Bay on a particularly tenacious basis. The same could be said of the Woodstock Coalition Against Poverty with regard to Oxford County. On the other hand, groups like Mothers and Others Making Change in Kitchener and the Scarborough Poverty Eliminators Committee chose to organize their own events and thereby put the Liberals in the hot seat.

6.   This document proposed such basic reforms as a policy of real rent control, the pegging of the Ontario minimum wage at 60% of the average industrial wage (about $7.25 at that time) and a significant hike in welfare rates. (The NDP had fully supported OCAP's call for a 25% increase, though this was not spelt out in their platform). In terms of revenue generation, the Agenda for People advocated such "tax the rich" measures as a minimum corporate tax, a wealth tax and a tax on speculation on property. None of the above has been implemented.

7.   McEwan's, Thomas. *The Forge Glows Red.* Toronto: Progress Books, 1974.

REFERENCES

Hannington, Wal. *Unemployed Struggles*. Laurence and Wishart, 1936. Reprint, London, 1979.

McEwan's, Thomas. *The Forge Glows Red*. Toronto: Progress Books, 1974.

Piven, Frances Fox and Richard Cloward. Poor People's Movements: *Why they Succeeded, How They Failed*. New York: Pantheon Books, 1977.

EUROPE'S GREEN ALTERNATIVE

An Ecology Manifesto

edited by Penny Kemp

While Europe is poised to enter the era of super-States with common markets, when most of the old ways are at the same time being questioned, the need for a new direction, not only for Europe but for the entire world, has become urgent.

Millions of people are suffering malnutrition in Africa, over a hundred thousand children are threatened with death in Iraq, child prostitution in Latin America has doubled, and the gap between the world's rich and the world's poor continues to increase. We have begun to decimate animal and plant species, and to disrupt food chains. We have put poisons into the ecosystem which will remain there for thousands of years. We now know the effects of pollution, we have all heard of the 'greenhouse' effect, the hole in the ozone layer, and politicians from all countries are making 'green' noises. But missing from the political agenda is a determination to question the existing political structures and systems under which we live and work.

The Green's alternative call for a 'new world order' that truly moves in the direction of a just and sustainable world is receiving the widest attention. To meet the challenges of rigorous definition of the nature of society's crisis and the ways that we can begin to emerge from this dangerous period in history, an international group of well-known authors gathered together to produce this exceptional guide through the labyrinth of ideas and social/political action.

Europe's Green Alternative is being published in English, German, French, Italian, Spanish, Portuguese, Polish and Russian, and it is the hope of the authors that the contributions made herein be superseded by a new dialogue, between nations, that will clear the way for a green, eco-socialist alternative.

Penny Kemp has been active and prominent in the Green Party in England, and was for a couple of years a co-chair of its executive committee.

200 pages, appendices
Paperback: 1-895431-30-1　　　　**$16.95**
Hardcover: 1-895431-31-X　　　　**$35.95**
Ecology/Politics

GREEN POLITICS

Agenda For a Free Society

Dimitrios Roussopoulos

It isn't easy to present the truth about the destruction of the earth without falling into the trap of apocalyptic despair, nor is it easy to challenge current assumptions about progress and what the future holds. This book courageously confronts these issues to suggest that we *can* create a new society that is ecologically sustainable, economically viable and socially just.

Widespread patterns of alienation are obliging us to re-consider both the neglected issues of community and of the individual. *Green Politics* is rooted in the conviction that there is a set of principles from which new and innovative solutions, based on a clear appreciation of our interdependent relationship with the environment, may emerge.

An international survey of various Green political parties is presented, featuring their programmes and progress. The result is a stimulating book that challenges accepted ideas about how the world should be organized and suggests the possibility of a safe and more satisfying future for all of us.

Dimitrios Roussopoulos is an editor, writer and economist. He has written widely on international politics (*The Coming of World War Three*), democracy (*The Case For Participatory Democracy,* with C. George Benello) and social change.

200 pages, index
Paperback ISBN: 0-921689-74-8   **$15.95**
Hardcover ISBN: 0-921689-75-6   **$35.95**
L.C. No. 90-83631
Politics/Ecology/Sociology

FROM THE GROUND UP

Essays on Grassroots and Workplace Democracy

C. George Benello

**Edited by Len Krimerman, Frank Lindenfeld, Carol Korty
and Julian Benello**
Foreword by Dimitrios Roussopoulos

Should today's activists aim for more than reformist changes in the policies and personnel of giant corporations and the government? In this collection of classic essays, C. George Benello persuasively argues that modern social movements need to rise to the challenge of spearheading a radical reorganization of society based on the principles of decentralization, community control, and participatory democracy. Integrating some of the best of New Left thought with more contemporary populist and Green perspectives, Benello's essays and the commentaries of Harry Boyte, Steve Chase, Walda Katz-Fishman, Jane Mansbridge and Chuck Turner offer important insights for today's new generation of practical utopians.

Surveying all of it, George's life, work, and thought exhibit an unusual and comprehensive consistency. He was a philosopher, educator, and activist who wrote about and practically promoted the implementation of his concerns for peace, social justice, local self-reliance, and economic democracy. He served as an inspiration to many organizers active in the social movements which have emerged in North America and elsewhere over the last thirty years...Arguably, George focused his most creative energies on developing a practical strategy for building models and precursors of the new society in the here and now.
— from the introduction

Where the utopian confronts the practical, Benello is perhaps most creative...From the Ground Up...is a valuable contribution to creating a new politics.
Z Magazine

C. George Benello, active in the movement for grassroots and workplace democracy from the early 1960s until his death in 1987, founded the Federation for Economic Democracy, the Industrial Cooperative Association, and the journal *Changing Work*.

251 pages, index
Paperback ISBN: 1-895431-32-8   **$19.95**
Hardcover ISBN: 1-895431-33-6   **$38.95**
Sociology/Politics

FIGHTING FOR HOPE

Organizing to Realize Our Dreams

Joan Newman Kuyek

The cheapening of the meaning of 'community' reflects a destruction of human relationships. As economic development—free-enterprise style—has progressed, its corollary has been the pillage not only of natural resources but of natural relationships. *Fighting For Hope* begins with an analysis of these forces and the ways in which resistance against them has been managed and suppressed. Activists in Canada have experienced dismal setbacks, unexpected victories and carefully planned successes. This book finds the common threads and weaves them into a guidebook for anyone who cares about social change.

Starting from the experiences of ordinary people, the author looks at how 'scientific management', in the form of political systems, educational systems, and communication systems, all work to diminish the power and ability of Canadians to determine their own futures. In *Fighting For Hope* there are sections on building the core group, structuring it, creating a vision, raising money, choosing strategies. There are descriptions (with examples) of various kinds of community organizing activity from popular education, to civil disobedience, to alternative investment funds.

Throughout, the book is infused with an understanding of how hard it is to keep a group together and motivated, but the message is clear. Even at this moment in history, when so many are struggling, *Fighting For Hope* shows that the best efforts of ordinary people to build a better life can be expanded and woven together to create a world where they do not have to fear for their children's future.

Joan Newman Kuyek is the author of *The Phone Book: Working at Bell Canada, Managing the Household: A Handbook For Economic Justice Work,* and numerous articles and pamphlets.

209 pages
Paperback ISBN: 0-921689-86-1   **$16.95**
Hardcover ISBN: 0-921689-87-X   **$35.95**
Politics/Sociology/Social Work

TOWARD A HUMANIST POLITICAL ECONOMY

Harold Chorney and Phillip Hansen

During the last fifteen years, the fundamental assumptions about the liberal democratic foundations of Western society have been undermined. The liberal consensus was based on a notion of a caring and humane society in which full employment and the welfare State played a central role. This consensus was shattered by a neoconservative wave that is only now beginning to recede. The wreckage of the past decade is visible to all in the streets of our cities and the desolation of many of our rural communities.

Guided by a critical theory perspective, Harold Chorney and Phillip Hansen focus their attention on the neglected cultural side of society in order to chart the progress of political change. They feel that the simple economic explanations and the old radical conventions can no longer be relied on in explaining and pointing the way towards a fundamentally reformed society. Instead they use as background some of the insights of writers as diverse as Hannah Arendt and John Maynard Keynes.

Toward a Humanist Political Economy is the fruit of a long intellectual and personal friendship between these two authors, and as such, sweeps a wide range: political culture, economics, political economy, public life, the crisis of socialism, and the critical theory of urban public policy. Essential reading!

Harold Chorney holds a Ph.D. in political economy from University of Toronto and teaches public policy and social theory at Concordia University, Montréal. Phillip Hansen has a Ph.D. in political economy from the University of Toronto and teaches Social Theory at the University of Regina, Saskatchewan.

230 pages, index
Paperback ISBN:1-895431-22-0 $19.95
Hardcover ISBN:1-895431-23-9 $38.95
L.C. No. 92-70623
Economics/Sociology/Politics

BLACK ROSE BOOKS
has published the following books of related interests:

SHOCK WAVES: Eastern Europe After the Revolutions, *by John Feffer*
MASK OF DEMOCRACY: Labour Rights in Mexico Today, *by Dan LaBotz*
SOUTHERN AFRICA: Post-Apartheid, *edited by Nancy Thede and Pierre Beaudet*
BRINGING THE ECONOMY HOME FROM THE MARKET, *by Ross V.G. Dobson*
VIDEO THE CHANGING WORLD, *edited by Nancy Thede and Allain Ambrosi*
PERESTROIKA AND THE SOVIET PEOPLE, *by David Mandel*
WOMEN AND COUNTER-POWER, *edited by Yolande Cohen*
GERMANY EAST: Dissent and Opposition, *by Bruce Allen*
VOICES FROM TIANANMEN SQUARE: Beijing Spring and the Democracy
    Movement, *edited by Mok Chui Yu and J. Frank Harrison*
THE NEW WORLD ORDER AND THE THIRD WORLD, *edited by Dave Broad*
    and Lori Foster
THE HISTORY OF THE LABOUR MOVEMENT IN QUEBEC, *the Education Committees*
    of the CSN and the CEQ
QUEBEC LABOUR, *CNTU*
THE BITTER THIRTIES IN QUEBEC, *by Evelyn Dumas*
THE TRADE UNIONS AND THE STATE, *by Walter Johnson*
WORKING IN CANADA, *edited by Walter Johnson*
ECOLOGY AS POLITICS, *by André Gorz*
SERVICES AND CIRCUSES: Community and the Welfare State, *by Frédéric Lesemann*
THE MYTH OF THE MARKET, Promises and Illusions, *by Jeremy Seabrook*
THE ECOLOGY OF FREEDOM: The Emergence and Dissolution of Hierarchy,
    by Murray Bookchin
TOWARD AN ECOLOGICAL SOCIETY, *by Murray Bookchin*
MEMOIRS OF A REVOLUTIONIST, *by Peter Kropotkin*
THE GREAT FRENCH REVOLUTION, *by Peter Kropotkin*
MUTUAL AID, *by Peter Kropotkin*
THE CONQUEST OF BREAD, *by Peter Kropotkin*
ETHICS, *by Peter Kropotkin*
FEMINISM, *edited by Angela Miles and Geraldine Finn*
THE LIFE AND WORK OF KARL POLANYI, *edited by Kari Polanyi-Levitt*
THE ANARCHIST PAPERS, *edited by Dimitrios Roussopoulos*
BUREAUCRACY AND COMMUNITY, *edited by Linda Davies and Eric Shragge*
DEMOCRACY AND THE WORKPLACE, *by Harold B. Wilson*

Send for our free catalogue of books
BLACK ROSE BOOKS
C.P. 1258
Succ. Place du Parc
Montréal, Québec
H2W 2R3

Printed by the workers of
Imprimerie Gagné Ltée